Prince Dracula

A portrait of Prince Dracula painted during the late fifteenth or early sixteenth century. The portrait is at Castle Ambras, near Innsbruck, Austria. *(Permission: Kunstmuseum, Vienna)*

Prince Dracula

Son of the Devil

DOUGLAS MYLES

McGraw-Hill Book Company

New York St. Louis San Francisco
Hamburg Mexico Toronto

1 2 3 4 5 6 7 8 9 DOC DOC 8 9 2 1 0 9 8

ISBN 0-07-072176-9

Library of Congress Cataloging-in-Publication Data

Myles, Douglas.
Prince Dracula.

Bibliography: p.
1. Vlad III, Prince of Wallachia, 1430– or 31–1476 or 7. 2. Wallachia—Kings and rulers—Biography. I. Title.
DR240.5.V55M94 1988 949.8′201′0924 [B] 88-12875
ISBN 0-07-072176-9

Book design by Patrice Fodero

For Thomas H. Quinn,
the author's good friend
and a prince among editors

Contents

	Introduction	1
1.	Dracula and the Cult of Vampirism	11
2.	Christendom Faces the Ottoman Empire	25
3.	Dracula's First Reign and Flight to Moldavia	45
4.	The Second Reign: A Policy of Terror	65
5.	The Deadly Game Grows Deadlier	91
6.	The Great Danubian Campaign against the Turks	115
7.	The Castle on the River	139
8.	The Prisoner of Vísegràd	161
9.	The Exile of Pest	185
10.	The Third Reign: A Gathering Darkness	213
11.	The Last Battle	235
	Epilogue	259
	Glossary of Foreign Words and Guide to Pronunciation	271
	Bibliography	275
	Index	279

I would like to express my love and appreciation to Elizabeth Myles for her endless encouragement and unshakeable faith.

Even Zeus was never so supported by Hera.

Introduction

The two naked half-brothers in the huge, ornate bed seemed out of place in their luxurious surroundings. Though they were princes and lay on the imported silk of fabled Cathay, a mere glance at their faces made clear their alienation from the men in the room. The younger one, a boy not much older than nine, was badly frightened. He was very good looking, a little too much so for a male, with a soft white body and full, sensuously curved lips that most girls would have envied. He cringed now, his face pale with alarm as he tried to hide his genitals with his hands, his dark eyes widening at the approach of the two turbaned harem guards with their powerfully muscled physiques and glistening black skins.

At a softly spoken command from behind them, the guards stopped and stood still, scarcely seeming to see the boys. The older brother, about twelve, gave no sign of fear. In him there was nothing feminine, nothing soft. His features were harsh for one of his age, as flintlike as his wiry young body was strong. In his eyes, very large and of a startling green, there was a warning. He would submit but he would retaliate. The Sultan Murad and the others could do to him as they did with so many captive youths, but the first chance he got he would kill them, kill them all. As the flaming torches on the walls cast their flickering shadows, he waited. He did not bother to cover himself. They would only jerk his

cry out or release the tears which shame and humiliation brought welling into his eyes. But there was no dignity left him now that it had happened, no maintaining his princely demeanor, no saving of his honor. There was only the acute sense of fullness to bursting, of being used unmercifully, of degradation and submission and defeat. It seemed to go on and on eternally, until sobs were wrung from him and childish curses flung at the damascened wall. And while they did this to him, commenting obscenely on his surrender and his helplessness, angry because they couldn't break his spirit, something changed in the boy, a subtle, nearly undetectable metamorphosis now, but destined one day to become a tempest.

Because of it—and other acts of viciousness yet to be perpetrated by his own people—a time would come in Eastern Europe when thousands of victims of both sexes would writhe in agony on stakes, poles thrust into them where the penises of these Turks had been, in their rectums.

Because of it, a madness that might have lain dormant would erupt into flame and fury, and battles would be fought without mercy, while the warlike ruler of the mighty Ottoman Empire, Mehmed, son of Murad, would be thwarted in his conquests for years.

As the last officer to satisfy himself withdrew from the exhausted boy he spoke laconically in Arabic, not the language of the Ottomans but of the universal Koran, the Islamic holy book. "Inshallah," he said. "As God wills."

The observation made in this fateful year 1443 was to prove prophetic. With the emptying of the janissaries' testicles into the bowels of the young prince the fate of a vast multitude was inexorably sealed.

The place was a motion picture theater in Southern California, the time the early 1930s. Outside on the marquee, the letters advertised the film *Dracula* and its sinister Hungarian star, Bela Lugosi. Inside, the house was full for the Saturday afternoon matinee, and at least one of the viewers, a very young boy attending on his own, might not in later years have been allowed inside for such a film without an adult escort.

By now the reader has perhaps guessed that the boy was the author and that this was my first exposure to the story of the infamous vampire created so many years earlier in the fertile brain of London's Bram Stoker. How did I feel about it? I remember being deeply impressed, half-mesmerized by Lugosi's slow, voluptuous delivery as the monstrous tale unfolded and the clever script and consummate acting lent the film a quality at once dreamlike and real. At that time, of course, I had no idea that Dracula had actually lived, and decades were to pass before I was to discover it.

I walked home in a sort of reverie, I remember, my mind full of macabre images: fangs biting into the tender throats of terrified maidens, blood-red lips on faces as pale as wax, humans who turned into bats and wolves, ancient castles with dungeons and torture chambers, and wooden stakes driven through the hearts of shrieking vampires. Were the shadows cast by trees and buildings that evening really deeper and blacker than before or did they only seem so? Shortly afterward, the film adaptation of Mary Shelley's *Frankenstein* was to have a similar, but not quite as profound, effect; it was not as horrific, despite the prodigious talents of Boris Karloff and Colin Clive. It was *Dracula* that was deeply etched on my brain. It still is.

The scene now shifts. The boy in the movie theater has become a man, has fought through World War II in the Marine Corps, acquired a degree, changed military services, and become an Army intelligence officer in postwar occupied Germany. I was very fond of skiing and pursued the sport at every opportunity, being conveniently stationed in Bavaria near the Austrian border. I skied the Zugspitze in Germany; at Zürs and Kitzbühel in the Austrian Alps; and at picturesque Innsbruck, the Tyrol's capital city. There never seemed to be enough time for all that I wished to do and see. Had there been, I might have visited the great castle that frowned above the River Inn that flowed through Innsbruck, seen Dracula's strange portrait there, and my awareness of his reality would have come sooner.

What would I have said if someone had told me about the painting, that I would some day write about its subject? Not very much, probably. The skepticism of youth often has little patience with the stuff of wonder and romance, still less with the supernatural revealed as fact. Yet Dracula had *lived.* Stoker's vampire was a myth, but not the fantastic figure from whom he was derived. I might have picked up his trace again in medieval Nürnberg had I but known. He was there more than once as a boy, he and his father, Prince Vlad, as guests of the Holy Roman Emperor Sigismund. But I had other things to do in that walled and moated city, and was unaware of my ignorance. The Army personnel of the Fürth Military Post were occupied with more mundane pursuits.

Actually, my discovery of Dracula's reality came about by chance some twenty years ago. I was out of the military service and teaching history and I spent considerable time in libraries. On one of my visits, seeking material on fifteenth-century eastern Europe, I came upon a book published in England in 1934, *A History of the Romanians* by the noted British historian, R. W. Seton-Watson. Because Seton-Watson was an old acquaintance, I took an interest at once and withdrew the book. Imagine my amazement on finding that Dracula, far from being a mere figment of Stoker's imagination, had actually existed. The revelation was somehow shocking but infinitely fascinating. I devoured the material. Then, as time permitted, I tracked down other volumes, thirsty for the information whose very existence had been unknown to me.

The Byzantine historian Kritovoulos of Imbros, a contemporary of Dracula, came to my hand with his *History of Mehmed the Conqueror*, the Riggs translation. So did *Memoirs of a Renaissance Pope: the Commentaries of Pius II*, translated by F. A. Gragg. Oscar Halecki, in his *The Crusade at Varna: A Discussion of a Controversial Problem*, provided material on Dracula's father. Constantin Giurescu, *Transylvania in the History of Romania: An Historical Outline*, justified his scholarly reputation in an excellent general overview. And there were other fascinating sources to come.

Among the latter were two excellent books published in 1973 by the American writers Radu Florescu and Raymond T. McNally, professors of history at Boston College. The first, *Dracula: A Biography of Vlad the Impaler, 1431–1476*, is scholarly and thorough, and benefits greatly from on-site research and the authors' conversance in Romanian, German, and Russian, the languages in which many of the old documents were written. The other, *In Search of Dracula: A True History of Dracula and Vampire Legends*, is less academic and more dramatic, emphasizing the vampire myth. Both books are well illustrated.

Yet despite these books the subject of Dracula remains underexposed, certainly one of the most neglected of all aspects of the history of Eastern Europe, a field which many more books would scarcely exhaust. In writing this volume I hope to contribute something important to arouse a greater general interest in the subject internationally, perhaps through added psychological insight into the character of Dracula himself; and, more specifically, to throw more light than has yet been shone on the vitally important role played by the Ottomans in the expansion into Europe of the forces of the Turkish Empire.

Yes, Dracula lived—but what was he? In the view of Seton-Watson and others he was a monster of cruelty and depravity with no redeeming traits whatever. Was this literally true? Research reveals that most contemporary accounts were written by his enemies or by scribes paid by his enemies, a factor damaging to many reputations, those of the infamous Cesare Borgia and King Richard III, for example. Was this Renaissance prince then the victim of a vicious smear campaign, his character blackened by fanatically prejudiced antagonists for political and military reasons? Or was he really the fiend depicted in the chronicles? Curiously enough, he appears to have been both. Vicious he certainly was, steeped in brutality and savagery. That enemy propaganda described him as even more diabolical than the reality may also be true. There is no question that the hatred he engendered among so many was incredibly virulent, but that fact, taken alone, is less than the full measure of the man. To see the other side of the coin it is necessary to delve deeply.

Dracula is a figure all but forgotten by history, one whose reality has been nearly totally submerged by myth and the inevitable ravages of time. It was not always so. In the regions under his power, and among those people who fell victim to his frightful cruelty, he was once well known indeed. He was a sadist, the bloody and unregenerate butcher of thousands, and quite mad. Yet if ever a psychopath had method in his madness it was Dracula. He slaughtered the guilty and the innocent alike, but he seldom struck at his victims without weighing every move on the scale of his ambition and the measuring rod of tactical or strategic advantage. Were you a possible ally in battle? He would woo you with all the ardor of a lover. Were you a potential or actual enemy? He would bring you down at any cost, by any method. And lucky was the foe who did not meet his end writhing and twisting on a stake, his every move unutterable agony as ruptured vitals led to eye-popping, inexorable death.

This was a figure larger than life, a macabre and horrendous purveyor of evil who was shrewd, ruthless, knew no pity, and who yet had within him, in some twisted labyrinth of the psyche, some of the elements of greatness. Certainly, great courage was his. There were many times in his strange and incredible life when death seemed as nothing to him, when indeed he appeared to welcome it, even to seek it. It may have come to him like that in the end, sought after, pursued, yes, *embraced* by a prince and general who knew he was insane, who could not stop himself, and who struggled desperately, blindly toward oblivion; a lost soul who knew he was lost, who found at last extinction and blessed deliverance among the unpitying arrows of a cold-blooded, relentless foe.

Dracula's homeland was in what is today Romania, northernmost of the Balkan countries. Wallachia, the domain over which he and his father and grandfather before him ruled as princes was in the southeast of that country. As depicted in Bram Stoker's novel, he held the noble rank of count. This is fiction. In that book, also, he was said to be from Transylvania, and this is fact. To most Americans, Englishmen, and Western Europeans, Transylvania is a mythical geographical entity like Ruritania in Anthony Hope's romantic novel *The Prisoner of Zenda*. Nonetheless, it is real. A region of western Romania, it is bounded on the north, east, and south by the Carpathian Mountains and the Transylvanian Alps. The terrain is heavily forested, well drained, characterized by Alpine grandeur. In the east, on a tributary of the Arges, itself a branch of the Danube, lies the walled medieval town of Sighisoara where Dracula was born. On the outside wall of the plain three-story house where the birth took place a bronze plaque hangs today, odd in that setting but less incongruous than the dwelling's electric wiring seen in modern photos. It says that in 1431 the house was occupied by Vlad Dracul. This was Dracula's father who five years later came to the throne of Wallachia as Prince Vlad II.

Dracula's name was also Vlad. He it was who with his younger half-brother Radu was taken hostage by the Turks in 1443, then held in the Ottoman fortress of Egrigöz as catamite guarantor for his father's future behavior. Dracula later ruled Wallachia during three separate reigns, very briefly in the first and third interludes, but for six years during the second. On each occasion he mounted the throne with the title Prince Vlad III of the royal house of Basarab.

How did he come to be called Dracula? It was a sobriquet, an unofficial title derived from the simple fact that his father was called Dracul. *Drac* means "devil" in Romanian. It also means "dragon." *Ul* is a suffix denoting the definite article "the." *La* is a diminutive ending meaning "son of." Dracula, therefore, son of Dracul, was also Son of the Devil or Son of the Dragon.

How can we reach a conclusion as to which epithet was intended to describe the father Dracul, "devil" or "dragon"? The former clearly denotes evil. Would that alone account for the nickname? Does it fit what we know of Dracul? He was wily, yes, a clever diplomat and negotiator who at various times was accused of duplicity and treachery by both the Christians on one side and the Muslim Turks on the other. But was he sufficiently evil to be notorious for this trait among his contemporaries? Research does not substantiate it. Duplicity was a way of life during the period, particularly for the highborn. Dracul walked a tightrope. Caught between the warlike and aggressive Turks moving ever closer on one frontier and the pressure of the militant Hungarians on the other, survival dictated that he play a double game, balancing the odds as best he could.

In 1431 (most historians believe Dracul's wife was pregnant with Dracula at the time) he left Sighisoara and made a difficult journey to distant Nürnberg, greatest of Germany's free imperial cities. The trip must have been carefully planned. The Holy Roman Emperor Sigismund, king of Hungary since 1387, had an abiding interest in his kingdom but little enough in the empire, and his sojourns in Germany (more properly "the Germanies") were brief and infrequent. It was therefore a question of timing. Dracul knew when the emperor would be in that city, for he had been summoned. He knew, also, that the reason for the summons was an investiture, that he, Dracul, was on the list of those imperial knights on whom the Order of the Dragon was to be conferred.

What was this order? The Order of the Dragon, like the Knights Templars, the Knights Hospitalers, the Teutonic Knights, the Knights of Malta, and the Knights of St. John of Jerusalem, was a crusading organization of sworn and devoted zealots dedicated to fighting the Muslims in general, as enemies of Christendom, and the Ottomans in particular. True, the Crusades had been over since the eighth and last effort, that of Louis IX of France, had failed against the Seljuk Turks in 1272. True, also, the Christian forces of the West were even more hopelessly divided now than then, split religiously as well as politically. Nonetheless, there were many in Europe who clearly saw the extent of the Islamic peril and the vital need to organize against it. Sigismund was one of these. When he invested Dracul with the insignia—a winged dragon recumbent on a cross, its tail encircling its head above a severed back—he ensured that his son, Dracula, if not Dracul himself, would inherit this solemn resolve and ultimately war against Islam to the death.

But the question repeats itself. Was Dracul "the Devil" or was he "the Dragon"? Clearly, in the minds of his subjects he was both. As a member of the order he was a Draconist, a prince consecrated to lead his knights in holy battle under the banner of the dragon. However, in the Romania of that day the dragon was something else as well, one of several manifestations of the Prince of Darkness.

To put Dracula into historical perspective it is necessary to fix him in time and balance the events of his life with those of a few of his better known contemporaries. In France, the saintly Joan of Arc was burned at the stake in 1431, the probable year of his birth; and the dreaded Italo-Spanish despot Cesare Borgia was born in Rome in the year of his death, 1476. Dracula, a man of the Renaissance, lived but forty-five years. However, during that brief span events of decisive importance kept all Europe locked in the throes of agonizing change as warfare was waged unceasingly and the last vestiges of medieval feudalism were drowned in contagion and blood.

In the West, England had momentarily ceased to play a role on the European continent. Having fought the Hundred Years' War against France, having won the great battles of Crécy, Poitiers, and Agincourt under such leaders as the Black Prince and Henry V, the Island Kingdom had nonetheless been beaten in the end when the French changed their strategy to one of gradual attrition. That end came in 1453, and all that was left to the English of French soil was the channel port of Calais. Two years later civil war racked the island, the opening of the Wars of the Roses between the House of Lancaster (the Red Rose) and the House of York (the White Rose), a struggle that was to last thirty years. When it ended in 1485 Dracula was already nine years in his grave. Joining him in death that year was the infamous Richard III, slain at Bosworth Field. It was the day of the Tudors in England. The reign that began with Henry VII was to usher in a resurgent strength which under his son, Henry VIII, saw the birth of British sea power.

The year 1453 was more important to the shaping of Dracula's destiny—and indeed to that of all Eastern Europe—than any other in the century. Not only did it mark the end of the Hundred Years' War, but it was also the year of the fall to the Ottoman Turks of the great Christian citadel of Constantinople, capital of the Eastern Roman Empire, which had endured for 1100 years. The sultan who took the city after a fifty-day siege in which he employed 150,000 men and the biggest guns ever seen was called Mohammed II in Arabic (Mehmed II in Turkish), Murad II's son, a man known to history as Mohammed the Conqueror. To Europeans, the psychological impact of the city's fall was devastating, rather as though today's Soviet Russia were to take Paris or London.

As it also happened, Serbian resistance to the Turks ended this year. Now at last the Muslim forces advanced to the line of the Danube River while all of the Balkans braced for the coming shock. And Dracula? Having already lost the throne of Wallachia once, he was in exile under the protection of János Hunyadi, the powerful and heroic Hungarian regent whose life was dedicated to stopping the Turks. At this time, the young

Wallachian prince, still in his early twenties, was a mere political and military pawn, a piece to play against the Turkish thrust when and as Hunyadi might choose. Neither regent nor sultan could possibly have foreseen the scope and power of the role he would fill.

They were fantastic times, these years of the fifteenth century. In 1448, the year in which a boyish Dracula assumed his throne for the first time, the Black Death (bubonic plague) struck Europe, again decimating the serfs as the frightful epidemic of 1347 had done, drastically reducing the labor force and damaging the waning feudal system even more. As epic voyages were made into unknown seas the earth shrank and the foundations of empires were laid. Among the navigators, explorers, and conquistadors one thinks of Cabot, Columbus, Cabral, Da Gama, Pizarro, Balboa, Magellan, and Cortés, to name but a few, all of them born in the fifteenth century. In humanistic scholarship the names of Erasmus, More, and Colet fairly glow. Torquemada, Savonarola, and Luther greatly influenced religious thought for good or evil. And because of such geniuses as Leonardo, Michelangelo, Titian, and Raphael the world of art was both glorified and forever changed.

But the soul of Dracula, like that of the deadly Borgia prince, or Ferdinand I, called the Beast of Naples, or Gilles de Rais (general under Joan of Arc and later notorious as the Bluebeard of France) was dark, darker than the souls of any of these; darker than that of Cortés who decimated the Aztecs or Pizarro who butchered the Incas. It was Dracula that destiny would select to throw in the path of the Turkish advance into Wallachia, a demonlike creature with the instincts of a headsman, yet capable of devastating, fanatically inspired leadership. He was an unfortunate choice for the Ottomans. Until nearly the end of his life his madness was to prove a frequent advantage. So was his sheer ferocity and unsurpassed élan in battle. *He was, in his one single person, possibly the most shocking case of military power wedded to murderous schizophrenia to be found in the human record.*

1
Dracula and the Cult of Vampirism

The *haiduc* Arghezi was a huge, hairy bear of a creature, and in the dimness of approaching twilight he seemed to the young man who looked at him even larger. The youth's name was Petru Calinescu. He was bound to a tree, a prisoner of Arghezi, held like the other five unfortunates because of the robber's belief that a ransom would be forthcoming. It did no good to tell Arghezi otherwise, as Petru had discovered. True, the captives were of a boyar family, all of noble birth. But even boyars experienced changes of fortune, up or down, and Petru's family was down, in disfavor with the reigning prince because they had supported his slaughtered predecessor.

Growing painfully uncomfortable in his rawhide bindings, he gazed steadily at Arghezi. The big man paid him no heed. Leaning languidly against the bole of a lightning-shattered oak, he seemed lost in thought, a study in brute power momentarily at rest. Slung at his hip was a short sword in a tooled leather scabbard, a weapon of foreign workmanship. Plunged into the ground beside him was a long spear, its haft and the shape of its head equally of foreign design. Petru considered them. Was it true then that in these "Mad Forests" of the lower Arges were to be found descendants of the ancient Dacians, tribes who down through the centuries had preserved the short-bladed *gladius* and long *pilum* wrested from their Roman foes? It seemed impossible. That sword and spear would have to be a thousand years old. He figured rapidly, hoping to take his mind off his growing fear. A thousand years? No, older than that by three centuries. Thirteen hundred years. It was incredible and he refused to believe it. Copies, yes, but never originals. The stories were mere *legende*. Myths. Almost as bad as the even wilder *doinas*, the folktales of the peasants who said that travelers lost in these forests went insane, that the few who ever survived were always hopelessly mad, raving, wild-eyed lunatics who dashed out their brains against walls or trees.

It seemed to grow darker suddenly. The bits of blue sky seen through the thick foliage were empurpling now as the sun fell rapidly and a chill invested the air. Petru shivered in his bonds. The thongs were cutting his circulation, he knew, making it harder for his blood to warm him. He glanced at the other captives, then focused on only one, his beautiful cousin Magda, tied to a tree some yards away. He wanted to call out to her, say something to comfort her, perhaps give her hope. But he knew it would be suicide. When they first were captured an hour ago a man had died like that, his father's *satrar*, Ivascu, cut down for daring to complain of their treatment.

As the young man watched, growing ever more desperate in his helplessness, Arghezi heaved himself erect and walked over to the girl. Hers was the true despair thought Petru. That *haiduc* dog could do anything he wanted to her and who would stop him? Even his fellow cutthroats were not on the scene now and only God knew what deviltry they were about. As he watched, his heart sinking within him, Arghezi, standing ponderously before the frail, cringing captive, drew a hunting knife and cut her bonds. Instantly she collapsed into his arms, a long sigh escaping her lips that Petru was sure was wrenched from her in a swoon. He saw Arghezi lay her on the ground, then cover her body with his own, fumbling with her clothing. It was maddening, unbearable. He jerked at the numbing rawhide but it held as he knew it would. Desperately his eyes shot right and left, trying to distinguish his fellow prisoners but seeing nothing in the gathering darkness, knowing them to be as helpless as himself. As Magda's ripped gown was raised by her ravisher he caught a glimpse of white, gleaming thigh, then what might have been a naked breast. Then no more.

Time seemed to stop. Petru had no notion of it, no way of reckoning. During a long interval he expected to hear the girl's groans, her cries of shame and outrage, but he heard nothing, not even the sounds of furious rut from the pitiless barbarian he knew had raped her. She had fainted, of course, her lovely lips sealed in unconsciousness. Then the moon suddenly appeared. It grew brighter as scudding clouds drifted across it. Brighter. Its shimmering light was filtering through the treetops. Petru caught his breath. It was not a man atop the girl, not the accursed Arghezi. Hovering above her now, only partly discernible in the deep shadows, was a thing of unbelievable loathsomeness; a thing not human; huge, black, covered with hair, with eyes of detestable savagery that seemed to glow in the night. He saw the long yellow fangs dripping saliva and blood in the moonlight, heard the slurping sounds of the hideous beast's lustful satisfaction. He struggled wildly, madly in his rage, praying for release. Too late. Too late...

This harrowing scene is not authentic. It was not taken from any known archive nor is it a literal rendering of folkloric legend or time-honored saga. It nonetheless illustrates one of the many ageless superstitions still prevalent today in the Balkans, a belief in the reality of that supernatural nightmare the werewolf; the phenomenon of normal human metamorphosed into hellish, carnivorous animal.

Few regions of the earth are as steeped in occult lore and mystery as the Slavic countries of Eastern Europe. The Balkans, which include Yugoslavia, Romania, Bulgaria, Albania, Greece, and European Turkey, are saturated with it. The Romanian peasantry, in particular, have clung to such beliefs since the time of the Dacians. To them, the werewolf is one of several forms taken by the vampire, the deadly aspect of the lycanthrope. Other aspects are those of the bat (very common), and occasionally the snake and the wild dog. Why these? Because since remote antiquity, indeed since before the Roman conquest, the peoples of Transylvania, Moldavia, and Wallachia regarded the bat as a symbol of evil, the venomous Carpathian viper as a harbinger of death, and the wild dog as a sign of dire misfortune.

In his famous horror classic *Dracula*, Bram Stoker wove such superstition into the stuff of spine-tingling drama; as for example, the electrifying scene in Chapter III where the visiting Englishman, Jonathan Harker, has his first proof of his host's true nature. Harker is already extremely apprehensive, as he says, "full of all sorts of horrible imaginings." Knowing himself to be a prisoner, yet not knowing why, one moonlit night he climbs high into the cold stone of Dracula's dreary castle to gaze upon he knows not what. He finds a narrow window giving access to open air—but let Stoker tell it in Harker's own words.

> As I leaned from the window my eye was caught by something moving a storey below me, and somewhat to my left, where I imagined, from the order of the rooms, that the windows of the Count's own room would look out. The window at which I stood was tall and deep, stone-mullioned, and though weatherworn, was still complete; but it was evidently many a day since the case had been there. I drew back behind the stonework and looked carefully out.
>
> What I saw was the Count's head coming out of the window. I did not see the face, but I knew the man by the neck and the movement of his back and arms. In any case I could not mistake the hands which I had had so many opportunities of studying. I was at first interested and somewhat amused, for it is wonderful how small a matter will interest and amuse a man when he is a prisoner. But my very feelings changed to repulsion and terror when I saw the whole man slowly emerge from the window and begin to crawl down the castle wall over the dreadful abyss, *face down* with his cloak spreading out around him like great wings. At first I could not believe my eyes. I thought it was some trick of the moonlight, some weird effect of shadow; but I kept looking, and it could be no delusion. I saw the fingers and toes grasp the corners of the stones, worn clear of the mortar by the stress of years, and by thus using every projection and inequality move downwards with considerable speed, just as a lizard moves along a wall.
>
> What manner of man is this, or what manner of creature is it in the semblance of man? I feel the dread of this horrible place overpowering me; I am in fear—in awful fear—and there is no escape for me; I am encompassed about with terrors that I dare not think of....

In fear? As well he might be. Dracula of course is without pity. To him, the Prince of Vampires, one of the undead who has existed for centuries, Harker is a mere tool to be used before being slain, fed upon, and cast aside. Harker is the real-estate agent the Count has hired to secure a piece of property for him in England, an appropriately decaying estate called Carfax Abbey. Once he has written the necessary letters to close the transaction he is merely food.

In Balkan folklore, no matter what shape he takes the vampire is always carnal, the way in which he uses his female victims invariably reflecting a lust for their flesh. This is seen in the frightful legend of the *incubus*, a derivative of vampirism, defined in *Webster's* as "an evil spirit supposed to lie upon persons in their sleep and esp. to have sexual intercourse with women by night." Of course, such creatures had their female counterparts, harpies out of hell going all the way back to ancient Greek mythology as in the Gorgon Medusa who was slain by the hero Perseus. *Succuba* is a Latin word for "prostitute" and denotes nothing supernatural. Taken from it, however, is the word *succubus* and that is something else. Again from *Webster's*, "a demon assuming female form to have sexual intercourse with men in their sleep."

With the advent of motion pictures it was obvious that efforts would eventually be made to adapt *Dracula* to the screen. The Germans were the first to achieve it. Directed by Felix Murnau and starring Max Schreck, the classic *Nosferatu* (Romanian for the "undead") is still considered by many critics to be the greatest horror film ever made. The harassed producers were forced to be circumspect, even devious. Bram Stoker was dead but the *Dracula* copyright was still valid. Permission had not been obtained to use the story and Stoker's widow had sued. When the picture was released in Berlin in 1922, five years before the first "talkie," not only its title had been altered but also its setting. Gone were the picturesque towns of Klausenburgh and Bistrita (Stoker called it Bistritz), the fateful Borgo Pass, the snowcapped grandeur of the Carpathians. The north German port of Bremen became the focal point of the plot, the time moved back to 1838. The main characters were all retained. However, in the unique interpretation of the leading role there was an almost Hellenic sense of immutable tragedy. This at least was certainly as Teutonic as it was Grecian.

Nosferatu is not easily described. There is nothing remotely suave or romantic about Count Orlock, as the vampire is called. Hideous to look upon, with enormous claws for fingers, he is evil in its most elemental and repulsive form, a hell-spawned demonic force divorced from all humanity. When he dies it is from exposure to the rays of the rising sun. But he does not die until the heroine, Jonathan Harker's gentle Mina, has voluntarily given herself to him in bodily surrender, staying the night with this frightful animal in order to expose him to daylight and save an unsuspecting world. Supremely sacrificing, she dies in the arms of her husband. The sense of human triumph over Satan is profound. The entranced viewer is left with the feeling of having experienced something incomparably sublime, grand tragedy in the imperishable mold of Aeschylus.

Fortunately, despite a court order that it be destroyed, *Nosferatu* survived and may still be seen in art theaters in many countries of the world. My viewing of it was in Los Angeles about 1940. Again fortunately, the erotically beautiful ending had not been cut.

In America, however, it was a different story. Little real eroticism could be shown on film, at least not in the days of the Hays Office and its successor, the Johnston Office. Sex had to be inferred from Bela Lugosi's famous leer as he hovered lecherously over his intended female victims, or from the nearly as effective expressions on the faces of such actors as Lon Chaney, Jr., Henry Hull, and Spencer Tracy, each of the latter two starring only once in horror pictures, *The Werewolf of London* and *Dr. Jekyll and Mr. Hyde*, respectively.

Appearing in later years, Dracula films imported from England and featuring Christopher Lee were allowed to be a little more obvious, as was a subsequent Hollywood release with Frank Langella as the vampire. However, generally speaking, it was not until the late seventies and early eighties that such films as *The Howling* (John Carradine, Patrick McNee, and a cast of relatively unknown supporting players) emphasized the sexual aspect of werewolves and the on-camera change of human into wolf in scenes of indescribable horror. In one scene, a man and a woman first change into wolves, then unite in a moonlit forest in very graphic coition, a savagely dynamic mating of wild beasts.

As was proved repeatedly, the emphasis on sex in *The Howling* and subsequent horror features sizably increased box-office receipts. However, in the hands of a creative genius imagined carnality, be it in book or film, can often be more arousing than its explicit counterpart. For example, Stoker's *Dracula* was published in 1897 near the end of the Victorian Era, a time known for its strict sexual repression. Yet witness the following. It's the scene in which Harker first makes the acquaintance of the Count's three wives, each of them athirst for his blood, and he yearns for their caresses despite the memory of his fianceé Mina.

> All three had brilliant white teeth that shone like pearls against the ruby of their voluptuous lips. There was something about

> them that made me uneasy, some longing and at the same time some deadly fear. I felt in my heart a wicked, burning desire that they would kiss me with those red lips. It is not good to note this down, lest some day it should meet Mina's eyes and cause her pain; but it is the truth. They whispered together, and then they all three laughed—such a silvery, musical laugh, but as hard as though the sound never could have come through the softness of human lips. . . . The fair girl advanced and bent over me. . . . There was a deliberate voluptuousness which was both thrilling and repulsive, and as she arched her neck she actually licked her lips like an animal, till I could see in the moonlight the moisture shining on the scarlet lips and on the red tongue as it lapped the white sharp teeth. Lower and lower went her head as the lips went below the range of my mouth and chin and seemed to fasten on my throat. Then she paused, and I could hear the churning sound of her tongue as it licked her teeth and lips, and I could feel the hot breath on my neck.

In a scarcely subdued frenzy of anticipation, helpless to save himself, Harker waits breathlessly until spared by Dracula who wants him for his own. This is true to the legends. In them the victim is often willing, longing for the nameless ecstasy of communion with the vampire even while knowing it means certain death. However, the legends seldom speak of male victims. Ever and again down through the dusty ages it's the female the vampire strikes, the female who lies waiting, vibrant with spine-chilling expectancy, who at once gives herself and is taken in the most abject and utter slavery possible to imagine.

Before Universal Studios signed Bela Lugosi to star in the film *Dracula* (released in 1931), he had played the part on the stage in New York and Los Angeles, achieving major successes and widespread notoriety. He said that "over 97 percent" of his fan mail was from women. In a book entitled *The Count: The Life and Films of Bela "Dracula" Lugosi*, his American biographer, Arthur Lennig, quotes the actor in interviews following his Broadway stage appearances, as follows:

> It is *women* who love horror. Gloat over it. Feed on it. Are nourished by it. Shudder and cling and cry out—*and come back for more.*

> Women wrote me letters. Ah, what letters women wrote me! Young girls. Women from seventeen to thirty. Letters of a horrible hunger. Asking me if I cared only for maiden's blood. Asking me if I had done the play because I was in reality that sort of Thing. And through those letters, couched in terms of shuddering, transparent fear, there ran the hideous note of—*hope*.
>
> They hoped that I was DRACULA. They hoped that my love was the love of DRACULA. They gloated over the Thing they dared not understand. . . .
>
> It was the embrace of Death their subconscious was yearning for. Death, the final triumphant lover.
>
> It made me know that the women of America are unsatisfied, famished, craving sensation, even though it be the sensation of death draining the red blood of life.

While making allowances for the dramatic hyperbole to be expected from an intensely emotional actor in such a role—he said more than once that it exhausted him and he attributed his drug addiction to it—this is still quite a statement. However, in significant measure it seems to be supported by known fact. Without women, it appears very doubtful that the myth of the vampire would ever have found a lodging in the human imagination, for the mystique of male-dominant carnality over female helplessness and surrender is deep in the race. It goes back to the time of the cave. For all the efforts of "enlightened" modern men and women to deny it, and they are many, it is still very much with us today.

But what else do the legends say? It all began with the Dacians. Called *Getae* by the Greeks and *Daci* by the Romans, they were a loose confederation of pagan tribes living roughly within the boundaries of modern Romania with some slight encroachment into Hungary. They were warlike by nature. The Roman emperor Augustus claimed them as tributary allies but could not bind them to Rome. They fought the veteran legions of Domitian to a standstill. Not until Trajan defeated them in two campaigns in A.D. 101 and 106 (their greatest chieftain, Decebal, killed himself to escape capture) did Dacia finally become a Roman province and accept Roman colonists. It was these Latin-speaking invaders who gave the region many of its early customs and established among the native stock the Romance language of Romanian.

The Dacians believed in vampires and in a fire-breathing dragon, their primal god, who was thought to have the power to slay them. Over the centuries a rich and varied culture developed that in some respects was similar to that of the Celtic Druids of pre-Roman Britain. The priesthood created the myths. *Devil* and *vampire* became synonymous terms. In time, a spreading cultism, more and more deeply entrenched, became the seemingly imperishable folklore that still exists today.

As regards the weird occultism of the *undead*, it teaches the following beliefs. The ancient legends speak of *the right of passage*. A vampire cannot enter a house unless asked to do so by its occupant nor will a vampire take an intended victim by force. In the novel *Dracula*, Harker unknowingly encounters this in the very beginning, in the first words spoken by his host when the Englishman arrives at the castle. "Welcome to my house! Enter freely and of your own will!"

Christian crosses, garlic, and wolfbane will ward off vampires. They cast no reflection in a mirror. (Harker discovers this early with Dracula.) Becoming incorporeal at will, without fleshly substance, they have the power to pass through walls or even spiderwebs without damaging or disarranging them. They can be killed by a wooden stake driven through the heart. If this is used, the terrible deed must be done between dawn and sunset when they are asleep in their coffins. Other things fatal to them are immersion in water and exposure to sunlight. Once dead, to prevent satanic resurrection they must be buried at a crossroads, preferably by a priest qualified in the holy rite of exorcism.

Again in legend, the most striking thing about vampires, what makes them humanity's most deadly and implacable foes, is the circumstance of their very survival depending on the drinking of blood. This is found in nature in several creatures, the vampire bat, the leech, and the mosquito coming immediately to mind. But in the Romanian *doinas* (peasant folktales), *basme* (fairy tales), and *strigaturi* (rhapsodic poetry) still being told or sung from the Danube to the Polish frontier, the blood that is sucked and drained is always human, and therein lies the crux of the most dire threat ever created in the fecund imagination of men and women. For it is not merely the body that the vampire imperils, but the soul. According to the age-old belief, those unfortunate wretches killed by vampires become vampires themselves and are damned without hope of redemption. Regarding the mixing of the victim's blood with the infernal blood of the vampire, Harker has this frightful prospect indelibly impressed upon him when at last he opens Dracula's coffin.

> Then I saw something which filled my very soul with horror. There lay the Count, but looking as if his youth had been half-renewed, for the white hair and mustache were changed to dark iron-grey; the cheeks were fuller and the white skin seemed ruby-red underneath; the mouth was redder than ever, for on the lips were gouts of fresh blood, which trickled from the corners of the mouth and ran over the chin and neck. . . . It seemed as if the whole awful creature were simply gorged with blood. He lay like a filthy leech, exhausted with his repletion.

Is the average human being then so boundlessly fascinated by the supernatural? Are parapsychology and the dark secrets of the occult so endlessly intriguing? Note the number of people the world over who patronize conjurors or the practitioners of the Black Arts, who witness the otherworldly trances of mediums at séances, who join witches' covens or the often lethal sects of crazed devil worshipers.

What is the most enduring form of motion picture? With the western said to be in decline, it is the horror film. From *Nosferatu* to *The Cabinet of Dr. Caligari;* from *Dracula* and *Frankenstein* to *Dr. Jekyll and Mr. Hyde* and *The Werewolf of London;* from *The Fall of the House of Usher* to *House of Wax*, it is this form of escapism that most totally captivates audiences. Who is the most famous film actor in America? With the older generation it is probably Vincent Price. Who is the most successful American novelist today? Surely, Stephen King ranks close to the top. People want it, seek it out, and are gripped by it. In many cases they are more shaken and influenced than they know. It was so when Oscar Wilde wrote *The Picture of Dorian Gray*, when Edgar Allan Poe wrote *Tales of Mystery and Imagination*, when Henry James wrote *The Turn of the Screw.* It does not change. All matters dealing with the soul, be they of the natural world or the supernatural underworld, are and will remain of the deepest concern to humans. It is simply a fact. It's the way we are.

And in the ancient beliefs, then, was suffering humanity always at the mercy of the vampire? Usually. Except for very rare instances it was not until modern times and the two gripping novels *Carmilla* and *Dracula* that the balance was seen to alter. In *Carmilla*, really a novella in the short length class of *Dr. Jekyll and Mr. Hyde*, the woman of the title is the passionate drinker of blood, already a century and a half dead when she encounters the heroine Laura and comes very close to claiming her.

However, as told by its Irish author, Sheridan Le Fanu, this jewel of a horror story, maintaining nearly unbearable suspense to the last, ends with the fatal stake through the vampire's heart, decapitation and cremation, and so alluring is the beautiful, Sapphic-minded Carmilla that many a reader must have regretted her passing.

As for Dracula, there is no question that Stoker was influenced by Le Fanu's earlier tale. Indeed, there are those who have credited *Carmilla* with being the prototype for Stoker's Gothic masterpiece. In Stoker's powerful rendering it is Professor Abraham Van Helsing, the Dutch authority on vampires, who valiantly defies Dracula, thwarts him in his efforts to gain mastery over the heroine, and eventually destroys him. Van Helsing, not Harker, is the true hero of the story. It has been suggested by more than one critic that Van Helsing may have been Stoker's alter ego; that the fact that they shared the same first name was more than mere coincidence. This is entirely possible. Stoker admired heroism. On one occasion he met Sir Richard Burton, a man who was at least half a mystic as well as a renowned explorer, writer, and linguist who shared with John Hanning Speke the discovery and mapping of unexplored central Africa's Lake Tanganyika. Burton was to write a remarkable English translation of the fabled *Arabian Nights* in sixteen volumes. But to Stoker, ever the romantic, this incredible feat would have been overshadowed by another. For Burton, master of Oriental languages, with his skin darkly stained and with great daring, was the first non-Muslim ever to penetrate the forbidden Arabian cities of Mecca and Medina, literally risking his head. He did it alone. Stoker would have understood that.

As this is a biography of the historic Dracula, it may be asked why I have felt it necessary to say so much about the fictitious one. It is because the two are inextricably interlocked, perhaps for all time. If the real prince had not possessed such a bloodthirsty and vicious character, Stoker would not have selected him as the logical figure on whom to base his vampire. Conversely, if Stoker had not created his sanguinary Count, largely from legend aided by the imagination, the real Dracula would have remained more mythical than historic and such books as this would probably never be written.

What in essence, then, is the contention? Is Bram Stoker the true discoverer of Dracula? No, he is not, at least not in the sense that a painstaking scholar may discover a once important person who for some reason has been swept into the dustbin of history. But in this modern epoch he is in a very real sense Dracula's chief publicist, the man whose remarkable novel raised the dread Wallachian from virtually total obscurity into the light of public awareness. It doesn't matter that for long decades Stoker's creation was just a story, its main character thoroughly fictitious in the eyes of millions. Without it, without the widespread publicity it attracted and the many films it later inspired on both sides of the Atlantic, it is highly doubtful that the Dracula who lived and breathed would ever have been revealed.

But what of this bloody prince in his own era? Was he not infamous in the fifteenth century, his name notorious not only in the Balkans but in the expanding Ottoman territories, parts of the German Empire, and south Russia? Was he not known even to Pope Pius II in Rome? Yes, all this is true. Very largely due to the work of printers of the time, such as the Englishman Caxton and the German Gutenberg, the Dracula horror tales were widely disseminated, very popular reading of the day, and doubtlessly often embellished for maximum effect. But though the Germans and Turks might have savagely condemned him during his lifetime, and the Rus (Russians) regarded him as harsh but justified, once he was dead he was quickly forgotten by all but the peasantry of his native Romania. To them he was a hero who fought for the land and its people, fought as few had ever done, and gradually his story was woven into ballad and legend. For them it was easy to overlook his cruelties, especially as most were inflicted on foreigners. In the end, curiously, they paid him what is perhaps the highest tribute of which a people are capable. In Britain it had been paid to the sixth-century Celtic king Arthur Pendragon; in Germany to the twelfth-century crusading emperor, Friedrich Barbarossa. It is the ultimate accolade of immortality, the belief of the common man and woman that when the people are in need and the land in danger, the once-buried sovereign will return.

Dracula, the cold-blooded sadist and grim, remorseless genocide, clearly did not deserve such a signal honor despite his undoubted value as a bulwark against the Turks. But perhaps we shouldn't be too hard on Romania's long-suffering people. Invaded by Greeks, Romans, Goths, Huns, Avars, Bulgars, Magyars, Pechenegs, Cumans, Saxons, Mongols, Hungarians, Russians, and Turks, perhaps they can be excused for giving their loyalty, even their sadly misplaced regard in some cases, to one of the few of their number in centuries who not only held a vastly superior enemy in check for a considerable time but very seriously bloodied him.

So let us to the task then. Goethe, the German poet and dramatist of the Enlightenment, the philosopher who brought a deeper insight to the curious legend of Faust than any other, once said that we should explore the explorable and quietly revere the unexplorable. But he also believed that knowledge must be sought with unrelenting persistence, for otherwise human beings would cease to explore. Surely this credo is applicable to the pursuit of the historic Dracula.

2
Christendom Faces the Ottoman Empire

They were far from the coast now, so far he knew he would have to climb to the highest of these white, windswept summits to view once again the waters of the Black Sea and the port of Varna in whose God-accursed outlying marshes he'd lost much of his army. For it was *his* army, never the king's. Ladislas had won battles last year, had bled the Turks because of *his* tactics, the tactics of János Hunyadi. But this was another time, this ill-omened year of 1444, a day of resounding victory for the Turks and crushing defeat for the Christians. Ladislas, King of Poland and Hungary, was twenty years old but he would never be twenty-one. He lay somewhere on the battlefield, torn by the Muslim swords and spears, maybe pierced by their arrows, and not even an intact fighting force to find him and take him back to distant Buda.

Seated as he was in the snow, shaking with cold, Hunyadi shifted his weight against the enormous granite boulder and tried to ease his back. For a long moment he gazed at his war-horse. Tethered only yards away, the black gelding was caparisoned in white and gold, but his saddlecloth was streaked with blood. White stained with scarlet, as he had seen him spattered before. And he, Hunyadi, *voivod* of Transylvania these three years, warlord, the most powerful man in the kingdom—no, in all of Eastern Europe, saving not even the Byzantine emperor and the pope himself. He had been called the Savior of Christendom—the White Knight. Would they ever call him that again? What was he now but a beaten, hunted fugitive in these frozen wastes of Dobrogea? Murad was victor. He'd defeated Murad before, but now the sultan had avenged those losses. Oh God, how he had avenged them! And the voivod was fifty-nine, already old by any standard. That's why the Wallachians had let him stop here to rest. They didn't dare kill him yet. He was known to have left the battlefield alive and Dracul could not risk it, not until he knew their thinking in Buda, *Hungarian* thinking. Dracul was not the man to gamble on a Magyar invasion. He was calculating and cool. Damn him. *Damn* him!

His black thoughts screwed his brow into a frown. What an irony to be saved by these men when his own Hungarians had fled the field. The Magyars and Poles had been outflanked, broken off the action and fallen back, many of them drowned in the marshes—but the Wallachians had held. They had held longer than anyone, then retired by another route. They were as valiant as any troops he'd ever seen.

He heard a rustling noise, saw a Hungarian officer approaching through the whiteness. It was Ferenc Arany, one of the very few of his countrymen who was still with him. Hunyadi got to his feet.

"Arany? What is it? Do they want to move on?"

The tall young man came up to him and bowed slightly. He was clearly embarrassed for his leader's plight, the once-powerful man subject to the whims of such as these. "Not yet, my lord," he said. "Their leader, Karadja, thinks their main body may be behind us somewhere. He has scouts out. He wants to give them a chance to catch us up."

"Who commands their main body?"

"I think Prince Mircea."

"Ah. Dracul's whelp." Hunyadi straightened his back. "He survived then. In the absence of his cowardly father he commands the entire Wallachian contingent, such as it is. How can they know his whereabouts now?"

"I don't think they do, my lord. But they assume the main force is somewhere to our rear. Mircea would likely be with them."

"If he didn't cut and run like the cur he is."

Arany frowned and chewed at his lip. "Your pardon, my lord, but I must speak the truth. I saw him on the battlefield. He fought bravely."

"They are the reason we lost."

"My lord?"

"The Draculas play a double game. They always have. One foot in the Christian camp, the other with the Ottomans. Dracul could have committed his entire army to this crusade, at least 30,000 men, and led them himself. And what did he send us? Four thousand soldiers, and commanded by a stripling who does not believe in our cause, who was spreading defeatism in Tirgoviste before we took the field if my agents spake sooth. Oh I know they blame me and the king for breaking the Peace of Seghedin, but only a craven fool would pretend it was ever real. Murad's mind is on conquest. If Europe doesn't bestir itself, mark you, a day will come when his janissaries will stand at the gates of Buda and Vienna. Yes, it will come, captain. You may count upon it. And if not by the hand of Murad, then by that of his son, the one the Turks call Mehmed."

"Mehmed, my lord?"

"In Arabic, Mohammed. Our spies say his father may step down for him. It could happen at any time."

"On the heels of the father's victory, my lord?"

"Possibly. Murad's goals are likely to change. Despite what happened to us yesterday, he has more the reputation of a lover than a fighter."

Arany beat his hands together against the cold. He seemed to be watching the congealed moisture of their exhalations. "And both of the royal pair are in a position to kill Dracul's hostage sons, I believe. The Turks lay careful plans."

"Do you make excuses for Dracul?"

"A son is a son, my lord. Two sons—"

"Are two sons."

"Yes, my lord."

"Yet Dracul sent his 4000 men. A sufficient provocation to the Muslims."

"Maybe he thinks the sultan will forgive that paltry gesture. Dracul is both a Christian and a Draconist. He is bound to the crusade—up to a point."

"He's bound to hell, Arany. He'd sacrifice his sons in a minute if he thought it would favor his political position. It's infamous!" Feeling his voice ready to break, Hunyadi paused to get control of himself. "It's infamous, Arany. History—history will record that yesterday, the tenth of November, the White Knight of the Magyars—lost Hungary."

"My lord—"

"It is true. Even the Pope will say that God was not with us. I know Eugene IV, a true ascetic but a scheming Venetian nonetheless. He will take the death of the cardinal as a sign from heaven."

"The cardinal, my lord?"

"Giuliano Cesarini died in the battle. You did not know?"

"No, my lord."

"The armor of a papal legate is no thicker than ours. I'm told his body is lost to us as well. Unrecovered." Hunyadi was looking at the deep dent in Arany's breastplate, apparently the result of a pike thrust. "I am cold," he said. "These mountains will freeze us all if we tarry here any longer."

"Or the Muslims will kill us more quickly."

Hunyadi had begun to walk toward his horse and Arany went with him. Both men had exchanged their icy steel cuirasses for Wallachian sheepskin shakos and jerkins, and were slapping their arms to increase their circulation.

"Murad will have lost valuable time," said Hunyadi, "delaying their pursuit. He holds with Turkish tradition. He will stay three days on the battlefield burying their dead, then dine among the Christian slain. By the blood of the martyrs, may the stench rot his nostrils!"

"It's a stupid custom," said Arany.

"Yes, it is stupid." Reaching his charger's side, Hunyadi stopped to smooth the dark fur of the animal's neck with a loving hand. "But when his turn comes, Mehmed will not adhere to it, I can tell you that. From what I know of that young devil he would not lose an hour, not for his dead or ours or anyone's. He'd stay on our track like a demon out of hell and bleed us for every foot of ground. No quarter, you understand? Slaughter to the last man."

"Is he so formidable, my general? An unfledged hawk, is he not? A callow boy without battle experience."

Hunyadi shrugged. "Now, yes. It's just a feeling I have about him. He is fifteen and thinks only of war and killing. His own janissaries call him Wolfeyes behind his back. Some of them think he is mad." He loosed the rein, tossed it over the horse's neck, and mounted. "I know this breed of Turk. He has sworn to take Constantinople after he ascends the throne, and before a beard can grow long enough to be sworn on in the name of the Prophet. And who is to stop him now, Arany? The Emperor Constantine has courage but the Byzantines are finished. Their walls are strong but their will is said to be weak, and the city is their last stronghold. They think all Christian Europe will rally to their cause, especially Genoa and Venice, but it will not. The Paleologus dynasty will perish in the city and Wolfeyes will trod on the cross on the altar of Sancta Sophia. So their *imams* have prophesied—and so he has promised."

As Hunyadi rode his horse slowly toward the troops waiting nearby, Arany kept pace at his stirrup. It was starting to snow again. Ordinarily, this might have concerned Hunyadi but he wasn't thinking of it. He was seeing the frightful carnage of that stricken field, hearing the triumphant shouts of the victors, the dying screams of the vanquished as the remorseless steel of the blades and lances and arrows cut through them. History would call it the Battle of Varna because of that port's proximity. There the Bulgarians had crushed the Byzantines nearly eight centuries ago. There the Ottomans had defeated the flower of Christian chivalry and slaughtered a Christian king—only yestereve.

"Karadja comes to meet us," said Arany, gesturing in the Wallachian's direction. "I think we can trust him only until he gets new orders."

Hunyadi did not respond to the remark. As the snow fell faster, he was dimly aware of Karadja's approach but his mind was far away. Hungary, the land of his fathers. Buda, the city of his power. Would he ever see it again? And if he saw it, would he be able to rally support after this bloody debacle? He was sure of only three things. First, if he survived and retained enough influence he would break Dracul as he'd done before, giving the crown of Wallachia to the rival Danesti claimant, Prince Vladislav. Second, it was only a question of time now before the Turks unleashed their promised offensive against Eastern Europe. Third, now that his darkest hour was upon him, his life, his fortune, and his two little sons at hazard, he must think and plan and struggle as never before; and when the time was ripe, he must gamble all on one throw of the dice.

He heard Karadja address him and nodded to that officer half-uncomprehendingly. What did it matter what route they took, up the Danube to Buda or to his castle of Hunedoara in Transylvania? The Wallachians would soon abandon them anyway, or kill them. He was a fatalist and had always been so, believing that what was to be would be. Had the scouts found the main body? Probably. Would they try to join it now despite the renewed snowfall? Very likely, for the Wallachians were a mad lot and stubborn. He saw Karadja's mount release dung, saw it fall steaming into the universal whiteness. Other horses were whinnying as the cavalry took to their saddles. Arany rode up to him on his gray and raised a gauntleted hand in salute. The old élan.

"We know it's Mircea now, my lord," he said. "The scouts have come in. He's only a mile or two behind us. The riding will warm us up, I think."

"Yes," said Hunyadi. "Lead on, Arany. I'll keep your crupper in sight."

Mircea. The name lapped at the edges of his mind as they moved out. Prince Mircea of the House of Basarab, eldest son of Dracul. A sixteen-year-old boy to whom a fool of a father had given the equivalent of a general's rank, then sent to fight a seasoned and wily enemy. Wasn't it enough for Dracul that two of his sons were already prisoners of the Turks in Egrigöz? The older one, Vlad, had the same mother as Mircea, so they said. The father might as well forget them. He, Hunyadi, could probably save his children from being murdered even in defeat, but Dracul could never save his. After this, the Muslims would cut off their heads and send them to him pickled. Blind them at the very least. This being so, what good did it do Dracul to hold back, to send his ally so little help when so much more had been desperately needed? Either way he would pay the same price, and now that the whole campaign had been lost the crusade would drown in its own blood.

Somewhere wolves were howling in this land of defeat and desolation. The beasts would find shelter in caves soon. They were smarter than men, he thought. Maybe that was why they called Mehmed Wolf-eyes, because he was like them.

Hunyadi half-turned in his saddle, trying to ease his left leg. He knew the calf was open again and bleeding. Not deep but painful. A scimitar slash that had cut between the steel greaves. As the pain bit harder his features twisted into a scowl. Then he saw the bitter irony and spat disgustedly into the snow. Untended by chirurgeons, with nary a leech to bleed him properly and drain off the poisonous humors, maybe the wound would mortify in this howling wilderness, rot him, fell him like a bludgeoned ox, in the end claim his life. That would save the scheming courtiers in Buda the trouble of assassinating him, wouldn't it? Maybe they would expect him to fall on his sword like King Saul after Mount Gilboa or Brutus and Cassius after Philippi. They would be disappointed.

He began to whistle softly to himself. Fate could reverse its remorseless course again, and yet again. He was the White Knight of Christendom, bloody but unbowed. He had beaten the Turks more times than he could remember. Even their vaunted general, Mezid-Bey, he'd destroyed only two years ago at Sibiu. In Buda they would crown a new king and he, János Hunyadi, would still be needed. All he had to do was to avoid being murdered at the hands of this boy, Mircea. He'd deposed Dracul once. He'd depose him again. Maybe the Draculas would hesitate to act and thus undo themselves.

By the time they sighted Mircea's mounted vanguard he had controlled his dark mood of depression. He was resilient he reminded himself, none more so, and could survive defeats. He was good at intrigue, nearly as adept as Sultan Murad. All he had to do was to outwit Dracul and his whoreson, take control in Buda before the next coalition could unite against him, then recruit a new army and train it in time to meet the Turk. The game was invigorating and he'd played it for years. He *liked* the game.

As they topped the next rise in the trail he actually smiled. The game? Since when was it impossible to turn it to ultimate victory? Seen dimly through the falling snow, Mircea's now visible horsemen were a welcome sight.

The thing that had brought a Christian army under Hunyadi and Ladislas III so far to the east to fight the Turks on the shore of the Black Sea was neither coincidence nor accident, as battles so often are. The Crusade of Varna, as it was later called, was carefully planned. In spirit it had the support of Pope Eugene IV. Yet, as it was fought only short months after his final victory over the Council of Basel, the Pontiff had found himself too domestically preoccupied to vigorously preach the crusade and too politically weak to effectively support it.

The trouble was Christian division and Turkish strength. The trouble was a world west of the Bosporus that claimed to believe in Christ but could not agree on how to worship him; and a world east of that strait in warlike, fanatical unity under Allah and his prophet Mohammed.

The Christians made heavy swords that sometimes could cut through helmets and chain mail, and they often turned them against other Christians. The Muslims made "scimitars of light" as they called them, blades wrought in Damascus that could slice through floating silk. But every Muslim weapon was made to kill Christians, not the Sons of the Faithful, the Children of Allah. Muslim did not fight Muslim.

The horses of the Christians were tall and strong, unusually heavy and not very fast. They carried armor as nobly as the knights who rode them. The horses of the Ottomans were smaller and much lighter, a desert breed of usually white Arabians, "the drinkers of the wind." No armor slowed their pace. In battle they galloped circles around the stalwart Percheron of the foe. On long campaigns they outpaced them by ten miles to one.

Christian leaders were occasionally murdered by their own men, so easy it was to settle an old score with an arrow or crossbow quarrel in the back. The punishment was hanging. Turkish officers were seldom so assassinated. The punishment was to have the eyes removed by a pair of thumbs, then to be sewn up in the skin of a pig until dead of shock and loss of blood. Contact with the pig was denial of paradise, an absolute assurance of descent into the Muslim hell. That was why Christian prisoners did the skinning. The satisfaction of killing a comrade in arms was scarcely worth it.

Between the two sides perhaps the most vital difference of all was one of a deeply ingrained belief, an article of faith. When the Christian was killed in battle he might go to heaven—or he might not. It depended entirely on whether he had been a good son of the Church and had given ample demonstrations of his faith. But with the follower of Islam there was no such requirement. If he died fighting the infidel salvation was certain and the Koran guaranteed it. No matter what his past life had been. No matter if his faith were sufficiently proved. Let him but fall at the hands of the enemy and within moments he would lie in the soft arms of the *houris*, most beautiful of women, transported by one of ten thousand angels. Allah's reward was gratification of the flesh.

The rise and development of these two forces that were now set on destroying each other makes a fascinating story. We must tell a little of it. For to understand the demon personality of Dracula one must know something of the world that produced him and of how that world came to be.

As has been said, the Romans conquered Dacia very early. However, by the late second century Roman strength was already in sharp decline. With Commodus (A.D. 180–192), self-indulgent and brutal son of the illustrious Marcus Aurelius, began irreversible internal decay and increasing anarchy, to the point where the laurel wreath of the Caesars went to the highest bidder. The process continued unchecked. In 265, the emperor Valerian fell prisoner to the Persians, an unprecedented catastrophe. In the following reign, that of Aurelian, the increasing pressure of barbarian German tribes forced the legions to abandon their trans-Danubian holdings and to cross that river into Moesia, today called

Bulgaria. The withdrawal was permanent. Never again would Roman power be felt north of the Danube.

A thousand years passed. During this time the Daco-Romans, as the Latinized natives of the land came to be called, settled extensively in the Transylvanian plateau, a region noted by Hungarian scribes as Transsilva or the "Land beyond the Forest." Some did not stay. As the legionaries had once moved south for sound military reasons, so in the course of several migrations did thousands of Transylvanians move southeastward through the mountain passes to escape the aggressive Hungarians. The land to which they came they had called Muntania or Greater Wallachia in the east and Oltenia or Lesser Wallachia in the west. Now as emigrants encountering more Latin-speaking people than ever before, they gave the entire area a new name more befitting the Romanized tongue, "the Land of the Romanians," Tara Romaneasca.

This area southeast of Transylvania was the homeland of the Draculas. Though in theory a march or border region of the Byzantine Empire, from the sixth to the eleventh centuries it was occupied in succession by the Lombards, the Avars, and the Bulgarians. By the twelfth century it had fallen to the Cumans, a wild Turkic tribe related to the Avars, who were then defeated by the all-conquering Mongols in the year 1240. Even this wave of savage conquest eventually receded. When it did, the native population left their mountain retreats, descending to the more heavily forested river valleys to found the principality of Wallachia in 1290, their first prince being Radu Negru or Rudolf the Black.

At roughly this time, the sister principality of Moldavia came into being to the north with its capital at Suceava. Campulung, on the southern watershed of the Transylvanian Alps (Prahova River Valley) was Wallachia's first capital. Curtea de Arges (on the Arges River) was the second; today an all-but-forgotten town, it was the burial place of Romanian kings.

By 1310, when Basarab cel Mare (the Great) came to the throne of Wallachia as the second prince of the line, a state in being had definitely been established, something that did not occur in Moldavia until the accession of Prince Dragos in 1352. But little is known about Basarab and his title of distinction remains an enigma.

From the standpoint of documents that can be verified, the history of the Wallachian dynasty really begins with Mircea cel Bătrîn (the Old), Dracula's grandfather, who came to the throne as the seventh prince in

1386. He was an excellent soldier. He was also an expansionist who broadened his holdings through successful military operations. In the course of time he crossed the Carpathians with his army to invest and take the duchies of Amlas to the west and Fagaras to the north. The Banat of Severin fell to his attacks. And everywhere he built defensive strongholds against the Hungarians on one frontier and the Turks on the other.

Ultimately, this prince extended Wallachian power to the Danube River, where he built the fortress of Giurgiu as a bulwark against the Ottomans. In Dobrogea (the land along the Black Sea in which János Hunyadi was eventually to lose the Battle of Varna), he launched an offensive in 1389 and again was victor, thereafter continuing the construction of fortifications. Few men saw more clearly the ever-present threat of Islamic invasion or reacted with more vigor. In this year the stubborn Serbian resistance against the Turks collapsed. In this year, also, the Ottomans won the bloody battle of Kosovo, defeating the Christian host and with it the small Wallachian force that Mircea had committed. For a while he stood on the defensive and made the Muslims pay in blood. Then, recognizing the situation as hopeless, in 1391 he became the first Romanian ruler to pay tribute to the Porte, the government of the Ottoman Empire.

Throughout his entire reign Mircea had but one respite from Turkish pressure though it endured for fifteen years. It began in 1402 when the Mongol ruler Tamerlane (Timur-i-Leng or Timur the Lame), having conquered Turkistan, Persia, and south Russia, having taken Delhi in India and the Caliphate of Baghdad, invaded the Ottoman Empire. The decisive battle was fought at Ankara. Sultan Bayezid I was defeated and captured. Only Tamerlane's territorial ambitions in China and return to his distant Asian capital of Samarkand saved the Turkish Empire from utter destruction.

Predictably, the Turks reestablished their power. By 1417 they were once more predominant and again Mircea paid them tribute, 3000 ducats annually. He did not lose all sovereignty. Wallachia was not forced to become a *pashalik* (Turkish province) as defeated Bulgaria had been, nor was the principality's land confiscated. Even the Wallachian nobility, the boyars, remained intact as a class. Unusual? Perhaps, but hardly the "miracle" that some Romanian historians have called it. Military occupations are costly in treasure and sometimes in blood; the Ottomans knew the danger of becoming overextended; still ahead lay their long-cherished goal of taking Christian Constantinople, all of the Balkans, and their even more ambitious plans for the conquest of Hungary, Austria, and Bohemia, in effect all central Europe. Wallachia could wait.

In 1418, the year after Mircea's final capitulation, he died. There followed a succession of short-lived princes, some of them illegitimate, more than one overthrown by violence. Mihail I (1418–1420) was the eldest of Mircea's legitimate sons. He was followed by Dan II (1420–1431), a nephew. Then came the broken reign of another son of Mircea, Radu II, called "the Bald," whose repeated tenures of the throne (1421, 1423, 1424, 1426–1427) give the clearest evidence of Wallachian political instability. Alexandru I, called Aldea (1431–1436), came next as brother followed brother. He was illegitimate. Born on "the wrong side of the blanket" also was Vlad II, called Dracul, the father of Dracula. Ascending the throne on Aldea's death he was to rule twice: from the winter of 1436 to the fall of 1442 and from the spring of 1443 to the winter of 1447. At the opening of his first reign he was forty-one years old.

Vlad Dracul inherited a situation ripe for disaster. Since the decline of the pagan Mongols the Muslim Turks were now fast becoming the most formidable military power on earth, with an army which in size, training, discipline, and fanaticism approached that of the nearly unbeatable Mongol *ka-khans*. In the Turkish capital city of Adrianople sat Sultan Murad II and his war council. They were sometimes at odds. The council maintained that all of Europe should be invaded and subjugated to Islam, first the east, and after its consolidation, the west. They believed it was possible. On the Danube River, once they had taken Belgrade there was no fortified city of any size until they got to Hungary's capital of Buda and laid siege to it. Murad hesitated. He visualized a hostile European coalition of enormous size: Hungary, Poland, Bohemia, the Holy Roman Empire, possibly even France, and all of it ranged against them. The fighting emirs of the council shook their heads. Paris would never ally itself to Vienna. Smash the Balkans first, they advised, then defeat the states of central Europe in detail, Hungary, Austria, Bohemia. Ultimately, further resistance could be paralyzed through the use of terror.

According to what the imams preached in the mosques, endless conflict was inevitable. They prophesied this to the multitudes. Once they had fanned the flames of *jihad*, or holy war, Murad knew he would oppose it at his peril. Speaking with the voice of Allah, the prophet Mohammed had stated it clearly in one of the most compelling *suras* of the Koran. "Warfare is ordained for you." In the tops of the minarets the *muezzins* called the faithful to prayer and the faithful came. The glorious past was invoked. Had not Haroun-al-Rashid listened to the inspired imams of Baghdad and conquered the whole of the Middle East? Had not Mahmud of Ghazni heard the voice of Afghanistan's *mullahs* before reducing Khorasan and laying waste northern India?

Murad was not a conquerer born but he feared assassination.

Warfare is ordained for you!

Dracul caught the martial wind from the southeast and knew its meaning. And in the northwest lay militant, expansionist Hungary, known as the Arpadian kingdom. Their battle steeds were champing at the bit. In the capital at Buda the war party sharpened its sword and looked southward, waiting for the moment when the Turkish Porte's attention might be elsewhere. That sword's cutting edge was a fine army, Dracul knew, a Magyar army, high-spirited, professional in part, drawing its inspiration from fierce Magyar tradition. Why did both Buda and the Porte want Wallachia? To the Hungarians it was the only logical buffer against the Turks. To the Turks it was one of several important staging areas from which to mount an attack against Europe. Neither side could allow Wallachia to fall into the hands of the other.

To meet this double threat Dracul had neither more nor less strength than his father Prince Mircea. The Wallachian army, at most times numbering about 35,000 men, was drawn largely from peasant levies. They were not feudal. The boyar nobility did not control them. Fortunately for Dracul, Mircea had been a strong ruler and had broken feudal power. Fortunately also for him, no boyar leader had risen to restore it during the passive reigns of his brothers. It meant the boyars were nearly helpless, no longer able to retain private armies large enough to be dangerous. It gave the advantage to the princes. They could suppress the boyars. Yet let one weak ruler appear at a time of boyar strength and the entire picture could be reversed. Dracul could never afford to let down his guard. To do so would mean his death and that of every member of his family in the Wallachian capital of Tirgoviste, and the permanent eclipse of his dynasty. He must be nimble. He must be shrewd. Above all, he must be lucky.

Dracul had always accounted himself lucky. Years of playing at touch-and-go with fate had convinced him of the reality of his good fortune. But it was already late on the calendar of destiny. The handwriting was on the wall. Time was running out for him.

* * *

In its long and violent history the city had had several names: Uscudama, Hadrianopolis, Orestia, Adrianople, Edirne. Much had happened here since the Roman emperor Hadrian had rebuilt it on the site of an earlier Thracian settlement. Many battles had been fought. In A.D. 378 the emperor Valens had been defeated and killed by the Visigoths, opening the way for the barbarian invasion of Greece. The Greeks had defeated the Bulgarians in 1254. Avars, Bulgars, and Crusaders had invaded in turn. Now it was Turkish.

Seated on luxurious ottomans with his staff and three of his wives, Murad II thought of these things, for he was fond of history. On all sides rose the mountains of Thrace, beautiful in their primal grandeur. To his rear lay the city, sprawling across the Tundzha River at its confluence with the Maritsa. To his front lay a vast open field. The noise of the war games brought him back to the events of the moment. His eager emirs, generals all, were watching with the fixed attention of falconers on a hunt. Two of his wives did the same. Only his current favorite, the intense and lascivious Aminah, was vaguely aloof and disinterested. Perhaps it befitted her, he thought. After all, was she not the namesake of the Prophet's mother? Her business was not war but love and the begetting of children, her battlefield the seraglio and the divan, her weapon that of sweet exhaustion. Yes, better an Arab than a Turkish name for her. The name of Aminah must surely bring glory and luck.

Turning again to glance at her veiled face he saw only her eyes, their long-lashed lids darkened with kohl. Ah what sights they had seen in her sixteen years of life, those black, burning orbs. Slave to a whoremaster at nine. Dancer in a brothel. Palace concubine. Wife to a sultan. Half-bemused, Murad realized he was indeed becoming the voluptuary men thought him to be, devoted to delight, not slaughter. Was that an offense against Allah? After the death of his beloved Khadija, Mohammed himself had had many wives. When he died it was in the arms of Ayesha, most carnal of them all.

Murad frowned. Wife to a sultan? What did it matter? He was that no longer. After his victory at Varna he had voluntarily abdicated. Mehmed had ruled these two years. His son, who at seventeen was so sure of his position, could afford not to attend the games at will, afford to have his soldiers see his ottoman vacant, have them question his devotion to them. That was Wolfeyes, as they called him. Vain and arrogant he was, yet ferocious in his anger. He was respected only for his bravery, and even that was but newly acquired.

Suddenly, his attention was riveted by a commotion on the field and he raised his hand to shield his eyes from the glare. Another fight? Yes, it seemed to be. This time it was not the janissaries but the horsemen, the mounted *spahis*. He couldn't see them clearly. Already the sun was well above the main peak of the Istranca Dag, pouring across the Black Sea and the Marmara Denizi in blinding rays of gold. He turned to the tall emir closest to him.

"The army is restless today, Ilderim."

The general nodded. "Yes, my lord."

"The army is the Sword of Allah, I believe, as renowned for its discipline as for its valor. Is that not true?"

"It is true, O Light of the World."

"Issue orders to stop that immediately!"

The emir rose and bowed. "I obey, lord."

As the general turned to address a subordinate, Murad spoke to no one in particular. "By Allah, these are *games*. These are not war itself. If they can't get enough blood in local campaigns we'll send them to the Gobi wastes and let them fight the Mongols. Maybe the descendants of Hulagu Khan will accommodate them."

Though all had heard him, no one spoke. Hulagu, grandson of Genghis, had smashed the Abbāsid Caliphate and ended it forever. Turks remembered. Outside the walls of surrendered Baghdad the Mongol had made an enormous pyramid of 200,000 skulls.

Murad's interest quickened now. He saw a mounted herald ride out to the *spahis* who had already separated, speak to them briefly, then saw them rejoin their squadron. In the center of the field the janissaries had formed in a Greeklike phalanx. Now the *spahis* trotted away, 3000 of them, wheeled about at the north end of the amphitheater, then came on in a canter with lances at the vertical. Green pennons. Lanceheads glittering in the sun. They were charging the janissaries. As their blooded Arabians broke into a gallop the lances were lowered. The janissaries stood like rocks, waiting, rank upon rank in their white felt caps, rank upon rank of shining chain mail and shields behind bristling spears. To their rear were their own corps of archers, bows raised and drawn, the nocks of the arrows against their jaws. They would shoot over the heads of the *spahis*. Arrows jutting from the ground would be broken by cavalry; horses felled by them could break their legs. Skill was the thing, and timing. If shot accurately the shafts would fall just behind the thundering horsemen, who would break away to right and left. The janissaries would then alter front to defend their flanks while the *spahis* reformed and the mock warfare would continue.

To a man the emirs were now leaning forward on their cushions, hands clutching crossed and booted calves, some pressing down the hilts of scimitars. As the cavalry swept past they shouted in their excitement. Bowstrings were released. Arrows hummed through the air in a long whining crescendo of sound. Behind the charging steeds, when the dust cleared, stood a riderless horse. A *spahi* was on the ground. At first he seemed unhurt. Then, as he staggered to his feet, the stump of a broken arrow was seen projecting from his shoulder. The unacceptable had happened. A skilled bowman of the janissaries had shot low by *several feet*.

Murad heard an emir curse. Behind him a group of favored imams and dervishes chattered excitedly as his wives muttered in huddled conclave. He got to his feet and everyone else rose with him. He spoke to the officer standing nearest him.

"Emir Osman."

The officer bowed. "Yes, my lord."

"The games are ended."

"My lord?"

"End them, general."

"Yes, my lord. Immediately."

As the man strode hurriedly away Murad spoke to another. "Emir Ilderim."

"Yes, my lord."

"'Tis a strange day, a day of ill omen. The janissaries are sullen and making mistakes. Their commander Ibrahim is frustrated. Anyone can see it. You have as many spies as I do. Tell me what is happening."

Ilderim looked abashed, hesitant. "My lord, I—"

Murad heard the rumble of the kettledrums now, huge iron caldrons with their drumheads covered with rawhide. That tattoo, so often dreaded by their enemies, summoned the janissaries to war or council but was beaten now to restore discipline. That this should be necessary shocked and appalled him, making his lip curl in anger.

"Speak, general. I'm losing patience."

Framed in its black beard, Ilderim's mouth grew thin. "It's the sultan, O Great One, may Allah defend him. The janissaries—the—"

"Yes?"

"There was a reported incident last night, my lord."

"Yes?"

The tall emir frowned his reluctance to continue. "The sultan—"

"My son. Yes?" Murad felt himself short of breath, as always when he was nervous. He sucked in his paunch and tried to stand taller. "Yes? Yes?"

"The sultan, may he live forever, had a slave, a young Circassian boy I believe recently acquired."

"Yes, I know of him."

"Last night some janissaries were restive. I'm told they were smoking hashish. One of them took the boy to his tent and, well, enjoyed him. The boy talked to a harem eunuch. The eunuch told the sultan. When the janissaries were questioned by the sultan's *tsaushes* not one of them informed on the wrongdoer. They said the royal bodyguard had no right to interrogate them, and quoted military regulations. The sultan—the sultan then summoned a body of archers, chose three janissaries at random, and had them executed. We think this is why the Exalted One is not here today, my lord. The whitecaps are licking their wounds, full of menace and lust for revenge. Perhaps—perhaps even mutinous. I believe the Grand Vizier advised him not to come."

Murad was thunderstruck. To kill janissaries like this without trial was worse than breaking the laws of the state. It defied the laws of Allah. Oh why had it been his favorite son who drowned, his beloved Al-ad-Din? Why could it not have been this one? This vicious, sadistic... he found himself choking on the word that came to his tongue and swallowed it down. He imagined he could see the condemned janissaries, the *tsaushes* with green kaftans as their judges. The tall caps of the doomed men were removed as they tied them to the posts. As the arrows tore through their chests their shaved heads fell forward, the long scalplocks hanging down in front. The Sword of Islam they were and Mehmed cut them down like chaff, *unjustly*. What would *this* do to army morale? What would it do to the most famous fighting corps Asia had seen since the *predoomed battalions* of the Mongols? Mehmed's mother was wild and willful. Murad despised her now. Why could she not have been like his Christian wife Mara, his tender Serbian? Ah the black day that he had been conceived. Better than his mother's womb should have shriveled and her breasts given no suck.

He thought of the lines he'd composed after his victory at Varna. His lips moved silently.

Cup-bearer, pour me again of yesterday's wine;
Music, play on! Forgetfulness bring to my heart.
Brief is our life, though sweet its rest and its mirth,
Soon shall a hand unknown
Level my dust divine with the dust of earth.

He said aloud, "When the Crusaders approached Varna he hid himself in my harem here, as though its inviolability would protect him. He was still something of a child with a child's fears, yet I gave him my throne. Now—now he hates Grand Vizier Khalil because he advised against enthroning him, and because he's the leader of the peace party. He hates his own janissaries. He despises the Koran."

These words spoken of the sultan of the Turkish Empire shocked Ilderim, who said nothing. Nor did Murad glance about to see who might be listening.

"Send a courier to the Emir Selim Mejid," he said, "and to Emir Osman, and summon the war council to meet after the noon prayer. I will teach Mehmed there are more manly pursuits than murdering our soldiers."

Ilderim bowed. "Your command, O Lord of the World."

He left at once. The short time interval passed quickly. In the early afternoon the council convened as Murad had ordered. Janissary and *spahi* generals, renowned imams and dervishes, Khalil and other senior officials, and the ever-present *tsaushes*, all of them gathered in the great gilded hall of the war room bright with its captured battle flags. The assemblage quickly fell into silence. As Murad took the central position on the carpeted dais, Turhan, the oldest imam in the court, intoned from the Koran.

In the Name of Allah, the Compassionate, the Merciful. Will you not fight against those who have broken their oaths and conspired to banish the Apostle? They were the first to attack you. Do you fear them? Surely Allah is more worthy of your fear, if you are true believers.

Make war on them: Allah will chastise them through you and humble them. He will grant you victory over them and heal the spirit of the faithful. He will take away all anger from their hearts: He shows mercy to whom he pleases. He is wise and all-knowing. Blessed be the name of Allah.

There followed the expected rejoinder from the council. Then two black slaves entered, one carrying a white silken cushion, the other a very large rolled parchment closed with a wax seal and ribbon. On the cushion was the green turban of state with its egret feather and diamond and emerald clasp, not worn by Murad since his abdication. It was laid before him with the scroll. Taking off his white one he put the green on his head. It would not surprise them, he knew. Rumors had gone about. Their continuing respectful quiet confirmed his belief. He spoke with sufficient force so that all might hear.

"As all of you know, I placed my son on the throne of the Ottoman Empire. *I* put him there. None other. If he behaves in a way that diminishes the state I will unseat him and resume my rightful place as leader of the Osmanli people, Allah's temporal representative on earth. My assumption of the turban of state confirms this. He has already been informed and has sworn me his fealty."

Breaking the seal of the parchment, he unrolled it with the aid of retainers, revealing a large map of central Europe, the Balkans, and the Near East. Then he resumed.

"Oh my children, favored of Allah and his Prophet, do you think I am too old to be sultan once again? I am *not* too old! I am still the one who humbled the Venetians at Salonica, the conqueror of Serbia, the victor over the Hungarians and Poles at Varna." He drew a jeweled dagger and placed its point on the Peloponnesus. "Can you see this map? If not, you may examine it when I am finished. We will invade Greece and base our forces here at Mistra, outflanking the Byzantines and driving a wedge into southern Europe, a wedge shaped like a *crescent*. Even Constantinople is not beyond our reach. By the beard of the Prophet, because I failed to take it in my youth does not mean I will fail again! That effort was twenty-four years ago and this is the dawn of a new and glorious era for Islam, the dawn of a new jihad. Go to the mosques, my children. The imams will tell you this. Let every emir who supports this venture, and myself as sultan, rise in his place and put his hand on his scimitar."

To a man all rose and complied.

"Good," said Murad, and for once his nearly perpetual look of melancholy had dissipated. "That is settled then. We will meet here tonight after evening prayer and confer, if necessary until dawn, until a black thread can be distinguished from a white. This meeting will adjourn after the imam from the Great Mosque has again recited from the Book."

Once more the old man stood up, his white beard hanging limply in the incense-scented air. Once more he spoke the words of Allah as revealed to the Chosen One.

> In the Name of Allah, the Compassionate, the Merciful. Men, have fear of your Lord. The catastrophe of the Hour of Doom shall be terrible indeed.
>
> When that day comes, every suckling mother shall forsake her infant, every pregnant female shall cast her burden, and you shall see mankind reeling like drunkards although not drunk: such shall be the horror of Allah's vengeance.
>
> The faithful and the unbelievers contend about their Lord. Garments of fire have been prepared for the unbelievers. Scalding water shall be poured upon their heads, melting their skins and that which is in their bellies. They shall be lashed with rods of iron.

Murad could see the effect this was having. That the imam chose passages at random made no difference. Either he, as sultan, would control the jihad or it would control him. Either he would ride at its head or follow in its wake like a helpless puppet. He was tired of war and longed for the energy of his youth, yearning for peace and comfort as never before. No matter, he intended to lead.

Of all the Muslim forces now massing for renewal of war against Europe, the janissaries were the most remarkable. No other military organization in history was ever quite like them. Founded by the fourteenth-century Ottoman sultan Orkhan, father of Murad I, they were an elite corps composed entirely of levies of Christian youths and prisoners of war, and were trained and indoctrinated under iron discipline. In the case of male children of Christian captives, when raised under the strict theocratic code of Islam they were often more zealous in the faith of Mohammed than even the Turks, and it was said their fanaticism knew no equal.

They were restricted to their cantonments and had no other existence. They lived for war. No janissary was permitted to marry or to form any attachment with a woman, for it was held that such relationships weakened a man's fighting spirit and made him yearn for hearth and home rather than the rigors of campaigning.

Under these conditions, of course, homosexuality became a way of life, for the popular western notion that it appeals only to very effeminate men is false. Alexander the Great, a redoubtable warrior in combat, was bisexual and had his male favorites, the most noted of whom was the general Hephaestion. Richard the Lion-Heart, equally renowned in battle, was the same and had his minstrel, Blondel. The system came from the Hellenes originally. Achilles and his Patroclus come instantly to mind. From them it was adopted by the Byzantines and so eventually by the Ottomans. In ancient Greece, the formidable *hoplite* infantry was based on thousands of pairs of soldiers who were literally mated for life. Even in modern times we find a parallel. In the seventeenth century, such *matelots*, as the French called them, were frequently found among Caribbean buccaneers, the infamous Brethren of the Coast. Still more recently, they are seen in the French Foreign Legion.

To make the janissaries' lifelong dependency on the army total, they were denied any opportunity to learn a craft or enter trade and were taught to despise such civilian pursuits as unmanly. The indoctrination went deep. To them, only the profession of arms could win the highest favor in the eyes of Allah. The Prophet had been a warrior. Of all the many possible ways to depart this life only death in battle was a guarantee of paradise.

Had Europeans understood the true nature of this host now arrayed against them, janissary and ferocious Turk together, they might have given more thought to mending their endless quarrels. As they wrangled, fought, and undermined each other, their time grew shorter. Their monks and other ecclesiastics, some of whom were historians, gave warnings that went largely unheeded. There had been a people like this centuries before, the pagan Vikings of Scandinavia, the ever-predatory Norsemen with their far-ranging longships and their war god Odin. They too believed that to die in battle sword in hand was to be taken immediately to paradise, a place they called Valhalla. They too were fatalists, fighting with a wild, insensate daring that few could match.

And the Christians might have remembered this. The Viking warrior called himself *berserkr*, meaning "he who fights in a frenzy." It was the way the Ottomans fought. Such half-crazed paladins of bloodshed and violence considered themselves unbeatable in *any* war that lasted long enough. If this belief were an illusion—it could be a very dangerous one.

3
Dracula's First Reign and Flight to Moldavia

The dungeon was cold, frightfully, paralyzingly cold. Through the semi-darkness surrounding him he felt it chill his spine as though it came from within him, first investing his bone marrow, then radiating outward to the ragged edges of his bloody, pain-filled flesh. Yes, it came from within, he knew. What month was this? Late November or early December, with snow everywhere and the Carpathians locked in ice, yet this sensation of freezing was *inside* him.

Dimly, he realized that he lacked the strength to stand and was held upright against the stone wall by shackles, spreadeagled, pinioned at wrists and ankles. They had tortured him. They had burned him with hot irons and torn his flesh with pincers and stretched him on the rack. Thank God they had so far spared his eyes. He knew this because he could still see dimly through the mist of his own blood and sweat. They had left him his vision. They had spared him the boot, also, which meant he could still walk if released, at least as far as that wall out there where they probably intended to kill him. And why? Because they hated his father, Dracul? These traitor boyars were Wallachians, not Hungarians. Yet they served Hunyadi the unforgiving, Hunyadi who hated both father and son, who had never forgiven Varna or its aftermath, who had attacked them now three years later and defeated them.

He spat blood. He saw again the scene of yesterday's battlefield; their soldiers falling everywhere, overwhelmed; Dracul fleeing the pursuing enemy as he, Mircea, was surrounded and taken prisoner. And now where was Dracul? Dead, probably. And his son was here in Tirgoviste, Dracul's own capital, chained to a wall in the bowels of this keep while the treacherous enemy within tore him to pieces.

He felt himself on the edge of despair. It was hard to die like this. The thought kept coming back to him. Hard to die when not yet twenty, a prince who should have had all of glorious life before him, Dracul's crown prince, heir to the throne of Wallachia. Was he afraid of death? Yes, if he were honest. Yes, he feared it. Oh not a death in battle, not an honorable exit from this world. But *this* kind of end, this agony which could unman him, break his spirit if they tormented him again, reduce him to a whimpering coward begging for mercy from those who would never grant it. Dear Christ, he deserved better from life than this, did he not? He was Mircea of the House of Basarab, his grandfather's namesake, not some dull-witted hind who had never worn a sword or ridden a horse or flown a falcon. He was Mircea. Mircea. MIRCEA.

He heard his name being called frantically, then recognized his own voice crying out in his dire anguish. He must think of his brothers captive in distant Turkey, Vlad and Radu. Radu would break rather easily, he believed, to be expected in a child so young. But never Vlad. That one was the bravest of them all, as hard as flint, as impervious as steel. They could hack him in quarters and he'd spit on them. They could cut off his head and he'd spit again before that head hit the ground. Where did he get the iron in his soul? You could see it in those green eyes of his and hear it in his voice. And Vlad was but a boy himself. He could be proud of him. They were full brothers born of the same parents. Vlad had a streak of obvious cruelty, but what did that matter? He was every inch the budding soldier. He must remember him, concentrate on him, do his utmost to emulate him. If they came again with the tongs and the fire he must try to be worthy of him. Yes, his younger brother Vlad... yes...yes...

He was plunged in a kind of reverie and his mind was wandering. He was still lost in it when they came for him, spoke to him, unshackled him. He was only vaguely aware of what they said. The voices seemed to float in and out of his consciousness, grow loud, then fade, then return.

"Hunyadi...Pay us well...Dobrogea...council of war...Demand

Hunyadi's life? This one will make no more demands...with arrows? Upon my faith, Conduratu has a better thought...yes...Look at him. Dracul is better off than he...the pig...Royal blood is red, as you see."

Demand Hunyadi's life? Yes, he had made that demand after Varna, he and his father together at the council of war in Dobrogea. With Hunyadi in their power they had made it, accusing him, blaming the defeat on him. A death sentence had been passed. Then Dracul had relented and let him go, given him escort to Transylvania. But Hunyadi remembered. Hunyadi never forgot.

He could hear laughter. Raucous. Mocking. He was being forced to climb steps but had no sense of rising. Had they injured him so badly then? The cobwebs seemed to disappear suddenly and he heard them again.

"You'll like this throne we've prepared, Mircea. Of course, you'll lie within it rather than sit, but a prostrate position will make it easier to lick the Turkish boots. Be of good cheer, therefore. Royalty was never so well served."

He didn't understand. Nothing they said made any sense. One of them babbled about the death of Dracul, and that he could believe. But this pitiless journey into the icy courtyard, this melancholy walk into oblivion, did they hope to frighten him by it? They had done their worst. What would death matter now? Would they hang him or kill him with arrows? Maybe decapitation was their pleasure. Within the walled rectangle at last he glanced about, half-expecting to see a headsman with sword or axe, but all he saw was a wooden coffin. It lay close to the outer gate in readiness, near it a horse and sledge as though waiting to receive it. He shuddered involuntarily and shook his head, trying to clear his dazed mind. A coffin. *His*, was it not? Of course. Of course. That would be the way of Conduratu and the others. Let the victim anticipate it. The final touch of cruelty. His grim bier waiting for him in the springtime of his life.

"Tie him well," said one of them.

Vlahuta this time. He recognized the voice. They were rough in their handling of him. The knots were pulled tight as they bound his wrists. Suddenly he knew what they would do. He *knew* it. A shout of anger and fear and soul-shriveling outrage swelled in his throat and hung there as he choked on it, freezing the blood in his veins. He struggled. Someone struck him a blow on the side of the head but he scarcely felt it. Burial *alive!* "Oh God!" his mind screamed. "Oh my God!"

"No!" he shrieked aloud then. "No, Conduratu! Not that! Not that, for the love of Heaven! No! No! No!"

They paid him no heed. Quickly the lid of the coffin was removed and they thrust him inside it. His blood seemed to be boiling now, pounding in his head like the waves of a raging sea. He saw a leaden sky, the cold winter sky of Wallachia. His brain reeled, clutching at the vanishing thread of life.

"Conduratu! Mercy! Mercy!"

"Mercy? We'll show you the same mercy we showed Dracul! That's mercy enough!"

The laughing faces of his assassins hung over him like demons from the Pit. Diabolical. Without a shred of humanity. Swollen with viciousness and savagery. Grinning faces that taunted him. Leering faces with mouths that spat on him. Then the lid was raised above him, the sky suddenly and forever blotted out. It was lowered. Blackness enveloped him, a stygian murk admitting not the faintest gleam of light. Down. Down. Down into the unimagined depths. Lost for all time.

"Turks," said a voice strangely like his own. "Why do they hate you for the Turks? You fought the Turks, supported the Burgundian galleys on the Danube, drove the enemy from Giurgiu. Why? Why? *Why?*" It was getting all mixed up. It *couldn't* be real. They were mummers enacting a pantomine, a troop of strolling players who had come to this place and would presently leave.

"It's black! It's *black*, damn your souls! Give me light! Give me light, I tell you!"

But there was no light. Vaguely he was aware of being lifted and swung through the air. Wood scraped on wood. He heard the sounds of muffled voices, a pause, the crack of a whip and the neighing of a horse. They were taking him out of town. They'd dig a hole some place and put him in it. Then they'd fill it with earth, smooth the ground above him, and leave. Lying there in the darkness as the runners slipped wetly through the snow below the swaying sledge, he wondered what it would be like to suffocate slowly. Could he possibly bear it or would he go mad before the end? What difference since the end would be the same? He wondered how long the air would last, if his lungs would collapse in the final, hideous, gasping moments. What did it matter? Death was death, the shroud of death all-encompassing. Conduratu would die some day and hell awaited him. It most surely waited for them all.

For what seemed a long interval, he tried to count the minutes as though by determining elapsed time he could judge distance, make a guess at his final resting place. Then he stopped. The Draculas were all believers. His remains would never be found but God knew where he was. God would note the spot and the heavenly angels would come for his soul. It was enough. On this violent earth with its beastly, heartless humans he would never get beyond his teens—but it was enough. He could face what must be faced. He was Mircea of the House of Basarab, Prince of Wallachia.

In his final realm of eternal night, helpless and doomed, he struggled in his unyielding bonds out of blind instinct. "Oh Father!" he cried in his desperate wretchedness. "Hear me! Oh hear me! I have not greatly sinned! Succour me in my last moments! Receive my soul, O God! Receive, I implore you, the soul of thy servant, Mircea!"

So died Dracula's older brother, buried alive, his death following hard on that of his father. The time was late November, 1447; the scene of Dracul's violent end somewhere south of his capital of Tirgoviste. No one can say what became of him. The archives are scanty. In his flight southward he apparently crossed the Dambovita River, in flood at that time of year, then entered the dangerous Balteni marshes and urged his horse to take him through them. This is where his own traitorous boyars caught up with him and cut him down. His final resting place? Some Romanian historians believe he was taken to the Monastery of Snagov for interment, a journey involving another crossing of the swollen river, this time with a cumbersome corpse. Would these murderous renegades have been so considerate of the man they betrayed? If they were, the monastery has no record of it and its present monks cannot identify the grave. It is more likely that he was found by peasants and buried not far from where he fell, on the grounds of an old wooden structure called the Monastery of the Hill that has long since disappeared. Today the place is marked by the multistoried stone Chapel of Balteni.

Because he was illegitimate Dracul's early life had not been an easy one. After the death of his father, forced to stand aside while his brothers wrangled over the throne of Wallachia, he spent much of his time at the widely dispersed courts of Sigismund I of Luxembourg, a monarch who by the year 1436 was King of Hungary, Holy Roman Emperor, and King of Bohemia. Thus at various times we find the youthful Dracul in the Hungarian capital of Buda and the German imperial city of Nürnberg; perhaps even in the Bohemian capital of Prague, though we can't be sure of that. He was homeless. He wanted his father's throne. Fortunately for his ambitions, Sigismund and his advisors had him in mind for it. Dracul was carefully watched by the emperor's agents and his every move was known. In 1430 he was allowed to establish residence in Transylvania where troops guarding the Wallachian frontier were under his command. Still he remained only a candidate.

As has been mentioned, Dracul's house was in the walled medieval city of Sighisoara where he went to live with his first wife and his small son, Mircea. This woman was probably a Transylvanian but her name is unknown, as is the precise year of the birth of her second son, Dracula. The best historical surmise is 1431. It was a signal year for Dracul. Invested with the Order of the Dragon in Nürnberg, he was also given imperial recognition as prince of Wallachia and even allowed to strike his own coinage. Regrettably, this did not mean very much at the time. Only military power could actually give him the throne and he lacked this. Five long years were to pass before he could claim it in fact.

Dracula's early childhood then was spent in Sighisoara. His mother may have died in childbirth. In any event, she did not live long after his coming, for some time shortly after his return to Transylvania Dracul took as his second wife the Moldavian Musat princess Eupraxia, sister to the reigning prince. This was a shrewd move. True, any strengthening of the ties between Wallachia and Moldavia was bound to anger Hunyadi, for it could only toughen resistance to Hungarian plans for the domination of all Romania. On the other hand, the Moldavian army was strong, Dracul had no troops of his own, and he needed military force to overthrow his half-brother Aldea. He accomplished this in the winter of 1436, shortly before Christmas. Thereafter, he and his family occupied the palace in Tirgoviste and Dracul ruled as his illustrious father had done. He did not merely reign but ruled in fact.

As might be expected of the son of a prince, in Tirgoviste Dracula was trained for knighthood, the first step of which was to become a squire. While still a young boy he took to the life with a quiet, purposeful determination that must have surprised those who taught him. We know he learned to shoot a longbow and to fence with broadswords; to fight with quarterstaves; to swim, ride horseback, and joust with shield and lance. He may have jousted in light armor specially made for his size. Dracul would have indulged him in that. In fencing and horsemanship he showed a marked potential for one so young, and in later life was to demonstrate a mastery of both. It is also not difficult to believe that in armed combat he possessed what a later century was to call the "killer instinct," for this suited his character.

The training of his alert yet devious mind was another matter. Now on the throne, Dracul could at last afford to send his sons to Constantinople, to give them that classical Byzantine education so prized by boyars. He decided against it. Carefully selecting tutors of proven merit, he saw that the princes added other languages to their native Romanian: Italian, German, Latin, and possibly some French. They also learned the intricacies of the Byzantine Cyrillic alphabet used in the writing of Old Church Slavonic; court protocol; political theory as applied to statecraft; the tactics of battle and siege; and the general strategy of warfare. As he was a curious mixture of intelligence, innate savagery, and ever-growing vanity, it is interesting to note that the boy Dracula took to his intellectual studies as avidly as to his martial ones and seems to have surpassed his peers. His instructors had small cause to complain. Considering his vindictive character, the early signs of which must have been evident, it's more than probable they were reluctant to do so.

In the years following his assumption of the throne for the first time, Dracul sired at least three other sons, but only the first of these, Radu, was by his wife Eupraxia. Two of them were destined to rule Wallachia: Radu during the interval of Dracula's second fall from power, 1462 to 1473, and again briefly in 1475; and the illegitimate Vlad the Monk in 1481, then again, 1482 to 1495. The illegitimate second Mircea, a shadowy figure whom history scarcely mentions, seems to have left no impression of any kind. Dracul had several mistresses. Were all of his sons born only to his first two wives it is obvious that the names Vlad and Mircea would not have been repeated. And one thing else is clear. Even though Vlad the Monk eventually came to the throne, Dracul never acknowledged him as his heir. As concerned the succession, he recognized only the first Mircea, the first Vlad (Dracula), and the only son by his second marriage, Radu.

Some historians, particularly Romanian ones, have noted that Dracula's character was forged in the fiery crucible of political expediency, and this was certainly true. He must have been a careful observer of his father. Seeing Dracul dodge and backstep and shift position, change allegiances, lie and deceive and betray merely to stay alive was bound to generate cynicism in the son, to make him coldly calculating, indifferent to the fate of others, utterly ruthless. Add to this an inborn sadistic streak and you have a being who lacked only one thing to make of him a potentially very dangerous tyrant—the military power offered by a crown.

As has been indicated, Dracul was a survivor, and survivors are normally astute. Once in Tirgoviste it did not take him long to determine that Turkish strength was growing rapidly. Looking to the northwest, he saw a militant but momentarily quiescent Hungary which he reasoned would not be able to march against him in less than a year. But to the southeast he viewed a more alarming scene. There the Turks were restive and menacing. They had beaten the Serbs and Bulgarians and occupied their land, dividing it into *pashaliks* ruled by the Porte. They had long since recovered from the onslaught of Tamerlane. Already Murad II had neutralized the Black Sea and the Dobrogea, and isolated the Byzantines in Constantinople. An early and devastating Ottoman invasion of the Balkans was a certainty. The only unknown was the time factor.

Accordingly, Dracul threw in his lot with the Muslims, at least momentarily. It was the year 1437. King Sigismund had just died in Prague and been succeeded by his son-in-law, Prince Albert (Albrecht) of Austria. It was time to act. When Murad invited him to come to the ancient city of Brusa in Asiatic Turkey, Dracul accepted. There, with a large contingent of boyars, he submitted to the sultan near the foot of Mount Olympus, offering tribute at the seat of Bithynian kings. It was a fateful move. From this day onward Hunyadi would never trust him. The following year when the Turks raided Transylvania, Dracul rode with the sultan, then, incongruously, upheld his Draconist oath by using his influence to save the Christian town of Sebes from the horrors of total sack. The gesture made little difference to the government in Buda. Hungarian plotting with Dracul's Danesti rivals increased. To turn his own people against him and foment rebellion was now a vital aspect of Magyar policy.

The earliest chance to do this came in the winter of 1441. In November of that year, having recently been appointed voivod of Transylvania, János Hunyadi journeyed to Tirgoviste with an extraordinary commission from the king of Hungary. The demand was nothing less than the renewal of crusade and immediate war with the Turks, with the Wallachian forces to play a principal role. The purpose of the visit was to hang Dracul on the horns of a dilemma. If he marched, his army would be the first to receive the brunt of the powerful Turkish counterattacks, his territories the first devastated. If he refused to march, well, he was a Draconist sworn to uphold crusade, to support the Christian armies in any and all endeavors against the Muslim enemy. Much could be made of such a refusal. Already Hungarian agents in Wallachia were calling him "the Apostate," spreading that word in the streets and marketplaces. Once raise the standard of revolt within his borders and Dracul must fall.

Dracul refused. As usual he prevaricated, carefully couching his phrases to disguise his true purpose. It deceived no one. In February 1442, the Turks alerted every garrison they had on the Danube, from Silistria in Dobrogea running upriver to Giurgiu, then as far west as Turnu by the tributary of the Olt. In March their general, Mezid-Bey, invaded Transylvania with his army and Dracul made no move to stop him. Rapidly the Ottomans thrust westward. The decisive battle of 22 March was fought on the southern border of the great Transylvanian plateau, near the ancient city of Sibiu founded by the Romans. Hunyadi was victorious. The Turks were disastrously defeated by the Christians. Among the dead on the battlefield was Mezid-Bey.

The White Knight of Christendom wasted no time. Considering Dracul's neutral position as tantamount to treason, he immediately invaded Wallachia in pursuit of the beaten Turks, mindful of his oath to depose Dracul, believing the latter's army was no longer loyal to him. In this he was probably correct. Dracul, at any rate, did not care to put it to the test and fled from his capital on Hunyadi's approach. Tirgoviste was occupied. In pursuance of the current Hungarian policy of supporting the Danesti claimant, Hunyadi enthroned that prince the following winter as Basarab II. In Buda there was much rejoicing. Among the Draculas there was only gloom and danger and the precarious lives of hunted fugitives as, frequently going into hiding, the family and a few loyal retainers crossed the Danube and entered Turkish-held Bulgaria. About the time that Basarab was crowned in December 1442, Dracul and his people were in Gallipoli (the ancient Greek Callipolis), called by the Turks Gelibolu. The Sea of Marmara was invigorating. So was the fact that Murad II was grateful for Dracul's neutrality at a time vital to Turkish interests.

It was not gratitude, however, that induced the Porte to restore his principality to him in less than a year. It was political and military expediency. The Danesti princes cooperated with the Hungarians. Dracul did not. It was as simple as that. The Hungarians could not hold Wallachia. They lacked the strength on that ground and could not effectively reinforce. The Turks could and did retake it. Thus it was by the winter of 1443, aided by the Ottomans, that Dracul once again sat on his throne in Tirgoviste.

This time, however, things were different. The Turks did not trust Dracul any more than any other Christian, and his past performance was unreassuring. They hedged him round with restrictions. He would pay the yearly tribute as before, recognizing the sultan as his overlord. He must swear fealty. Never could he join any crusade. To emphasize his submission, a proviso certain to make him hated and despised by his own subjects, henceforth Wallachians would join other subject peoples in filling an annual quota of male children to swell the ranks of Christian recruits for the janissaries.

Nor was that all. Not five months had passed before additional Turkish pressure for a surer guarantee struck Dracul heavily. He was known to love his family. His legitimate sons in particular were said to be close to him. By the summer of 1444 he was left with no choice. His eldest son Mircea would remain in Tirgoviste as heir to the throne. Vlad (Dracula) and Radu, ages twelve and nine, would be pledged as hostages. This was done. Long was the journey of the young captives, nearly 600 miles to the south-southeast as the crow flies, to the hill fortress of Egrigöz in the Anatolian principality of Karaman, the ancient Laranda. In this former lair of Isaurian pirates high on the shoulder of Mount Kociadag, Dracula was to be kept for nearly four years. Perhaps no other period of his life was to prove so influential in shaping his character.

As it happened, this year of 1444 was to be one of great significance for the history of Eastern Europe, for this was the year of Varna. In the fall, the fragile Peace of Seghedin was broken by the Hungarian boy king, apparently in the belief that the military successes of the year before could be repeated. He held two thrones. Therefore, Polish levies would join the Hungarian. The command was to be divided, frequently a mistake, with the successful general, Hunyadi, serving as co-commander in the manner of a Roman proconsul. The Roman pontiff would be represented by his legate, Giuliano Cesarini.

The strategy had the merit of simplicity. By virtue of their river fortresses the Turks held the entire line of the Danube and had thus driven a wedge into southeastern Europe. This bristling salient must be reduced. Considered equal to the task was a fleet of Genoese and Burgundian galleys equipped with deadly bombards and a crusading army of 20,000 men. Ottoman domination of the Black Sea was believed open to challenge. The port of Varna was the key. Once capture the Danubian redoubts and this vital harbor could be taken by assault; the south would be vulnerable; and in Constantinople the Byzantines would open the Strait of the Bosporus to the Christians. How then could the Muslims maintain their grip on the strategic coasts of the Sea of Marmara? And if they lost that, how then could they control the Mediterranean?

It was not a plan for the conquest of the Turkish Empire but it was ambitious nonetheless, excessively so for the limited forces available. Dracul had a part in it. His Wallachian army was desperately needed. The pope, Eugene IV, absolved him of his allegiance to Murad II and his oath of fealty, urging him to commit himself utterly. But now Dracul was trapped. A great crusade was about to be launched and his people knew it; it was holy war, the fanatical Christian counterpart of the Muslim jihad. But what could he do? A Draconist he surely was and pledged to fight the heathen, but in distant Egrigöz his two young sons were held in hostage to prevent his participation in this very thing. To join the crusade would be to seal their doom. To end on the losing side would ensure his own.

Characteristically, he chose compromise. Since the maintenance of strict neutrality was impossible, he would send only a token force, 4000 men under his heir, Mircea, with a veiled promise of more to come. Even this would cost him the lives of his sons, he believed, and said so in a missive to the Saxon burgomeister of Brasov (Kronstadt). He would fight to reestablish "the Christian peace" he declared, and ruefully accept the consequences.

The Crusade of Varna was predestined to disaster. Hunyadi escaped the battlefield. In the hands of his Wallachian "allies," brought to what amounted to a trial during flight in the Dobrogea, he was accused of incompetence by Dracul and his life was demanded by Mircea. Only his aura of greatness and distinction saved him by reversing the sentence of death. Dracul gave him escort home. Regardless, the grudge Hunyadi bore thereafter was implacable and deadly, and only blood could satisfy his thirst for vengeance.

He quenched that thirst three years later. Overcoming all obstacles, working with furious dedication, by the autumn of 1447 he had rebuilt most of the decimated Hungarian army units, trained and equipped them, and honed them to a fine fighting edge, meanwhile maintaining a formidable battle array at his Transylvanian castle of Hunedoara. With this force, in November he invaded Wallachia through the Transylvanian Alps and the Arges River valley, adding the advantage of tactical surprise to that of superior numbers. As he advanced on Tirgoviste, he was met by Dracul in the field. The odds were perhaps four to one. Overwhelmed, the Wallachian army disintegrated. Mircea was captured. Dracul was killed.

The frightful manner of Mircea's execution does not do credit to Hunyadi, great man that he was. True, he may not have specified the method, yet he must have known of the youth's plight, and to have left him at the mercy of his treacherous boyar captors was inexcusable. One assumes he must have lived to regret it. Basically he was a man of honor and to such as he a needless stain on the escutcheon is hard to bear. It tends to corrode the soul.

"Your seizure of the throne of Wallachia three years ago was ill-timed, cousin. I would have done it differently."

From where he sat in the gilded, high-backed chair Dracula watched the young man who spoke these words. The youth stood in front of one of the mullioned windows of the castle's great hall. In the fading light of this gray October afternoon his slender body was dramatically silhouetted against the leaded panes, lending power and stature to a martial air that already seemed regal enough. Should he take offense at these words, the listener pondered? No, for none was intended. Between blood-related princes all was in the intent.

"How differently, Stéfan?" Dracula's voice was very quiet, self-contained. "Remember I am twenty now and you still something of a stripling. Do you propose to advise me on statecraft or war?"

The young man turned to face him. The countenance he looked at, green-eyed and hawk-nosed, was determined and strong, but no stronger than his own. "Perhaps both," he smiled. "Have we not fought shoulder to shoulder under Prince Bogdan?"

"You speak of him as though he were not your father."

Stéfan shrugged. "I speak of him as prince of Moldavia. And here we are in his capital of Suceava, and the snow lies white on the ground once again, and I presume to advise you. Crasna alone gives me the right, my Vlad. Remember your words to me on that field? 'Today you have won your spurs,' you said. 'The Poles are in flight and no man of us fought better.' Remember?"

Dracula nodded. With his head bent, his black locks hung beneath his beardless chin and almost touched. "Of course," he replied. "That was fifteen months ago. The Poles were valiant but foolish. Now it is the fall of 1451 and many things have changed."

"You made a mistake," persisted Stéfan, "a serious tactical error."

"I expect to make more."

"It is our way to discuss such things, you and I, is it not?"

"Discuss."

"I mean, we learn from such things."

"Discuss."

"All right, Vlad. When you made your move you knew that Hunyadi and a sizable Christian army were headed south toward the Serbian border. You knew it was not merely a maneuver. It was a major invasion, a new crusade to avenge Varna."

"How could I have been sure of that?"

"Because of the direction of the thrust. Straight across the Danube. Serbian territory. It had to be an attempt to reinforce the Albanians."

"Iskander Bey?"

"You would call him that with your knowledge of Turkish. Call him what you will. Scanderbeg, George Castriota, or Beelzebub, it's all one. You didn't know the odds involved. You didn't know Hunyadi's chances, yet you marched on Tirgoviste regardless, knowing he would turn on you if he won."

Dracula's laugh was so soft it was barely audible. "He lost."

"But you should have waited on that event," said Stéfan. "You acted blindly, like a dice-thrower in a game. As I see it, war should be a matter of astute calculation. Mathematics."

"There is also room for intuition."

"Not much."

Dracula was unsmiling now. "It wasn't Hunyadi who dethroned me," he said. "He had already lost at Kosovo, been captured by the Serbian Brancovic, and was in chains in the dungeons of Semendria. It was that swine of a Danesti, that pig who dares to style himself Vladislav II, Prince of Wallachia. He never should have survived Kosovo. If the Turks had fought with their usual skill they would have slaughtered him and his army to a man."

"But they didn't," said Stéfan. "He escaped the battlefield and attacked you. He caught you by surprise. At such a crucial time you should have had scouting parties of cavalry on every road, your watchtowers manned day and night."

In a way that was characteristic of him, Dracula pursed his lips. The nether lip was abnormally full and protrusive so that the gesture looked almost grotesque. "I was seventeen," he said, still in his quiet voice. "My own boyars betrayed me—and not for the first time. You know this."

"Yes."

"The dice you speak of could have fallen either way and caution is not in my nature. Did the Black Prince of the English show caution at Poitiers? I held the throne—"

"For less than two months."

"But I *held* it, look you. This was not a wasted moment. In so doing I established my right to rule in the eyes of my subjects. I will return to Tirgoviste. The Danesti cannot hold Wallachia. The people hate them as poltroons, fools, and arrant knaves, the lickspittles of the Hungarians. The boyars play their own filthy game and always have. As for my people, even the Crescent of Islam would be preferable to them."

"Are you sure of that, cousin?"

"Indeed."

Stéfan took a chair opposite Dracula and regarded him levelly. "Remember our pact," he said. "Whichever of us comes to his throne first—"

"Will aid the other in coming to his."

"That is right, Vlad. And if it be within my power—I will help you avenge the deaths of Dracul and Mircea."

Dracula's eyes held a faraway look. No one but Stéfan dared mention their names to him, proving once again their closeness. It was odd he thought, odd that but one man in his life should be close to him. But why odd? Their families were interdependent. When he'd faced revolt, Bogdan II had been given protection at the court of Dracul, and Dracul's second wife was his sister. Bogdan was Dracula's stepuncle.

"I swear it on my mother's virtue," said Stéfan very seriously.

Dracula's sensuous mouth broadened slightly. *There* was an oath. The Princess Oltea was Wallachian and related to him by blood. It was she who *made* them close, really, he and this clever, calculating youth.

"I do not expect you to fail me, Stéfan. Hah! Sooner would the redoubtable Scanderbeg betray his Albanians than you fail your cousin Vlad." He paused. "What do you think of this trip your father has made?"

"What do you mean?"

"I mean I think he has made a more serious error than ever did I. He has insufficient escort. He exposes himself."

"To what?"

"To attack by his enemies."

Stéfan considered. "You mean the Aron faction."

"Them and others. A prince is ever at risk and his would-be assassins are everywhere. It's a matter of who strikes first."

"Petru Aron cannot take Suceava."

The frown that had begun to furrow Dracula's broad brow grew deeper and a hectic flush of color suffused his high cheekbones. "There are times when your hasty judgments betray your immaturity," he said impatiently. "If he lops off the head of state he can take anything. He can take all of Moldavia. Pray do not deceive yourself."

"Do you have a presentiment?"

"I'm sorry to tell you this. I do, and never stronger than now."

"What omens have you noted?"

Dracula shook his head. "None, my cousin. It's just a feeling. I wish the prince were better armed—with twice the number of men at his back. I wish—"

As though his words had struck the sonorous bell of fate itself, at that moment there was a commotion in the courtyard below, the sounds of shouting, a clanging gate, horses' hooves knifing through snow to scrape on cobblestones. Both men went to the window and looked out.

"Sentry!" shouted Stéfan. "Who goes there? What is amiss, man?"

Dracula saw the helmeted head turned upward. Instinctively he expected the worst.

"'Tis a courier and lead horse from General Lupescu, my lord!" came the excited reply. "His Highness Prince Bogdan—His Highness—"

"Yes?"

"Your father is dead, my lord! He's been murdered! One of Petru Aron's assassins!"

"Like Dracul," said Dracula softly.

Stéfan shook his head as though he'd been struck a blow. "What?"

"I said—like Dracul." From his large lower lip his teeth had drawn blood. "When they haven't the stomach to face us they bury their poniards in our backs. What a reckoning there will be when we find them. The world will tremble on that day."

Stéfan fell back from the casement, shuddering. "My father," he said brokenly. "Oh my God, my father!"

Dracula caught him in his arms and held him. "And mine," he said tonelessly. "Fear not, my cousin Stéfan, we will yet take their price in blood. For Dracul, Mircea, Bogdan, and all the rest whom lesser men have slain, we will exact a terrible toll. I swear it on my honor. Yea, upon the honor of Prince Vlad III of Wallachia I do swear it. It will be blood for blood. Torrents of it. Rivers of it. We will leave no man or woman of the accursed plotters alive. They love to inflict death. We will show them the grinning face of death as they have never imagined it. Easy, my Stéfan. Easy. Sit down awhile."

He helped the stricken youth into a chair and stood beside him, gripping his shoulder, his mind a seething mass of hatred for the killers who decimated them. "Stéfan," he said softly. "My cousin Stéfan."

From somewhere a woman began screaming and Dracula listened to her. The Princess Oltea? Yes, that would be she. Stéfan's mother would take this hard, for her love for Bogdan was well known. He thought of how Eupraxia had wept when news of Dracul and Mircea was brought to her. He hadn't been there to see it, but they had told him later. So many Olteas and Eupraxias in this world, a world full of widows. A world full of bereft mistresses, also, like Dracul's hot bitch Caltuna.

Unconsciously, his left hand fingered his sword hilt. The screaming had stopped. Only Stéfan's nearly soundless grief was audible. Dracula's green eyes that had blazed with a fierce light only moments before seemed to be slumbering, as though the fires burning behind them were momentarily dampened.

In the late winter of 1447, shortly after Dracul and Mircea were killed by Wallachian traitor boyars in the pay of Hungary, Dracula and his younger brother Radu were released from their Turkish mountain retreat of Egrigöz after nearly four years of detention. This was an extraordinary occurrence. Normally, Dracul's machinations would have been more than enough to ensure the destruction of both juvenile hostages but Murad II was too smart for that. The sultan hated the Hungarians and planned their conquest. He hated the Wallachian Danesti clan as well and knew he could never trust them. That left the possibility of Dracula as a candidate for the throne in Tirgoviste, and *he* was a youth who during these years of captivity had displayed remarkable fortitude.

Accordingly, the brothers were taken from wildest Karaman in the far south to debauched and decadent Adrianople in the extreme northwest by the Bulgarian border. Such a trip through the largely roadless mountains of western Turkey would have been virtually impossible. Therefore, although the archives are silent on the point, it must have been by sea in a naval galley rowed by slaves, possibly a double-banked bireme that left the bay of Fethiye Körfezi and threaded the entire Aegean northward to the Strait of the Dardanelles.

At the sultan's palace Murad himself told the boys they were free. Radu declined to go home. Bisexual, having become as much a voluptuary as any Turk, he reveled both in his role as catamite and his freedom to use the women of the royal harem. Assassination might await him in Wallachia. In Turkey all was licentious indolence, especially as he was now a favorite not only of Murad but also of his ambitious son, Prince Mehmed. It may have been the Turks who first called him Radu the Handsome. He was very much one of them. He was not destined to leave Adrianople until 1462, after his feared brother's defeat and capture.

Dracula, of course, was entirely another matter; his possible use as a future political pawn was uppermost in Murad's mind. He was offered and accepted a commission in the Turkish forces. Here the archives are unspecific, but considering the already high caliber of his horsemanship it was probably as an officer of *spahis*. Did he want the throne of his father? He was told it could be his for a price. First it required patience, the undetermined wait for the right time to seize it. And secondly? There was the guarantee to the Porte that he would govern Wallachia in the best interests of the Turkish Empire; with an unusual amount of freedom, to be sure, but essentially almost as a *pashalik*.

As wily as Dracul ever was and far more determined, Dracula agreed. He had not wasted these four years. Not only had he learned the Turkish language and customs but he was now conversant also with their religion, their military tactics, and even the application of their policy of terror as an instrument of war. Yes, he would be patient. Of course he would be loyal to the Porte and swear fealty to the sultan as his vassal. Was there a hint of insincerity in the voice, some sign of it in the large green eyes? Perhaps. If the Turks had learned their subtlety and cynicism from the Byzantines, Dracula had learned his from the Turks. They had told him of the death of his father and brother. If there had been no war with Murad they would still be alive. But he could wait. They would see how he could wait. Biding one's time until the right moment to strike was an art and he intended to cultivate it assiduously.

As it happened, his chance came sooner than he anticipated, in the fated autumn of 1448. Hunyadi was the prime mover. Believing the Christian invasion of Turkish-held Serbia would create a fluid situation, knowing that Vladislav II had joined the crusade and was thus badly out of position, Dracula abruptly made his move. He was very influential despite his youth, an officer of the Turkish army known to be favored by the sultan, known also as the Porte's candidate for the throne of Wallachia. This influence he used adroitly. The pashas of Varna and Nicopolis put soldiers at his disposal. Quickly he welded them into a small striking force.

Then, unopposed in the absence of the hated Danesti, he marched on Tirgoviste and proclaimed himself prince in a tense atmosphere of sullen watchful waiting by its citizenry. All this while Hunyadi, his army badly beaten by the Turks at Kosovo, languished in a dungeon of Semendria Castle.

Knowing that his despotic captor George Brancović hated him for turning Serbia into a battleground, aware that his life would soon be forfeit, Hunyadi made his daring escape in December. By then, having reigned less than two months and having suffered defeat at the hands of the returning Vladislav, Dracula had crossed the Danube, taken refuge with Murad in Adrianople, then, perhaps fearing assassination at the hands of Radu who despised him, had once again fled northward.

This was when he came to Moldavia, to its capital of Suceava, its ruler Prince Bogdan II, and to his cousin Prince Stéfan. It was a strange year that was ending. Already Dracula had won and lost his throne and the Balkans, with the exception of Albania, their cherished independence. The Son of the Dragon remained in Suceava until October 1451. Then, with the assassination of Bogdan at Reuseni and the sudden rise to power of his murderer Petru Aron, he fled with Stéfan into Transylvania. No move could more clearly indicate the degree of his desperation. Although he himself had been born here this was Hunyadi country. Dracula knew the part Hunyadi had played in the deaths of Dracul and Mircea. In any case, the appeal for asylum was rejected. Nothing could alter it. Finally, on the very edge of destruction, word reached the two youths that Aron had been overthrown and with all speed they returned to Suceava. The date was March 30, 1452.

In the course of time, presumably at his own request, Dracula was given a house in the town of Sibiu near the southern end of the great Transylvanian plateau. An early Roman colony, refounded in the twelfth century by Saxon colonists from Nürnberg, it was called Hermannstadt by its German inhabitants. It was here that he heard the earthshaking news of the fall of Constantinople. Mehmed had taken it as he said he would, the slinking wolf whom a large part of the Christian world called Mohammed II. Sultan of the Ottoman Empire since the death of his father in 1451, he'd laid siege with 150,000 men to the great city and ripped and cannonaded its 8000 defenders into submission in fifty-three days. No one before had ever seen such monstrous cannon and no walls ever made could withstand them.

This event staggered the civilized world. We may presume that Dracula took careful note of it. He knew Mehmed well and detested him.

Though historians are not sure, it is possible the Wallachian prince spent several months of his boyhood as a page at the court of the emperor of Byzantium. Now that man, Constantine XI Paleologus, was gone, having died a hero's death in headlong attack against the janissaries. His dynasty was gone with him and with it a symbol of the Christian faith that had endured eleven hundred years. Had Wolfeyes kept his oath and trod on the Cross of Christ on the altar of Hagia Sophia? Probably. Almost certainly if he knew him at all. And after this monumental victory? More than most, Dracula was aware of the Ottoman plan to conquer and subjugate all of Eastern Europe.

In 1455, when the warlike Petru Aron again usurped the throne of Moldavia, Dracula had no alternative but once more to withdraw to save his life, for he knew that all those related to Bogdan's family would be condemned out of hand. Again it was to Transylvania he fled. Again it was to Hunyadi that his courier rode with an urgent request for sanctuary. It was then that his luck changed. Hunyadi, having recouped much of his military and political strength since the successive debacles of Varna and Kosovo, was very firmly in power in Buda. Long Voivod of Transylvania, he now held several other important titles, among them Ban of Severin and Count of Bistrita, and with them vast tracts of land that had much increased his wealth. And other things had changed. In the pride of his newfound strength the White Knight of Christendom had violated Wallachia's territorial integrity, which was another way of saying he had entered that principality and taken what he wanted, the important duchies of Fagaras and Amlas. Naturally, this led to an immediate breech with Vladislav II. Therefore, war between him and Hunyadi was only a matter of time.

Knowing this, the great crusader admitted Dracula conditionally, for whenever the Danesti were out of favor, the rival house was invariably in. The errant son of the murdered Dracul was received at Hunedoara Castle, the ancestral seat of the Hunyadis, who were actually transplanted Transylvanians. Indeed, he appears to have been welcomed there with at least the outward signs of respect, first as an honored guest, ultimately, as time passed and the prince stayed on, as something more than that; as a student of battle learning the art of war from one of its masters; then (dare we believe it?) almost as a friend.

If friends they were, how did Dracula rationalize his strangely contradictory position? As house guest and pupil to the man chiefly responsible for the deaths of his father and brother, how did he allay his conscience? (For perhaps we may assume that at this stage of his life he still had one.) No one will ever know. Certain it is that Hunyadi confided to Dracula that the fortress of Belgrade was the key not only to Hungary's defense but to that of all central Europe against the Turk, the hard iron core on which the coming Ottoman tide must surely spend itself. Certain also is the fact that in March 1456 he gained an audience for his protégé with Ladislas Posthumus, King of Hungary and Bohemia, and hereditary duke of Austria. Dracula, he told the monarch, should be restored to the throne of his fathers, for he alone among Wallachian princes would fight the Turk to the death.

This was literally true. Perhaps Hunyadi reminded the ruler that all the Draculas were draconists and sworn to crusade. Perhaps he pointed out that the Ottoman scimitar hung poised over Europe this moment, that in the east only the redoubtable Scanderbeg and his Albanians fought on. What he may have said made little difference to Dracula's fortune. Within a short time Belgrade was under Turkish siege as the Arpadian kingdom fought desperately for its very life. Within five months, having broken that siege and turned the Islamic tide as by a miracle, Hunyadi lay dead in the Danubian city of Zemun.

His bravery legendary, his stamina incredible, his dedication sublime, no Muslim weapon had felled the White Knight. Rather it was something so small the eye could not detect it, a bacillus carried by fleas that infested rats, the deadly contagion of bubonic plague. His death checked Dracula in full stride. Could he prevail now with his mentor gone, his influence buried with the only powerful Christian he knew? The situation seemed hopeless. Yet, governed by a sure instinct to seize the initiative that again and again he was to display, he decided the time had come to take his greatest gamble.

His army, all Wallachians, was small, only a fraction the size of that of the enemy. Yet surprise could be his, nearly total surprise if his luck held, and that could win battles. He would use the mountain passes he had studied so thoroughly and enter Wallachia silently like a puff of smoke, be across the foe's lines of communication before they knew it. A desperate chance? He must have smiled at the thought, if grimly.

The first leaves of autumn had not yet fallen when they marched, down through the barrier alps, down and down, into the storied plain of Wallachia. They had come to win or die and every man knew it. There was no road back for them. King Leonidas had known the feeling. They were like the three hundred Spartans at Thermopylae.

4
The Second Reign: A Policy of Terror

It was a distant world she looked upon, a place unlike any she had ever known, a scene as alien to earth as something from an unbidden dream. Before her, illumined by what seemed firelight, were gently rolling hills of an alabaster whiteness, pink crowns, a tangled foliage between pale columnar cliffs set apart at obtuse angles. Directly ahead of her across that white waste something was in movement but she could not determine its nature. It advanced and receded like an errant tide. Now it seemed as black as night, radiantly black; now it had the semblance of a face, a pale feminine visage touched with a strained, intense beauty.

She knew instinctively that the scene was all wrong, unreal, the dream in possession as reality lay eclipsed. The undergrowth was dark brown rather than green, an unruly tangle. The distant girlish face was too large, dwarfing the curling flora it seemed to feed upon. The whiteness of the intervening ground was too white, as white as snow in a landscape where she knew somehow that snow could not be present. It made no sense. The two pink protuberances were out of place. They lost and regained shape as though kneaded by hands, her own hard-clutching hands in frenzied torment. Something bitter was in her mouth, a buzzing in her ears, the white expanse rolling away before her in infinitely soft paroxysmic undulations. She opened her mouth and screamed.

"Feliciana!"

Instantly the face that was beyond her rose between the pale, vibrant columns. A female voice touched with deepest concern spoke softly.

"My lady."

"Where are we, Feliciana? Where is this place?"

The voice grew softer still. "It is my lady's—it *was* my lady's capital. Tirgoviste. We're in your own bed chamber, mistress."

"I am naked."

"Yes, my lady. You have often been naked with me. I trust the fire in the grate will keep us warm."

"What have they been giving me?"

"Absinthe. They've been giving you absinthe for three days."

Ah, the odor of wormwood. The bitter taste. Her maid between her legs was a constant occurrence, for who could find tenderness with Vladislav? Who could love him with his arrogance, his coldly supercilious air, his selfish indifference both in and out of bed? But not with absinthe. Her beloved Feliciana did not need absinthe to take her pleasure of her, to open her for her tongue or be opened by her. She felt herself seized with a strange foreboding.

"That stuff will kill me. It is poison. It is *poison!*"

"My lady, he gives it. He forces it on you." As naked as her mistress, Feliciana rose from the foot of the bed and came to lie beside her on the coverlet. "I—I cannot help it, my lady."

She took the girl in her arms and held her very close, their soft limbs entwining. "Who am I?" she asked, still half-dazed.

"You are my mistress, my lady."

"What is my name?"

"You are the Lady Alceste."

"My full name?"

"Alceste Olteanu."

"The former whore of the boyars, am I not?"

"My lady was wrongfully accused."

"And the plaything of Prince Vladislav, that chilling bastard."

For a moment Feliciana went rigid in her embrace. "He—he has not returned, my lady. He did not come back from the battle."

Alceste sat up abruptly, bringing Feliciana with her. Very slowly she rubbed their breasts together stimulating their nipples, a thing she did unconsciously after three years of intimacy.

"Not returned? Who—? What—?"

"Prince Vlad's army is here."

"Prince *Vlad!*"

Feliciana clutched her tightly, a catch in her voice. "Yes, my lady. He has beaten His Highness. Everyone is talking about it. Everyone is full of fear. It's your old enemy Vlad, the son of Dracul. They say he won against heavy odds and now the throne is his again. No one knows what he will do."

Almost absently Alceste caressed her lover's vagina, half unaware of the extreme wetness, even of her own loins that tingled and flowed and filled her with unsatisfied longing. She gazed into the dancing fire. "He is no enemy of mine," she said. "I don't even know him. Why do they fear him?"

Feliciana was reacting to the intense digital stimulation, panting softly. "He is the Son of the Devil—the Son of the Dragon. They say no one but a madman would have attacked His Highness with only a token force."

"His Highness no more, I think. Where is my good Vladislav?"

"No one knows, my lady." Feliciana was writhing now. "I have not heard. Oh God! Oh my God! Your hand—"

Fully returned to reality and sensual awareness, Alceste thrust her fingers deep. "Yes, you love it, don't you? Were you preparing me for him?"

"My lady?"

"We are spoils of war, aren't we? Prince Vlad is a man—and a conqueror. He will take what he wants. You say three days? Why has he waited?" She stroked Feliciana's long black hair, pulling her closer, dallying with her in the ways they loved. "It is not like a man to wait. Is he such a boy he cannot claim what he wants?"

Feliciana stopped squirming and seemed to catch her breath. "I think he is not quite a boy even in years," she said. "He is twenty-five. He will be Prince Vlad III again now, when they reinvest him. Already the people are starting to call him—Dracula."

Alceste nodded. It was the people's way of recognizing his legitimacy as the son of Dracul. The Danesti had lost. Vladislav could be dead. Her imagination reeled at the thought of what her fate might be under Dracula. *Under* Dracula. *Beneath* him. *Spread wide to receive him.*

"Where is this Vlad now?" she asked.

"He has come here twice to watch us."

"Making love?"

"He watches to see that I obey him, that I do what he told me to do."

"Which is, my pet?"

From seemingly out of nowhere Feliciana produced a long ivory dildo. "He—he seems to show consideration, my lady. He seems to wish not to hurt you. He—he said I was to prepare you."

Puzzled, Alceste shook her lovely head slowly. "It is ridiculous, beloved. I am not a virgin. Nor is he one of those elephants the Muslims use in their wars in Africa. Prepare me for what?"

Feliciana seemed hesitant. "My lady—my lady did not feel any of it?"

"Feel what? Oh this cursed absinthe numbs my poor brain. Feel what, my love?"

"He would use my lady as a boy."

And now she knew what it was, the reason she felt a tenderness in her anus, the reason she drifted in and out of her dreams with a vague, half-realized sense of fullness and tightness. Feliciana's dildo, that cleverly carved marvel of Cathayan craftsmen, that always erect partner. This prince was indeed considerate—or not virile enough to force a tight entry. But why take her as a boy in this debauchery and bliss? Was it to make clear her utter submission, to humiliate her even further? That would be in character for a conquering prince, especially one in possession of his rival's helpless mistress.

"And you, Feliciana?" she asked.

Her devoted paramour made a little gesture of helplessness. "He has already had me, my lady, more than once. He did not show me—the same solicitude."

"I see." She released her maid and lay back. "Perhaps you will bear him an heir, my dear. I mean, he will not always be satisfied with your backside alone. Then you'll come up in the world. You even have some education, and a royal concubine has many privileges."

Feliciana did not reply. She was still breathing heavily with sexual arousal. Now she clamped her full white thighs around her own moving hand and groaned.

"What else did he put in my drink?" asked Alceste.

"Ah, you sensed it. *Imsak*, I think, my lady. It's a potion of the Muslims from Damascus and Aleppo. They say he knows of such things. They say he's half a Turk."

"A soporific drug? An inducer of sleep?"

"I don't know, my lady. It may numb the pain but I think it is also a love elixir, an aphrodisiac to make my lady's loins as hot as fire—like the cantharides of the Greeks and Byzantines. Oh your taste is in my mouth and your fragrance in my nostrils. Love me. Love me, I *beg* you!"

Alceste responded at once. But then, as they fell into close embrace once more, turning their nude bodies to lie reversed, a noise was heard in the outer corridor and they pulled apart, instinctively covering themselves with blankets.

"Who is it?" asked Alceste, half-breathless with loin-tingling excitement.

Feliciana seemed to be trembling. "It is *he*, my lady. I know his tread."

"Why do you fear him?"

"I don't know."

"Why do you fear him?"

"Oh my lady, I don't *know!* He is like no man I ever saw. He is so strange—and there is something in his eyes. Oh Lord God protect us!"

What Alceste might have said remained unspoken, for the intruder was at the door. She heard his hand on the handle, saw it turn slowly. Why did she feel this sudden dread, she wondered? She had more right in this palace than he. The Danesti claim was as good as his. It was better than his and she was Danesti property. Yet she felt his power, felt it through that oaken portal studded with iron, felt it like some elemental force, like wind or rain or flood. Implacable. Indomitable. Impossible to stop.

Dracula!

He came through the door and stood before them. She had expected him to be tall but he was not, though powerfully built. Except for silver shoe buckles and cut silver studs on his doublet he was dressed all in black. Black hair to the shoulders. A trace of black hair on the short upper lip, the beginnings of a mustache. Green eyes that caught the reflected light of the torches burning in the wall brackets, eyes that seemed huge beneath their long lashes, that glinted and sparkled above a prominant acquiline nose. The hand that pressed down the hilt of his broadsword glittered with diamonds. She thought she recognized the ornately damascened weapon from the royal treasury.

"Good evening, Lady Alceste," he said quietly. He had stopped halfway across the room and was standing motionless, staring at her. "I am glad to find you rested. You'll forgive my indelicacy. I'm also glad to find you can sit without discomfort despite—ah—Feliciana's tender ministrations."

Alceste felt the flush in her burning cheeks and was surprised at her own modesty. She actually stammered. "I—Your Highness is unkind to mention it."

"Maidenly indirectness?"

"I am not a maiden, as Your Highness well knows, but I have my pride."

He seemed to be laughing at her with his eyes. "And what is your pride worth?"

"Your Highness?"

"What would it fetch, say, in the Moorish slave market in Algiers when some huge black opens you for the bidders with the handle of his whip? Can I turn it into gold? How many ducats?"

"Your Highness jests. Would you sell me to Algerian pirates?"

"Sell you? Oh no. Not when the wine of your desire is scarcely broached. Yes, Alceste, I jest." He stepped closer to them. "Feliciana, you are fair to look upon and I'll make frequent use of you. Leave us now. I will send for you when I need you. Leave the artificial lover here. I may decide to amuse our lady with it."

The girl rose still gripping the blanket and abandoned the dildo. "As my lord wishes," she said.

Dracula laughed lightly. "You needn't conceal yourself," he chided. "I've seen it all, remember? Ah, the supreme illogic of women. You may take your gown and slippers with you, there's a good child. Indeed, I find you delightful."

As she started to pass him he ripped the blanket from her and dropped it on the floor, grasping her arm in a steellike grip and pulling her nakedness to him. "Have you prepared your mistress for me?" he asked very sharply.

Feliciana was rigid with fright. "I h-have tried, my lord," she stammered.

"I think it was kind of me, don't you?"

"Y-yes, my lord."

"Yes. I'm like that. Kindness and gentleness personified. A sort of saint, really, like that ivory one to titillate our lady's love passages. Yes. That's a saint, too." Suddenly he clutched one of her bare buttocks and squeezed. "A strong hand, isn't it? Even powerful you might say."

Feliciana emitted a startled cry. "Oh my lord! Oh yes, yes, your hand is very strong. Oh my good lord, please don't hurt me, I beg you!"

He released her. "Your softness enchants me almost as much as your submissiveness. Go now but keep my kindness in mind. Venerate my sainthood."

When she had gone he turned quickly to Alceste. She felt his eyes burning into her soul, eyes that seemed to speak with a command. She let the blanket fall from her body and sat very still on the bed, concealing nothing from him. *This* was what they all feared, she realized, her mind in turmoil. There *was* something inhuman about him, something terrible, diabolical. Gripped almost with a sense of panic, she wondered if he would kill her now or wait until he had raped her.

He came to her and sat beside her on the bed. Startlingly, with infinite tenderness, he caressed her pendulous breasts with both his hands, massaging them with the pale ghost of a smile on his lips. But now she seemed to dread him even more, finding herself unable to meet his glance.

"These are very nice," he said, stretching her nipples gently.

She said nothing.

"These are *particularly* nice."

She trembled, her moving lips appealing to him wordlessly, supplicatingly. She felt half-paralyzed.

He dropped her breasts and sat there appraising her, his strange green eyes missing no tiny detail of her naked, vulnerable body. "I can bring you great happiness," he said. "Do you realize that? Unimaginable ecstasy."

With a strong effort of her will she raised her face to look at him. "I am not in a position to think of it, my lord. Can a slave be happy?"

"Sometimes, if she uses her head. You have a very pretty head. Indeed, it's a match for your voluptuous and inviting body. You are wondering what happened to Vladislav, my dear, are you not?"

She could not stop the trembling and knew he saw it. "Yes," she said. "I am wondering."

Dracula nodded. "I will have the town crier announce the tidings tomorrow. Broadsheets and placards in the public square, all to bespeak his misfortune. He proved himself something of a fool. He fought well enough, but I had the advantage of a carefully prepared ambush and took him by surprise. It was a bloody affair, I'm afraid, rather like Hannibal and his Carthaginians when he destroyed the Roman army at Lake Trasimenus—although I faced greater odds. Vladislav fled the battlefield, which was on the plain north of Tirgoviste. He rode eastward across the Prahova River. I led my mounted flying column in pursuit. We caught up with him at Tirgsor. You're perhaps familiar with the place. There he was taken and he pleaded for his life. A Danesti begging mercy of *me!* Can you imagine the futility of such a request? I had him dig his own grave, and I confess to a certain pleasure in watching him do it. Then my newly appointed headsman simply shortened him a bit and tumbled him into it."

He paused. Now his hands stroked her bare thighs and soft, flaring hips. Very slowly, almost absently he caressed her. "I'd like to be able to tell you he died nobly but in sooth it was with an ill grace. Such is the way of Danesti princes, pretenders one and all."

Still she did not speak. As his fingers entwined in her pubic hair she inwardly gasped, feeling herself begin to sweat in sudden overwhelming arousal. As he continued to address her, the quality of his voice was like syrup, the pulsing of a distant drum from some unimaginable void.

"I considered bringing his head here and mounting it above the city's main gate. Yes. Or perhaps on the very top of the Chindeia Tower. However, it seemed like a pointless affectation. Don't you think? It would have elevated this abysmal varlet over the people he pretended to rule, and that he did not deserve. He is better left in his earthen hole and forgotten." He paused as though in reflection. "The tower is in disrepair, by the way, and I shall rebuild it."

She cared not a pin's fee for Vladislav and was glad he was dead. She found her voice suddenly. "Will my lord make love to me?"

"Of course."

"Now?"

"Certainly. It is why I am here. I know you are not ready. It takes at least two weeks of daily preparation, as I well remember, but your pleasure will be all the more exquisite for that. I am not Vladislav, that quaking poltroon. I am Dracula. I am *Dracula!* Do you understand that?"

She nodded. When she spoke, weighed down now by a sense of utter helplessness, it was just above a whisper. "I am yours, great prince. Yours to do with as you please. You do not need drugs to seduce me."

"Drugs? I am an opiate unto myself. Or an unbearable stimulant. It depends. Why do you tremble?"

"Because I fear you, lord."

Faintly, he smiled his satisfaction. "It is good, little slave. Yes. It is as it should be."

She was barely aware of his act of undressing. Reentering the bed, he appeared to come to her more like some metaphysical entity than as a man; with a burly, very muscular body; with a tongue that licked and licked and licked; and startlingly white teeth that seemed to tear at her, mauling her tender flesh, yet curiously without pain.

"I am Dracula," he told her. "Say it."

"You are Dracula."

"I will bring you ecstasy. *Say* it!"

"Y-you will bring me ecstasy."

Never had she dreamed that such utter mastery in a man was possible. She felt overwhelmed by his power as though her will was nothing, her womanliness all. She took the shameful position he wanted her to take without protest. When he entered her she gave a long, piercing cry. It seemed as though her soul poured out of her and flowed like wine. Red wine, the color of blood.

"You will rupture me," she moaned. "Oh my lord, you will *rupture* me!"

"Don't you want to be ruptured?" He was thrusting mercilessly, brutally. "Don't you?"

"Yes. Oh yes, yes, yes! Take me on this journey and into this madness! I will die for you!"

"Beg for it."

"I beg you."

"*Beg* for it!"

"I beg you, my prince. Oh my God, I *beg* you!"

After that the room seemed to dissolve, to flow magically into ever-receding distances. Alceste, once mistress to the dead Vladislav, received the subjugating cudgel of her conqueror, absorbed it, became one with it, and was borne away by the swirling, immeasurable tide.

From all that can be gleaned from the paucity of documentation and inferred through the use of logic, Dracula's victory over Vladislav II was won by speed, daring, and deadly surprise. There was nothing haphazard in his methods this time. When he took the throne before, he did not know how to protect it and had no plan. Now he had one. On the previous occasion, he was not really sure who his enemies were in his own court or how best to deal with them. Now he knew the identities of at least a few and thought he had found a way to uncover the others. The murdered Vladislav was buried at the Monastery of the Hill and may thus have lain close to Dracul. Even today the words on his tombstone have not been completely effaced. They give the date of his death as August 20, 1456.

Dracula's title remained unchanged. In the early fall of this year he came to his second coronation as Prince Vlad III. As though to stress the continuing political dichotomy that had divided Dracul's loyalties (and incidentally acknowledge the balance of military power), he was then immediately trapped into compromise. On September 6 he swore an oath of allegiance to Ladislas Posthumus, king of Hungary, and wined and dined the Magyar delegates from Buda. Then, before the month was over he was forced to surpass this cynical performance, conceding himself vassal to Mehmed II before Turkish plenipotentiaries from conquered Constantinople. As he hated all of them bitterly it is not difficult to imagine the emotions that seethed in him. It was as though the Hungarians and Turks had lighted the fuse to a powder keg, then sat down on it the better to stifle it. Beneath their weight the fuse continued to burn closer and closer to the powder. Ignition was inevitable.

As far as we know, Dracula was never able to find his father's body, though it is virtually certain that attempts were made. The remains of his slaughtered brother, Mircea, however, had been reburied in Tirgoviste's public cemetery long before the second enthronement, perhaps having been moved there by monks friendly to the family. The newly crowned prince ordered immediate disinterment after nine years of burial and was witness to this grim scene. He knew the wretched youth's fate then. Mircea had been asphyxiated. In his dying paroxysms, gasping frantically for air in the coffin in which they had sealed him, he had loosened his bonds enough to turn his face downward toward the little remaining oxygen. Thus the neck of the corpse was twisted. Thus rigor mortis had fixed it in time, immutable evidence of pitiless savagery. Was it then that something snapped in Dracula's brain? We shall never know. That something *did* give way at or about this time was soon to become evident from a change in the man that was at once profound and terrible.

The winter arrived, the year 1457 in its course. It would be a remarkable year. In Suceava, Dracula's cousin would become prince of Moldavia with Wallachian military assistance, eventually winning the title Stéfan cel Mare (the Great) and an important place in the history of eastern Europe. Times were changing. In Spain, a Dominican priest named Tomás de Torquemada was thirty-seven years old and still unknown, still ahead his founding of the most frightful instrument for religious persecution ever devised, the Spanish Inquisition. In the Italian city of Ferrara, Girolamo Savonarola, one of the greatest martyrs the Catholic Church was ever to know, was a boy of five. In the Italian port of

Genoa, a lad only one year older played in the flooded streets with wooden boats. His name was Cristoforo Columbo, but the English-speaking world would know him as Columbus.

Dracula bided his time. In the early weeks of the new year his regime seemed remarkable for its peacefulness and stability, but in reality such a conception could scarcely have been more misleading. He saw enemies on every side and lived in fear of assassination. His own barely subdued rage gnawed at his vitals. He was beside himself with wrath. Of all the creatures on earth, none is more dangerous than he who is both armed and beleaguered, who has the courage to strike and the patient craftiness to choose his moment. Such was he. Ever watchful and suspicious, fanged and envenomed, he was as lethal as a cobra in a thicket. He thirsted for blood. It is probable that at this time he was potentially the most deadly human alive.

Historians have speculated on why he did not destroy the boyars at once. Two reasons suggest themselves. First, his growing spy network of fanatical secret police—always the chief bulwark of tyranny—was not yet sufficiently organized or experienced to supply him with reliable information on boyar strength. Would the people support them against him? If so, to strike prematurely could spark the revolt that would bring him down. They were used to weak princes. His uncles had all been weak. Because of that they had backed the boyars before and might do so again. They needed to be taught fear, to be inculcated with the firm conviction that he and he alone could protect and sustain them.

The second reason for his delay concerned the army. How loyal was it? Could the officers be trusted in crisis? True, his victory over Vladislav II had raised his prestige very considerably. Yet he was well aware of what a few disloyal zealots could accomplish when they set their agents quietly to work among the rank and file. Such covert treason had spread disaffection before, toppled princely thrones, even imperiled kingdoms and empires. The Turks could vouch for that. He must wait and put the army repeatedly to the test, meanwhile ferret out the known disloyal and have them quietly disappear. He knew the day was not far off when he could flaunt the mailed fist openly.

On the surface, such machinations would seem to indicate a rational mind, more or less acute mental clarity, in fact a condition of perfect sanity. Yet events were to prove that this was far from true. Dracula had a breathing spell. In Albania, the victories of Scanderbeg over the Turks had slowed the Ottoman advance. Now that redoubtable fighter was uniting Albania and Montenegro, and the new pope, Calixtus III, had named him captain general of the anti-Turkish crusade, the new Hunyadi. It threw the Turks off balance, delayed Mehmed's timetable for conquest. Still more was the sultan chagrined when the powerful Republic of Venice began courting Scanderbeg for a defensive alliance against the Porte, offering to place Venetian sea power into the scale of balances in the Mediterranean. The Queen of the Adriatic was still to be feared. With Turkish energies momentarily concentrated elsewhere, the new ruler of Wallachia was quick to see his opportunity.

In Dracula's view what was needed was a sudden, unexpected thrust that would establish an iron rule, instill fear in the Romanian population, and launch a reign of terror that would paralyze all opposition. If economic as well as political advantage could be derived from it, so much the better. He would put it on a racial and patriotic basis. Romania for the Romanians; all others beware. If at the same time he could raise the native living standard he might even become a popular figure, at once honored and respected. But rule as an absolute despot he would and must. He was by nature imperious. Moreover, he was sure his survival depended on it.

Tailor-made for his purposes was the situation in neighboring Transylvania. Technically, except for the duchies of Amlas and Fagaras, the entire region was a part of Hungary, and even the two duchies had been independent of Wallachia since 1453. Dracula wanted them back and was prepared to kill the remnant of their ducal families to get them. He also wanted widespread economic changes that would favor the native peoples at the expense of the immigrant Germans, primarily the Saxon merchants whose wealth and strength were growing alarmingly. He regarded their guild system as a threat, their thriving centers of trade as "foreign" enclaves, and his knowledge of history was an ever-present reminder of what these people had accomplished before. In medieval times the Germans had been a great power in the Baltic. The thing that had given them that power was *mercantile* dominance, the suzerainty won for them by their formidable Hanseatic League. This once widespread organization was accursed in his eyes and all Saxons were swine. At any cost he must break them.

As it happened, on the day of the previous year (1456) that he had sworn fealty to Hungary he had also renewed a treaty of commerce with the Germans, and would now be false to both. The treaty was concluded with Brasov, which the Germans called Kronstadt; with the entire transalpine region of Tara Bîrsei (Bursenland); and a separate agreement had been made with Sibiu (Hermannstadt), his former residence at the foot of the Transylvanian Alps. Free trade had been guaranteed. Custom duties were to be kept low. Nothing was to impede the flow of Wallachian raw materials to the Saxon manufacturers or the reciprocal movement of finished goods. Even political interests were recognized. All participants agreed not to give asylum to an enemy of any of the signatories. Dracula, always magnanimous if he thought he saw an advantage, even offered to defend the German burghers against a possible Turkish invasion. Relations appeared quite amiable.

Now, less than a year later, all that was to change overnight. If he invaded Hungarian territory could Buda retaliate? He seriously doubted it. The capital city was in turmoil. Hunyadi's son Ladislas was dead. Having procured the feckless youth's assassination and lost power thereby, Ladislas Posthumus had fled to Prague (where the plague had since broken out) and at the moment Hungary had no king, only chaos and imminent revolution. It was time to act.

Quietly massing his troops before Tirgoviste, Dracula crossed the Dambovita River, then followed the valley of the Arges west-northwest through the passes of the alps, reversing the route he had taken to attack Vladislav II. Hastily recruited frontier guards swelled his force to an estimated 20,000. Not far beyond the point where the final pass debouched into the Transylvanian plateau lay the city of Sibiu whose citizens had given him refuge when he was desperate. He fell on them like an avalanche. Few Turkish emirs or *pashas* had shown such ferocity. Only the Mongols killed like this, slaughtering man, woman, and child indiscriminately. It mattered not in the slightest that the Germans themselves had founded the place three centuries before, that they and not the Romanians had colonized it. They were foreign vermin and must be obliterated. And now we see the diabolical metamorphosis, the infernal change of character that was fixed and unalterable and would endure to the grave. Everywhere the flames of pillage roared and crackled. Everywhere was butchery and rape, the surprised and hopeless defenders put to the sword. Then, the devastation and ruin complete, the Wallachian prince showed how he dealt with prisoners. Many of both sexes and all ages were burned alive. Many others were taken back over the border into Wallachia where Dracula had planned a grisly spectacle. By some accounts nearly 10,000 people died.

He was to win his most odious nickname now. Stakes driven into the ground were his chief instruments of death. After these first mass executions the news of the massacre spread rapidly. This man killed in the cruelest way of all, evoking scenes of Roman crucifixions in the long ago, terrible scenes out of legend. Rank or station did not matter. Sex and age were meaningless. The shocked Romanians themselves dubbed him Vlad Tepes—Vlad the Impaler. Before his course was run he was to set more victims writhing on pales than any tyrant in history.

It was Easter day of the year 1459 and the pleasant April weather to another person might have been a tonic. Dracula was unaware of it. As he stood on the ramparts of Tirgoviste, a solitary figure, the balmy atmosphere of late afternoon could have been filled with drenching rain and it would have made no difference, such was the intensity of his mental preoccupation. Only a fly took his notice. It landed on his face. He slapped at it, felled it, and squeezed it to nothingness between his fingers. He reflected abstractedly that he was quick, as his fencing master had noted more than once, so quick he could snatch such insects out of the air and destroy them on the wing.

He smiled a little wanly. He had not been quick with the boyars. Too many considerations had delayed him. Until now they must think themselves secure indeed. Until now they must be certain he was just another simpleton in princely trappings, capable of arousal on occasion but of nothing dangerous, nothing they need worry about. How smug they must be at this very moment in their silken finery and jeweled tiaras, all of them here at the palace now, all invited to the royal Easter feast by the very lord they plotted against and would seek to overthrow at the first opportunity.

He gazed across the city. Some of the boyar dwellings were nearly as imposing as his own. In the ostentation of their Byzantine domes they aped royalty. In the pretentiousness of their gardens and courtyards and private chapels they hurled a challenge at his autocracy, defying him in their accursed independence, spitting on his claim to rule by divine right, laughing behind his back because he knew they had killed Dracul and Mircea but could not isolate the full cabal of assassins. Were they *insane?* Since last year Hunyadi's son Matei Corvinus ruled Hungary. He, Dracula, was in this king's favor. Did they think they could survive without him? It was last year, also, that Mehmed took Athens. Did they believe the Turks finished? Why did they think the son of Dracul now fortified

Bucharest? Mehmed would pulverize them. He was already in the process of strangling Serbia. The Wallachian nobility were fools as well as traitors, the greatest fools in Christendom.

He turned his head from side to side. He spat to the east, then to the west, as though he had gagged on the foul taste of the boyars long enough and must expel them from his system.

"Time," he said softly between clenched lips. "Their time has run out, for the lord of Wallachia can no longer stomach them. A Richard the Lionheart would merely behead them. A Mehmed the Turk would open their leg arteries in the best Ottoman tradition. But I, by God, will *eat* them! I'll devour them whole, pass them through my guts, and excrete them like the stinking dung they are!"

He was inwardly raging now, fighting to contain the fury he believed would kill him of the falling sickness if left to burn unchecked. He pressed down the hilt of his broadsword until the long scabbard and blade were horizontal. They could not see him. They were in the banqueting hall stuffing themselves with capon and pheasant and roast lamb; quaffing wine by the keg; utterly absorbed in revelry while their strumpet wives wantonly displayed their breasts and cast flirtatious glances at every male from the virgin pages to the yeoman guards. Many of the latter when not on duty wore brightly colored codpieces over their genitals in the manner of western Europeans, some with fringes and tassels the better to catch the feminine eye. He laughed silently at that. Recalling his learning from history, he remembered how the Roman emperor Caligula had regarded the senators' wives as whores, even opened a brothel in his palace and sold them to strangers off the street for five gold pieces a turn. Codpieces to attract the eyes of *these* ripe bawds? Hah! They would still stare at the same full pouches if the objects of their lust were plastered with hay and horse manure!

He began to walk slowly along the high, crenelated wall. In his mind's eye he could see clearly all the points which already his men were covering. Though they did not know it, the boyars were surrounded, hemmed in by overwhelming military power. The palace was comparatively small. Not all of them could dine in the main hall. Some of the lesser nobility laid services of their own in the meadow outside the east rampart, well separated from the guildsmen and other members of the despised Third Estate who had also been invited. He could hear music. The gypsies played their lutes and viols; their women danced with the

Iberian castanet; in time the multitude would join them in the Romanian *hora;* and skirts would fly, and petticoats go astray, and the minds of all turn to amorous frivolity.

If he let them live that long!

He passed a sentry who came smartly to the salute with his pike. Moments later he was approached by Bratulescu, Captain of the Guard, in glittering morion and cuirass. This time it was the hand salute. In the officer's demeanor was a certain tenseness. Dracula addressed him quietly.

"Have you finished making your rounds, captain?"

"Yes, Your Highness."

"Is anything amiss? I detect a certain concern in your manner."

"No, Your Highness. It's just—it all seems too easy."

Dracula nodded. "That's the result of careful planning, Bratulescu. *My* planning. If you would catch a carp in one of our many lakes, you simply bait the hook. This one is baited and tipped with hemlock. The boyars have taken it but they will not shake it from their mouths. They will swallow this hook, look you, and pull and pull until it disembowels them. Do your men know what is expected of them?"

"Yes, my lord."

"Good. It is a wise man who knows his duty in this world. When my left hand covers the buckle of my sword belt Cantemir's troops will go into action. The boyars must be separately handled. I offer no violence to merchants or craftsmen, and none to the priesthood—yet. Any who resist are to be cut down but I wish to avoid slaughter if possible. Remember, I have a very special use for the able-bodied among them, both men and women. Am I understood?"

"Perfectly, my lord."

"Excellent. I'm going down now to rejoin my guests—who I am sure have missed me the while. This will be lively sport, captain. It will be dusk in two hours. I promise you an evening to remember."

The officer saluted again. "God grant Your Highness success."

Dracula descended the steps leading down to the courtyard, then passed through the guarded corridor giving on the great hall. Now everything changed suddenly. All was noise and wassail and ostentatious display as the boyars sought to outdo each other in ribaldry and eloquence. He tried to join them unobtrusively but failed in this as a watchful herald announced his entry by trumpet. As he resumed his place at the head of one of the long silver-laid tables, a silence ensued. Then, as he swept the masses of his guests with a seemingly kindly and benevolent eye, the frivolous behavior was continued as flagons were drained and all drank more deeply than ever.

The prince bided his time. An hour passed, then nearly double that interval while he laughed and joked, displaying the charm that many had noted but few fully trusted. As twilight approached, he visually checked the positions of his soldiers, noting each carefully placed man. There would be no exit for his victims, no sanctuary, no place to hide. When he struck the obsidian butt of his carving knife several times on the table an alert chamberlain called for immediate quiet. Very quickly the tumult subsided. The sweeping glance of the host now included everyone.

"My honored guests," he said, "I've been sitting here regarding you and an amusing thought has struck me, something that I know will take your interest and give you reason for pause in your festive celebration. You know, there has never *been* such an Easter as this before. When this day is done I'm sure you will all agree with that."

His gaze took in the robed ecclesiastics before him. "Even my most pious lord the Metropolitan will come to agree with me, I think. And my lord abbots, and my lord bishops. You see, it is a question I am going to pose to you. Oh nothing difficult. A mere matter of mathematics. The question is this. How many reigns have you, my loyal subjects, personally experienced in your lifetime?"

That the query was pregnant with malice was not immediately apparent to the listeners. There fell a momentary quiet. One or two snickered self-consciously.

"'Tis a jape!" said a stalwart cavalier. He was Ion Sima, a nephew of the Ban of Lower Wallachia. "My lord does but jest."

Dracula's smile was as cold as ice. "I jest not, good sir, for jesting would be frivolous on such an auspicious occasion, almost insulting to this august assembly. Withal, I'll ignore your observation and repeat my question. How many reigns have you lived to see here in Tirgoviste? You may answer simply."

Nicolae Slavici rose in his place to speak. He was old and white-headed, once *spatar* or cavalry commander under Dracula's grandfather Mircea. "As my lord is in earnest, may I ask a question?"

"Ask, noble friend of the throne."

"Does my lord include *all* reigns, both Draculesti and Danesti, or does he speak only of his own lineage?"

Dracula laughed tonelessly. "The memory of him who was once Master of Horse to Prince Mircea grows dim. We are all related, all of the

Basarab line. Dan II was cousin to my grandfather. Include the Danesti by all means. That they serve Satan and we Draculas God is of no concern at the moment."

"Then I have served many," said Slavici. "I am too old to remember their number. Perhaps twenty."

"Twenty princes. Twenty sovereign lords in one man's lifetime. How quickly they rose and how briefly they survived." Dracula's piercing gaze fixed on another. "And thou, Octavian Mille? You were *postelnic* in the time of Mircea, were you not? You're as grizzled and slack-jowled as Slavici. As court chamberlain under Mircea, even minister of foreign affairs for my father, Dracul, you also must have seen many reigns. Is it not so?"

Mille nodded. "It is true, lord," he replied. "There are less than two inches of my beard for every reign and my beard is long. Twenty or twenty-one."

"Twenty-one. Possibly even more if you nudge your memory. All dead now, is it not so? Dead and buried and forgotten. Like Dracul whose grave I cannot find. Like my brother Mircea, who first was murdered—then flung like dirt into potter's field." Suddenly Dracula's eyes became huge and seemed to flash with green fire. "And thou, Barbu Cosbue, *logofat* under Aldea! Thou, Titu Asachi, *vornic* under Mihail! Thou, Dinu Feraru, *vistier* in Dracul's first reign and under Basarab II! And thou and thou and thou!"

He rose to his feet, thrusting his stiffened forefinger at them like the blade of a dagger, the muscles of his face working spasmodically as a nervous tic pulsed in his temple. "Do you think I am both blind and a fool? Tell me, how do you explain the fact that you have had so many princes in your land? The guilt is entirely due to your shameful intrigues! No, don't speak. I will speak now."

He had drawn his poniard from its sheath, a wicked looking *main gauche* of French origin, its blade glittering in the newly lighted torches. "They are dead because of your plots! They are dead because of your *treason!* Who was it among you who betrayed my father and hounded him to death in the marshes of Balteni? Do you think I don't know who you are? Who murdered my brother by burial alive? Do you think I can't identify you? Do you think all these months I've been idle, that my police do not have your names? I tell you, vile traitor dogs, *you* are the fools, not I! But you've been found out! It is over! I say to you it is *over!*"

Even the most drunken among them was alarmed now. Some of the boyars' wives began to scream. Men rose up from the tables, weaving and dizzy with inebriation. Dracula's left hand went to his sword belt. Pandemonium reigned as armed troops closed in at the noted signal, brandishing their gleaming weapons. Badly frightened and unprotesting, the clergy were led away.

Even at the height of the uproar Dracula's voice was louder than them all. "Let none escape!" he thundered. "He who vouchsafes passage to any one of them will take his place on a stake!"

Shifting the *main gauche* to the left hand he drew his sword. With the agility of a hound he leaped over the table and attacked the first boyar he could reach who was trying to defend himself, cutting him down in seconds.

"Die!" he shouted as he jerked free his blood-streaked blade. "You and those who fall with you are the lucky ones!" He turned to a corpulent boyar without recognizing him in his rage. The man's bloated face was sweaty with his exertions, yet he'd abandoned all defense and was standing motionless beside his hysterical wife, his useless hanger dangling from a bleeding hand. "Dost yield, traitor?" Dracula demanded.

The boyar looked confused, as though his drink-befuddled brain could not take in the situation. "Yield, traitor," he repeated numbly. "I—yes, I yield."

Dracula raised his blade and pointed it at him. "Then drop that sword!"

The weapon clattered to the floor where many others already lay.

"They are finished, Your Highness!" cried an officer. "They haven't got the skill to fight trained troops!"

"Nor the balls," said someone else.

He looked around him. There had been little resistance. Taken completely by surprise, the disheveled nobles were disarmed and dazed, most of them shocked into soberness now, some already shackled. Their morale had been utterly crushed. He saw that at once. There was no fighting spirit in them. Their wives and children wept in fear and panic. A few of the women had already collapsed in swoons and were lying on the floor. His triumph was complete. Including those who had been captured outside he estimated their number at more than 500.

He turned to the small man who now approached and saluted and was waiting for orders, the battle-hardened Vasili Luca. "My congratulations, General Luca. You have done well."

A grin spread over the officer's flushed countenance. "Thank you, Your Highness. Uh—did you say *general*, my lord?"

"Indeed. You are the senior surviving officer after Lazan and he will soon be worm bait. Had you failed you would be gracing the end of a stake within the hour, but I reward devotion and success. You now hold general rank and are my *spatar*, commander-in-chief of the Wallachian army, subject to no order but mine."

Luca bowed. "Overwhelmed, Highness. If I may say so, my lord, you spin a very pretty web."

"The better to ensnare these insects, eh?" Dracula kicked at the remains of the man he had killed. He recognized him now. He was Titu Blaga, considered a lady's man and a wit, even something of a minor poet. "Take Blaga's head, and those of any others who died, and mount them on pikes on the Chindeia Tower. I regret that their deaths were quick. I should have taken particular care to save them for something special. Well—my father and brother will forgive me."

Still aglow with his promotion, Luca bowed again. "In paradise the souls of your distinguished kin rejoice, Your Highness. Shall I—?"

"Yes. The old and unfit are to be impaled in the morning. There are enough stakes already emplaced. Segregate the young and the strong, then iron them in the dungeons to await my pleasure. By the eternal God, before I have finished with them they will wish they had died with the rest!"

"My lord's command."

"And Luca."

"Yes, Your Highness."

Dracula had been holding his slowly dripping sword under his arm, not wanting to foul his scabbard. "Have this blade cleaned and return it to me," he said, giving it to the other. "The weapon of Wallachia's prince must not remain stained with the blood of a treacherous dog."

"At once, Your Highness."

As Luca turned to go, Dracula caught his arm. "A moment," he said. "You are a man of refined tastes, general. I think you may have an appreciation for high drama, something in the classic mold of Aeschylus and Euripides. Have I judged you aright?"

Luca, a simple soldier who had no idea of the identity of either man, could only nod and smirk a little. "I like to consider myself partial to them, my lord."

"Say you so? Good. Then tarry a moment to view what I shall show you."

Dracula had made sure that the frightened boyars and their wretched families were watching his every move. Now he strode to the center of the room between the long dining tables and raised his hand imperiously. In that stricken hall of the dead and the all-but-condemned the silence was absolute, for even the children were stunned and cowed into muteness. His voice broke that silence.

"Now that your well-known cowardice has rendered you as meek and mild as so many kittens, it would be unseemly of me as your host not to give you some notion of the fate that awaits you." His eyes became fixed on a bound boyar in scarlet doublet and hose. "Ah Tudor Vlahuta, how your fortune has changed since you helped to murder my brother Mircea. This will be especially interesting to you."

Hangdog and sullen, trying to conceal his fear, Vlahuta said nothing. Dracula's gaze shifted to another man similarly restrained. "Miron Conduratu, isn't it? The torches fail somewhat of their service but I see you, thou miscreant swine. You were the leader of the murderers. Did you enjoy Hungary's gold or was it thirty pieces of silver? Speak softly and tell us, thou foresworn filth."

Conduratu's vicious face was very pale. Yet knowing his fate was certain he had somewhere found the courage of defiance. "If I am filth," he said, "what are you but a prince of scum? I should have let air into your jester's belly long ago."

Dracula's face was like a flame but he saw the intention. The insult was of the worst. Conduratu hoped to enrage him and thus gain a quick death.

"The air you denied my brother, isn't it? Hah! Mark you this, thou sputum of a sick whore, in any trial of battle I would spit you like a capon! But now enough!"

All during the day and evening, curtains had been drawn and the inner courtyard effectively sealed from the view of the guests. At a sign from Dracula the curtains were now opened. Flaming brands lighted the outer darkness. There in the center of the rectangle, greased with tallow that made it seem to glow in the reflected light, was a single stake. No writhing victim hung upon it. No corpse lay slumped in death. The bare pale just stood there, waiting, the torchlight playing on it as though it were a fang from the bowels of hell.

Beside it stood something else. It was apparently alive, for it moved slightly. It may even have been human in its filthy rags, but so bent and twisted was it, so blackened and covered with filth, that no one of the captives who saw it could be sure. It was just there—like the stake. People looked and did not fully comprehend. Then Dracula was speaking again.

"What you see before you is a vision of the future, the immediate future. For those who are old or infirm there is the stake. Many such pales are already planted in the Valley of Retribution. They are waiting for you. On the morrow you will go to them, receive them in the preordained orifice, and grace them with a noble dignity befitting your high station."

He paused for dramatic effect. "For the more physically able there is another destiny. It is represented by this curious gnome from my dungeons. Some of you may recognize the thing. It had a name once. Perhaps you remember it. It was Eliade Eftimiu, once called the Sage of Moldavia. I think he should have stayed in Suceava, but he chose to come here and join the conspirators against me. *Look* at him! Burn the pitiful sight of him into your memories. Is it a man? A beast? Whatever it is, it's of noble aspect compared to what you will become, I promise you. For I have something singular in mind for you. Ah, the poetry of the thing bemuses and enchants me. You will be struck by the beauty of it—when you know what it is. Indeed, my honored ones, a great artist was lost when I became a statesman."

At another sign the curtains were closed. Some children were crying. Uncomprehendingly they cried, their mothers weeping also as they tried to comfort them. And that was all. As his new commander departed to obey, Dracula's gaze followed after him.

"Luca!" he called.

The general swung about. "Your Highness?"

"Don't ever lose a battle."

"No, Your Highness."

"Carry on, my *spatar*."

Luca bowed and was gone. Dracula found himself sweating and wiped his brow. He glanced at the shambles around him. So it was done. At last the boyars had tasted humiliation and defeat, something to lay against the score. He could never balance the scales. He knew that. Yet it was a token. Tomorrow their elderly would embrace slow death in the mile-long gorge to the northwest of the city. And in the near future? Why then the wine of fate would be poured again and the present survivors would quaff it. They would drink the cup of despair and agony to its dregs.

Vlad Tepes, as he now was called—Vlad the Impaler—was as good as his word. For a long time he had had a plan. It had to do with a fortress, a castle which would be impregnable, giving him ironbound security against his enemies, possibly saving his life should he be defeated. He had selected a site. It was on a high bluff above the left bank of the Arges River, 50 miles to the west-northwest of Tirgoviste. Here, within close proximity to each other but on opposite sides of the river, lay the ruins of two once-powerful redoubts, the Castle of Poenari and the Castle of Agrish. His idea was simple. He would use the stone and brick from the first to rebuild the second. Boyar sweat would be the tools and boyar blood the mortar. He envisaged a masterpiece. When it was finished it would be the most secure and commanding stronghold in all of Wallachia.

He was not long in getting started. Hardly had the corpses of the elderly chosen stiffened on their stakes before the hundreds of younger men and women, chained with their offspring, came under the lashes of their overseers on the long, deadly trek to the west. It was through rugged wilderness country along goat trails. The demoralized victims were not in condition for it. Years of luxurious living had made the boyars soft, impairing stamina and muscle tone. It was brutal. Their wives and children were particularly unfit and many did not survive the rigors and cruelties of the journey.

Characteristically, Dracula had planned ahead. Near the base of the high rock extrusion on the summit of which the new castle was to be built lay the village of Arefu, which still exists today. His agents had gone there early. Already prepared were the kilns for firing thousands of bricks, cut wood with which to fuel the flames, even a large number of horse- and mule-drawn carts to transport them as close to the construction site as possible. This was one prime source of building material. Another was Poenari across the river, by far the larger of the two ruins. The bricks it supplied would have to be rafted across or carried precariously over a temporary rope bridge. Both methods were used. Nonetheless, despite all possible ingenuity, carrying heavy loads up the steep and treacherous mountainside was another matter. It was quite beyond the strength of the women and children, impossible for them. The husbands and fathers labored at this. We can imagine them using crude leather carrying bags borne on their backs and slung from their foreheads, see them struggling and sweating with as much misery and pain as any hapless slave who was worked to death in the building of the pyramids of Egypt or the Great Wall of China.

For death was their lot in the end. Many died of exhaustion and beatings before a month had passed. Disease and malnutrition took heavy toll. Some, more hardy or with a greater will to survive, lasted longer, bearing their burdens with ever-diminishing fortitude in more and more grueling despair. How long did the construction continue? We do not know. Five months. Six, perhaps. We are told the prisoners' clothes rotted on their backs and fell away, leaving them naked in their helpless wretchedness. So that those who had arrived exhausted in Arefu still in the tattered remains of their Easter finery, doubtless presenting a rare sight to the wide-eyed villagers, ended with nothing but torn flesh and nudity.

Dracula got his castle. Apparently, all the prisoners who lived to see it completed were slaughtered. The records show that hundreds of names disappeared suddenly from the census of the noble ranks in Wallachia, only to be replaced by hundreds of others drawn from the less illustrious members of the Third Estate. It had happened many times in history and was to happen many more. It was the way of vendetta, of blood feud, the way that counseled if you kill a man you had best kill his wife and children also, for to fail in this would invite revenge. The ancient Greeks practiced it. So did the Caesars, the Huns, the Mongols, Turks, and Afghans, indeed the blood-gorged dynasties of half of Europe. Long after Dracula's time, the Sicilian Mafia would make such total extermination of one's enemies a fixed operational credo, first on the island of their origin and the mainland of Italy, then, only decades ago and still continuing, in such seemingly unlikely places as the larger eastern cities of North America.

The ruthless Impaler had done what he set out to do. He had leveled a crushing blow at his foes, more than decimated the boyars, filled their places with others of more humble origin who owed their positions entirely to him. It is possible he was well satisfied with this signal accomplishment and could afford if he chose to rest on his laurels. But not for long. Already his morbid paranoia was in control. What he had done, though bloody and decisive, was only a foretaste of what he planned to do. They would see. He had *eaten* the boyars as he had sworn he would but still saw himself as a ravenous pike among elusive, nimble minnows. His many enemies could swim but they could not hide. It was only a question of time before he devoured them all.

5

The Deadly Game Grows Deadlier

As he walked unsteadily over the broken ground, the stout, middle-aged German priest was sweating profusely. Suspended from a chain around his thick neck was a silver cross which he held in his hand. A small cross. Unassuming. It glittered in the rays of the late afternoon sun as he tried to shield his eyes. It seemed to burn his fingers as his very soul was burning this moment, as his soul fled away from him down some dark corridor of time and the infinite. The words in his mind were from Mark 8:36. Even under the crushing weight of the dread that bore him down he still remembered the bitter, forlorn question.

"What shall it profit a man if he should gain the whole world and lose his own soul?"

His own soul. His soul besmirched and irredeemable. He sometimes stumbled, and each time it happened a voice inside him said it was inevitable, for he had lost his way. Often he lurched sharply as some jagged stone tore into his sandal. Lost his way the voice mocked. Lost his way. He could smell the blood now. From the northwest a light breeze had sprung up and the nauseating, gut-wrenching stench of the impaled victims on the hill was growing stronger. The priest intoned from the litany.

"Hail Mary, full of grace. Blessed be thy name and the fruit of thy womb, Jesus. Hail Mary, full of grace. Hail Mary— Hail Mary— Hail—"

The words were all running together like the vapors of the wine of evil which were in his nostrils, like the sins of the fathers and of the world that racked and twisted him, allowing no respite from torment. All running together... running together...

"Hail Mary, full of grace..."

What day was this? What year? As he plodded on he tried to remember, to put his agonized mind on anything but the terrible love-imposed duty before him. It was the second day of April, wasn't it? Fourteen fifty-nine? Yes, he would think about that. But how useless to imagine that date chiseled on his headstone or inscribed on the honored scroll of the church fathers. And his name. Father Heinrich Lessing. He could not be buried in consecrated ground. He knew that. He had broken his vow of chastity and all the penance in the world could not undo it. And *this* day, O pitying God of Hosts, before the sun had set he would do far worse than anything done yet, be even more in a state of mortal sin and sure to incur damnation.

The ground was beginning to rise now and he rose with it, climbing with labored breath. Still holding the cross, he pressed with his fingers the knife concealed in his robe, so appalled by the chilling, impossible task he had set himself he could feel his pulses pounding in his temples as though they would burst his skull. He glanced at the crowd of spectators. They were just above and to his left, on a stretch of almost level ground cleared for the occasion. Their leader was still with them, that devil Dracula. He felt his demon eyes burning into him, soulless eyes of deepest emerald he would never forget.

"Go and shrive them, father," the Wallachian had said to him in German. "They are Catholics, these Saxons of yours, and I have no priest with me but my own Orthodox clergy. Go with my blessing. You come late to this hill of vengeance, but the more recently impaled are still alive and thirst for your benediction. You are free to minister the last rites."

The last rites... Extreme Unction... What had the people done that the Almighty should send this hellish scourge against them? What had they done to merit the attack of this modern-day Attila, this murderous, ravening wolf? Attila? An infernal reincarnation perhaps, but now there was no Pope Leo I to face this chilling Mephistopheles and turn him back. The citizens of Kronstadt had failed. Call it Kronstadt or Brasov as did the enemy, they had let themselves be taken by surprise and now they were dying by the thousand.

He bore away to his right, then began to climb with increasing difficulty as the gradient steepened, half-closing his eyes in the sun's stupefying glare. He knew he could have come by the footpath that led to this Golgotha, the way used by the Wallachian troops and executioners, but he'd told himself that this would be shorter, that God would give him the strength because it was Calvary all over again. Calvary...oh yes, surely that again, though a myriad now hung where only three had been of old.

He spoke softly. "Forgive me, O Lord, that I compare this hill with thine. Yet were not these, thy children, born in thine image? Succour them, Father. Withhold not thy hand from them in this the hour of their torment."

He was nearly there, he believed. All the condemned were blotted from his view because of the ridge that now lay between him and them, but already his sandals were on that ridge. Already...As he struggled, feeling his weight and gravity unite against him, gradually a scene was coming into focus in some dark corner of his mind. It was a cemetery. At first he thought it was here on the Kappelenberg, on this very prominence the Slavic Transylvanians called Tîmpa Hill with the chapel of Saint Jacob just above him. But no, it was not here. The picture in his mind's eye was not here. It was the graveyard of the Church of Saint Bartholomew he saw, *his* church, now already desecrated by the Wallachian madman. Even the chalices stolen, even the vestments themselves, for to the Orthodox it was the Catholics who were the heretics and outcasts.

He looked around, confused. As though he gazed through a tunnel his eyes focused on only two graves close together. They came nearer to him. He did not seem to be moving. The graves came to him. He saw the names. *Father Heinrich Lessing, priest of this parish. The Lady Karla von Arnim, widow to Graf Helmut von Arnim.* Her late husband was not here. No stone for the suspicious, jealous, cuckolded count who had taken his own life. Only the two of them with the dates of birth and death. The death date was today but he already knew that. Why were they *together?* What could such a thing as this mean? As it faded he was struck by a sense of timelessness, of precognition, as though all this had happened before in some other existence. He and the woman. He and Karla. He and his own parishioner in God-accursed, hell-spawned *adultery!* Was he responsible for her husband's self-destruction also? Oh God! Oh dear God!

He stopped and closed his eyes. He could feel himself swaying on his feet still holding the little cross. God had forgiven Magdalen. God had forgiven *Magdalen!* But *when* would He forgive the slayer of the innocent? The vision was gone now. He climbed on. As though by magic the ridge had been topped. And there they were. Hundreds of them. Thousands of them. Spread around the ruthless invader and his diabolical entourage in a vast circle of agony and death. They were *close* now, overwhelmingly, paralyzingly close. He'd seen them before. He'd stood over there with Dracula the Accursed as he and his Satan-spawned followers ate their meat and drank their wine. But *this!* To be here with them, *among* them!

"Oh Father!" he breathed in his pain. "Oh my Father!"

The smell of them struck him like a blow in the face. The horror of it. Men and women. Even many children, God help them. Most were already dead. He saw that at once. Even he who hung on the tallest stake in the center was only a corpse, the hapless courtier the devil's lickspittles had talked about. He'd complained of the terrible odor they said and Dracula had overheard him. "For that you will die!" the tyrant had told him. "I'll honor you with the longest stake of all. I live here. You live up there yonder where the stench cannot reach you."

He was looking for *her* now. She'd been to the left of this one. Ten yards. Fifteen. Yes. He found her at once. A great lump burst in his throat. The tears flowed, leaving vertical trenches in the caked dust on his haggard face. He crossed himself, trembling, quaking in the very heart of him. His legs had gone to water and he could hardly walk. As he approached her he begged for the strength to reach her side. Was she still *alive?* He could not know. Her head was slumped like the rest.

"Oh Karla! Karla, my love!"

Dared he say these things? Dared he go to her as to a *woman?* "I am coming! I am coming! Oh merciful God, where is thy pity? Withhold not thy hand from us, O Lord, for we are naked in the wilderness! Succour us! Oh succour us!"

As he progressed through the maze of stakes in this forlorn landscape of the dead and dying he raised the crucifix repeatedly to give the benediction. But it was *her* his eyes dwelt upon. He saw the others only peripherally, was aware of them only on the margins of consciousness. He was a priest here only to perform his duty. The tyrant must not think otherwise. The tyrant's archers were always ready, their bows close at hand. And Father Heinrich *must* reach Karla. He must live long enough for that. Must live . . . must live. . . .

Was he a prelate who came to her in her extremity? Was he a man?

He did not know. He covered the ground like a somnambulist. He knew only that at last the stake stood before him, *her* stake, its merciless shaft rising above him. How could he climb it? It was slippery with blood, the blood of the woman he had loved—the woman he still loved. Yes, he understood it at last. The cloud over his mind was gone. *This* was love. It was death *because* it was love. It was redemption, too. He had not acted for the sake of vile lust. He had lusted because he had loved. And God would take him. God would take them both. He turned to face the watchers on the hill. He raised the cross, but in defiance, not blessing.

"May the divine strength of the Lord God of Israel strike you down! May you die, Dracula Voevod, and be sucked down unto the ninth level of hell, there to burn in the agonizing flames throughout eternity!"

He knew they couldn't hear him. The breeze was blowing toward him and would not carry his voice. He saw an arm waved at him from among their number, not Dracula's but that of someone else. They suspected nothing yet. But in moments they would be all alertness. A slight hesitation while their minds grasped the significance of what they saw. Then the prince would give an order, and on the strength of it Heinrich Lessing would depart this life.

He turned to the stake. Again he crossed himself, this time for the sake of his own imperiled soul. Was she *dead?* It didn't matter. He would do this regardless, because he loved her and she had loved him. Jehovah must understand that. He *must!*

He kicked off his sandals. He placed his hands on the long pale before him, the pale that rose to God. Then he came against it, struggling with it, fighting it, trying to grip with his bare feet. He climbed. He was half the height of a man above the ground before he slipped and fell back, defeated by the blood, *her* blood. He turned and looked at the spectators again. The archers yet? No, but the Wallachians were on their feet, every eye fastened on him. Maybe they would make a sport of it he thought, the hated Saxon ecclesiastic seized by madness, seeking to find heaven by ascending a stake. It was possible they would do that. He prayed for it, for the time such a foolish error would give him. But how could he overcome the *blood?* How could he *get* to her?

He turned again to the pale and grasped it. Again his feet and hands gripped and he rose upward to the same height, knowing he would slip again. *But not if the blood were removed.* He began to lick the flowing wood. His tongue worked frantically, for he sensed how short was the time. As though from a thousand miles away he heard someone shouting. Vlad the Devil? He knew not and cared not. Other voices joined the first in a swelling chorus. There was laughter. Yes, even that he could distinguish. They were enjoying themselves like revelers on holiday, the incredible scene like a tonic to their jaded appetites. Let them he thought. Her blood was in his mouth as he licked and licked, moving slowly, steadily upward. At first, its fast-clotting viscousness seemed to choke him as he tried to swallow it but he would not spit it out. It was *her* blood. He was closer to her now than ever they had been in sexual congress, than ever on the three shame-faced occasions when they had met as lovers. Closer to her now. Closer.

He looked up as he climbed. She was just above him. He thought he could hear her groan but could not be sure, for others still breathed in this Gehenna, still clung despairingly to life, still murmured in hopeless agony. She was naked. Most of them were naked. But that didn't matter either. Victims were stripped when impaled, the anus exposed and penetrated as hers was, the... the... He was shaking so hard his strength nearly failed him. But now his face was at the level of her feet. He shifted his weight, corkscrewing to the rear of the stake. Oh God, he must not grasp her, torture her by adding to her torment! Where were the archers? He heard the voices, the shouting. It seemed louder now. His face was beside her beautiful white buttocks, the cheeks smeared with gore. His feet slipped, then found purchase where he had licked. He straightened his body. The small of her back appeared. Her shoulder blades. He saw that her head was still fallen. Beyond her, a hazy outline in his sweat-filled vision, was the opposite hill and those who had condemned her.

"Karla!" he breathed. "Oh Karla, my love! Karla! Karla!"

She was *alive.* Her dark head lifted slightly, then fell back. "Heinrich. Heinrich."

He was struggling for breath. "I am here, beloved. I love you. I love you so desperately. I will go with you. Do you understand me? We will be together—as we should have been long ago. Paradise awaits, my Karla. Are you ready?"

He thought she might be in extremis. For long seconds she made no sound. Then, very close, ascending over the unfeeling, vicious cacophony of the viewers, she spoke to him for the last time.

"I... ready... liebchen. Take me... with you."

He hung on with his feet and one hand. He clutched the concealed knife. But no! No, no, no, he could not shed her blood to add to this blasphemy! He reached forward and took her very tenderly by the hair, entwining his fingers in her sweat-matted tresses, softly caressing her. He was powerful. The sinews of his arms were like steel. He had not always been a priest. For years before his ordination he had worked as a woodsman swinging an axe. Now he was heavy and slow but his hands could still break fragile things. Beautiful things. She would bless him for it even as he made to her this final gift of love. As he turned her head toward himself he would see it in her eyes before the light in them faded.

"I love you," he said again.

Then, with a sudden movement of his hand, he broke her neck.

"I love you, Karla." He was choking on his tears. "I love you."

No word spoke she nor ever would again. It was over. He pulled himself above her on the stake, swung his body to one side, and faced the multitude who had brought them to this.

"Do you mock us, you fiends?" he shouted. "Then mock and be damned! I have drunk the blood of the martyrs... *her* blood... the wine of God! I am free of you... and she is free!"

Adultery. The driving of a husband to suicide. Failure to forgive his enemies. The killing of his love. Sin heaped upon sin. It didn't matter. None of it mattered, for her love had made it meaningless and redeemed him. But now the archers understood. He saw the body of bowmen move in front of the others and unsling their weapons. The first arrows were close but missed. Their whine was incredibly loud. Then one grazed his shoulder and tore his habit. He drew the knife, the one he had brought for her that had failed its service.

"God bless you, my love," he muttered. "Depart not from me, for I am thine."

He turned the blade toward his diaphram, then slanted it upward into his chest. "O Father, accept, I pray thee, the soul of this fallen priest who has failed thee! Forgive, O God!"

His descent through the air seemed timeless, as though eons and ages passed, and color and light and the faint laughter of children. When he landed on the knife he was dead. The darkening vault of the sky looked down on him. The world rolled on. Only Father Lessing and his Karla had departed.

One would have thought that the terrible massacre at Brasov might have been enough to appease Dracula but that would have been to underestimate the full measure of his hatred and blood lust; to underestimate, also, the scope of his plan to subdue his opponents by terror. Other atrocities were to follow, the scale and savagery of some of them almost beyond belief. He was always lashing out with lethal venom. His whole adult life had been based on it. Everywhere he imagined that plots were being laid against him or saw pitiless aggressors poised to strike him down. But the motivation behind his raids into Transylvania went deeper than that. His foreign policy alone was certain to involve him in conflict. The key was the situation in Hungary.

Recklessly, almost from the opening of his second reign, he became embroiled in Hungarian internal politics. He was truculent, enormously vain, threatening and abusive whenever he reckoned such tactics to his advantage. His demand for the return to Wallachia of the Transylvanian duchies of Fagaras and Amlas angered Buda, for Transylvania was Hungarian territory. Dracula came to his throne the second time in 1456. In the following year Hungary's king, Ladislas Posthumus, was to die. The arrogant Wallachian prince came under the heading of "unfinished business." Ladislas opposed him vigorously. The traditional way to do this was to send out agents to foment unrest in Wallachia and, above all, to support the rival Danesti claimant to Dracula's throne.

The Danesti branch of the family was prolific. As Dracula's uncles had done, they too jockeyed ceaselessly for position and power. Among their number, Basarab Laiota (the Old) was still alive. So was his brother Danciul, who as the "Old Pretender" was sometimes still referred to as Dan III. Both Laiota and his son, Basarab the Young (later known as Tepelus, the Little Impaler) would come to rule in Tirgoviste in the unknown future. But relatives even closer to Dracula coveted his throne and he knew it.

One of these was Radu, his half-brother grown to manhood in Constantinople, now as much a Turk as Sultan Mehmed himself. Another was also a half-brother, Vlad the Monk, the illegitimate son of Dracul's mistress Caltuna. The Turks backed Radu for the throne of Wallachia. Ladislas Posthumus backed the other. When Dracula came to the throne his priestly namesake fled into Transylvania and was given asylum by the Hungarians in their basically German city of Sibiu. In 1457, when he attacked that city and slaughtered its helpless population, one of Dracula's motives was to capture Vlad the Monk and execute him, almost certainly by impalement. Apparently forewarned, the intended victim fled, yet he must have known the lines were drawn. Ultimately, one of the brothers must die.

It has already been observed that Ladislas Posthumus lost the struggle in Hungary, that he fled to Prague and was there struck down by the plague. Noted, also, was the fact that Matei Corvinus, son of the late János Hunyadi, replaced him in Buda as king. Dracula had rallied to Matei from the start. He had done it by backing the nobleman Michael Szilagy, a trusted cohort of Matei, a man into whose family he, Dracula, would eventually marry. Matei was grateful. Crowned as King Matei I of Hungary on June 24, 1458, he made it clear he would oppose the Holy Roman Emperor Friedrich III, a monarch who had been the ally of his predecessor. Then Matei went further. He wrote a letter to the Saxon burgomeister of Sibiu, instructing him and his followers to forgive Dracula for his infamous raid and frightful slaughter—as though forgiveness could be legislated.

Brasov was smashed on April 2, 1459. Shortly thereafter, Dracula's agents in Transylvania cautioned the Wallachian merchants to secretly evacuate their homes and flee for safety across the border. Apparently, this was carried out in the dead of night so as not to alert the Saxon authorities. It should have been a warning to the Germans. Incredibly, they ignored it. Their response was to send some 400 teenage boys (and 30 coachmen) into Wallachia, ostensibly to improve relations and trade by learning the language. Their declared intention may or may not have been genuine, but in Dracula's view the youths were spies sent to gather what today would be called "economic intelligence." His troops took them prisoner. All of them, boys and drivers alike, were herded into an old building and there burned alive.

When it was reported to him, this incident must have shaken Matei and made him doubt his own judgment. But Buda was far from Wallachia and the Magyar sovereign, crowned less than a year and harassed by deadly intrigue in his own court, had problems enough just to keep his head on his shoulders.

Throughout the first half of the year 1460 Dracula's reign of terror did not abate. Because the roads were usually dry and firm at that time of year he favored the spring and summer for military operations. In April, he cut off and cornered the pretender Danciul (Prince Dan III of the House of Basarab) and made him captive. It was an unexpected bit of luck. That the Danesti would suffer the same fate as the late Vladislav II was inevitable. This time, however, a refinement was added. A written valediction was handed the condemned. Standing at his own graveside he was forced to read it, then given time to pray (Dracula's self-proclaimed piety made this imperative), then beheaded. It was now very clear to Dracula's foes that to fall into his hands was virtually certain death.

In July he went on campaign in Transylvania again, this time striking directly at the city of Fagaras on the Olt River, the capital of the dukedom of the same name. As at Sibiu and Brasov, the inhabitants were unprepared for him. Surrender meant virtual annihilation and once more he taught a vanquished opponent the frightful meaning of defeat. Every wretched citizen his troops could lay their hands on was impaled or killed by other tortures; men, women, children, the elderly and infirm, gypsies and beggars, both native and itinerant. One almost has the feeling he would have butchered the very pariah dogs that roamed the streets if they could have been taken. The place was ravished, burned, looted of all transportable goods, very nearly erased. Unlike the murderous Hunnic king Attila many centuries earlier, he did not sow the ground with salt, probably because he never thought of it. Fagaras would be long in recovering. Although he accounted it his own enclave, he made sure that if he could not have it no one else would consider it worth the taking. This was conquest with a vengeance. Historians have estimated the number of slain to have been between 10,000 and 15,000. A great many more were destroyed in the gutted outlying villages.

Every student of the history of Western Europe knows of Catherine de Medici, Regent of France, and her infamous mass destruction of the French Protestants (Huguenots) in Paris on the night of August 24, 1572, an event remembered as "the Massacre of Saint Bartholomew's Eve." In the plot carried out by Catherine and the Catholic zealot Henri, Duc de Guise, not only the Protestant chiefs and their principal leader, Gaspard de Coligny, were struck down (together with some 2000 Huguenots in Paris itself) but spreading violence in the following days accounted for many more. This is common knowledge. Numerous books have been written about it. But how many know that Eastern Europe had seen a bloody parallel to this over a century earlier and something on a much larger scale?

Again, of course, it was Dracula. The town of Amlas (Humilasch in the German) lay some 25 miles west-southwest of Sibiu in the great Transylvanian plain. On August 24, 1460, not much more than a month after the sacking of Fagaras, the Wallachian despot fell upon Amlas with his army, overwhelmed its meager defenses, and brought the nightmare of his own merciless brand of fire and sword to the inhabitants. Again the devil-spawned stakes were planted in the ground. Again a peaceful Saxon community was burned, its surviving citizens of both sexes and all ages horribly tortured before virtual annihilation. Again, as in the case of Sibiu, Brasov, and Fagaras, all the outlying district was ravaged and put to the torch, for this was a Saint Bartholomew's Day the Impaler swore would be remembered. From archival evidence it is probable that at least 20,000 died.

Holding themselves to be descended from such demigods of the Dark Ages as the heroes Siegmund and Siegfried, the Germans have always been a very brave people. Had they had an army with which to defend themselves there is no doubt they would have resisted with fury, possibly defeating Dracula in the field and invading Wallachia to overthrow him. History might have been quite different then. As it was, they were largely unarmed and helpless. They could only flee or die. However, those who did survive to become refugees fought back strongly with the one weapon they had, that of propaganda. Over the coming years they besmirched Dracula's reputation and made it stink from one end of eastern Europe to the other. They turned public opinion against him, alienated possible allies, and in general made his name such an abomination that a day would come when he would find himself almost alone. So successful were they in this endeavor that it is probably no exaggeration to say that in the end it was they who defeated him. Their cloistered scribes vilified him endlessly. It was they who dubbed him *hosti generi humani*, a term that eventually found its way even to the Vatican in Rome. It was largely accurate. As news of his depredations spread, in the minds of many thousands he had indeed become the enemy of all mankind.

After much study and consideration, the only thing that seems to account for Dracula's nearly unbelievable butchery and cruelty is schizophrenia, the psychiatrist's term for a split personality. How can we infer this? Because the madman capable of committing such frightful crimes was also capable of reasoned statecraft, highly effective combat tactics and strategy, and very unusual leadership in the larger sense of control over others.

We are dealing with at least two personalities, perhaps with three. For who was the strange ascetic who so often visited monasteries and frequently endowed them with riches? What the identity of the inconstant theocrat who like all the Draculas even went so far as to repeatedly found such institutions? Was this the second personality in action, aiding the church in penance for the grievous sins of the first? Or was it a third and distinct entity entirely? Was it perhaps a man divorced from his other selves, briefly committed from time to time to a world of severe austerity, quiet contemplation, and self-denial? If this third man existed he could hardly be in greater contrast to the first. But it can happen. They say that Chicago's notorious gangster Al Capone delighted in being nice to flower girls and others in a state of poverty. But this same mob leader was responsible for dozens of killings, including the infamous Saint Valentine's Day Massacre. On one occasion, when two of his hired *mafiosi* were found to be betraying him, he had them forced to their knees under aimed guns, then personally beat out their brains with a baseball bat. The Jekyll-and-Hyde syndrome is not especially rare in the human animal.

The truth seems to be that Dracula's multiple personalities overlapped in a sort of weird psychological mélange. For example, the theory of breaking German economic power in Transylvania through repeated invasions would appear to have originated in the mind of the soldier-statesman. But could this harsh but clear-thinking realist have been the same man who impaled thousands of men, women, and children with nearly unparalleled barbarism? Could the man who quietly sat down with Saxon representatives to sign economic treaties be the same who turned his torturers loose among an overwhelmed and helpless population? It is this incredible contradiction that resulted in such confusion among the chroniclers even of his own time. Nothing was understood of psychosis. Such terms as "paranoid" would not be coined for centuries.

In eastern Europe, in particular, the emergence from the darkness of the Middle Ages into the Renaissance and the rediscovery of the medical knowledge of the ancients (Egyptian medicine, for example) were late in coming. Thus multiple legends arose to fit multiple personalities. The homicidal maniac seen by the Germans, Hungarians, and Turks was not the stern but essentially just "father figure" of the Romanians. The sadistic pervert who had the sex organs of women cut out and their breasts removed could not be the same (many scribes and historians were certain of it) as the devout Orthodox Christian who built monasteries and lavished money on abbeys. It was simply too incredible to believe. To many, the renowned soldier Prince Vlad III and the incarnate demon Dracula were and had to be *two different men*. The very lengthy elapsed time between an event and its reporting had a tendency to substantiate this myth.

Although some historians have tried to deny the truth of the Dracula atrocities, there is one very cogent piece of evidence in support of that allegation. It lies in the fact that accounts written long distances apart, and by people who could not possibly have been in touch with one another, essentially agree about events. Who became involved in the telling of these tales? In addition to the Germans, Turks, Hungarians, and Romanians already mentioned, Byzantine historians wrote of them in Greek; Catholic and Eastern Orthodox monks in Latin and Greek; and Serbian, Croatian, and Italian travelers in their own languages. In those days, literary collaboration between such diverse peoples of different tongues was rare.

The deplorable inhumanity of one human to another is as old as the race. From the Carthaginians and Romans who crucified their victims to the more sophisticated present-day tormentors in many countries, the picture has altered but little. To be sure, methods have changed through advancing technology but the *will* to do evil remains very much with us. Whether it be the Japanese army using bulldozers in the streets of Nanking to bury Chinese alive in the bomb craters, or the Nazis at such camps as Dachau and Auschwitz loading the ovens with human freight, or the Soviets driving prisoners insane in the Gulag as this book is being written, it is the same instinct for tyranny and butchery that impelled one Neanderthal to crack the skull of another with a club in the long ago.

Impalement has not been uncommon in history. One finds it practiced in ancient Persia, Scythia, and Afghanistan; among the Turks until fairly recent times; in the Balkans by some of Dracula's contemporaries such as Stéfan of Moldavia; even in nineteenth-century South Africa by the Zulu chief Shaka and his half-brother and successor by assassination, Dingane. In Russia it was also used, where it was called "the death of the hook." Here the technique was not usually to impale the anus but rather some other part of the body, normally the back or chest, the ribs being counted on to sustain the victim's weight. Dracula, too, employed such methods but seems to have abandoned them later in favor of inflicting a slower and more agonizing death. To prevent immediate and massive hemorrhaging he ordered that the stakes be rounded at the ends and greased, thus ensuring a gradual rupturing of the viscera over a much longer period.

At first view, it might be wondered to what degree Dracula's incredible sadism may have been unique. The simple truth is that it was not. If he outstripped most others in the number of his victims, he was still equaled in moral degeneracy by innumerable tyrants throughout the ages. Take the Roman emperor Gaius Caligula, for example. According to the historian Suetonius and others, there was virtually no length to which this demented despot would not go to satisfy his cruelty, including the insensate slaughter of his own close relatives. "Kill him slowly," he told his tormentors. "Do it so he will *feel* he is dying."

Whether it be Nero in Rome, lighting the gladiatorial games at night by using Christian prisoners as living torches; or Gilles de Rais, the fifteenth-century Bluebeard of France, strangling and sodomizing kidnapped children in his castle at Tiffauges; or the Nana Sahib in the Indian Mutiny, cutting off the feet of British women and children and leaving them in neatly arranged pairs of shoes for the husbands and fathers to discover (Cawnpore, India, 1857), it is not difficult to find Dracula's peers. Primarily, it is the sheer magnitude of his crimes that make them spectacular, that and a personality that is almost unbelievably diabolical.

Again and again we come to it, far more in the German tales than anywhere else, this disposition to sadistic madness. Impalement was king but it did not stand alone. According to the chroniclers, Dracula's victims were often mutilated in every conceivable manner: blinded, maimed, disemboweled, skinned alive, boiled in oil, burned, hanged, garroted, and roasted over slow fires. Occasionally he crucified them. Occasionally, too, he used the hook as in Russia, as a number of Saxon woodcuts graphically illustrate. Imitating the Roman emperors, especially Nero, he even exposed helpless captives to the attacks of half-starved wild animals, particularly the Carpathian wolf. Indeed, there seemed no limit to his devilish ingenuity.

At this time there was in the Vatican a very unusual man, the Sienese intellectual, Enea Silvio de Piccolomini, known as Pope Pius II. Most steadfast of all papal opponents of Ottoman expansion, the only pope in history to write his autobiography, he had three chief concerns. They were Turkish plans for the conquest of Europe; a means of controlling Louis XI, the "Spider King" of France; and a way to maintain the papacy's militant alliance with Hungary, the country Pius considered the key to the defense of what was left of the Balkans. In the interests of the last named he sent to Buda as legate one of his most impressive representatives, Nicolas Modrussa. It was a good choice. Nearly as much courtier as prelate, this worldly ambassador quickly came to friendly terms with King Matei. When the legate wrote to his overlord in Rome he spoke of Dracula's genocide, an estimated 40,000 dead.

> He killed some of them by breaking them under the wheels of carts; others, stripped of their clothes, were skinned alive up to their entrails; others placed on stakes, or roasted on red hot coals placed under them; others punctured with stakes piercing their head, their navel, breast, and what is even unworthy of relating, their buttocks and the middle of their entrails, and, emerging from their mouths; in order that no form of cruelty be missing, he stuck stakes in both breasts of mothers and thrust their babies onto them; he killed others in other ferocious ways, torturing them with varied instruments such as the atrocious cruelties of the most frightful tyrants could devise.

Nearly unbelievable? Almost. Virtually unparalleled for sheer fiendishness? Quite possibly. Yet consider the following lines from the book *Khyber* by Charles Miller, words referring to one of the most celebrated rulers in Afghan history.

> The Amir Abdur Rahman Khan once told an Englishman named Frank Martin that during the course of his reign he had ordered the execution of more than 100,000 Afghans. Martin served for some years as Abdur Rahman's chief civil engineer, and the book he wrote about his experiences with the Amir included a chapter entitled "Tortures and Methods of Execution," whose subtitles read: "Hanging by hair and skinning alive... Beating to death with sticks... Cutting men in pieces... Throwing down mountain-side... Starving to death in cages... Boiling woman to soup and man drinking it before execution... Punishment by exposure and starvation... Burying alive... Throwing into soap boilers... Cutting off hands... Blinding... Tying to bent trees and disrupting... Blowing from guns... Hanging, etc." Martin also noted that "there are other forms of torture... but these cannot be described."

The author adds, "The most revolting aspect of these barbarities was that they were perpetrated in a good cause." By which he means the formulation of a stable government and incorruptible law for Afghanistan, and the suppression of brigandage. It cannot be doubted that this, too, was achieved in Dracula's Wallachia. Crime was nearly extinguished. The punishments for it were so savage that very few criminals considered it worth the risk. Even morality was legislated, for Dracula's ethos for *others* became more and more rigidly puritanical. Female adultery was punishable by death. So was "proven" immodesty of any kind, and the evidence required for proof was slender indeed. Thus did the righteous Impaler rule his principality.

Mustapha Inonu Pasha was proud of his physique. As he stood naked in the lavish quarters Dracula had provided him, he admired his body reflected in a large mirror, turning very slowly this way and that as he indulged his narcissistic pleasure. Yes, it was good for a man of fifty. Very good. His chest and stomach were still firm, his arms corded with ropelike sinew. Even his legs were impressive in their development, bulging as they did with the great riding muscles that bespoke his equestrian prowess. It was unusual in a political emissary he told himself, but then his appointment as Turkish ambassador to the Court of Tirgoviste was only recent. He was an officer of *spahis* on temporary leave from the army, not a diplomat. Apart from his credentials, it was as such that he would present himself and his retinue to this lunatic, this pretender to royalty, and may Allah restrain his urge to cut the Wallachian's throat.

A final time he flexed his biceps and tightened his abdomen, smiling with his white teeth at sight of the long black hair of his head which like his beard was only slightly touched with gray. He was a *soldier* and let none forget it. Let them remember his valor in battle, how Sultan Mehmed himself had conferred on him a kaftan of honor in the great square of fallen Constantinople, rewarding him on the same day he ordered the death of Grand Vizier Khalil and other traitorous members of the peace party. Peace? What peace could there ever be with the Christians? Dracula would find out. He would not slaughter Turks as easily as Transylvanians. This was the year 1462. In 1459 the Porte had finished Serbia; in 1460, taken Mistra and Thebes; in 1461, all of the Trebizond, that part of the ancient Greek empire long claimed by the Byzantines. Now it was the turn of what remained of the Balkans. Already the sultan stood firmly on the Danube.

He laughed softly. Those of his staff believed that Dracula knew this. He himself believed it, for Wallachian spies were everywhere. So be it. This blood-crazed dog must now humble himself or fight, accept Ottoman rule or wage suicidal war. He turned away from the mirror, then paused in the middle of the room in grim reflection. If the swine chose war, perhaps no more than the head of Inonu Pasha would ever return to the Turkish capital. So be it, also, if it were ordained. The way of the true believer was submission to the will of Allah.

Still nude, he walked into the sleeping chamber. There on the great bed amidst hangings of damask and silk his two little pages, as naked as he, disported themselves amorously in eager fellatio. The blonde, Achmed, was seven years old; his darker lover, Yousuf, about ten. Both were the sons of Christian captives, both destined for the janissaries. They would probably be mated for life unless otherwise paired. As he watched them and listened to their moans he felt the familiar tingling in his groin and slowly began to erect. How marvelous they should know such ecstasy before the age of orgasm. Shortly, their daytime dalliance must end, he reflected, for this year the holy month of Ramadan would begin in three days and only the like of soldiers and the sick were exempt from its restrictions. But there would still be the nights. He wanted to enjoy them this moment but knew there wasn't time. He must array himself for the royal audience.

"Yousuf," he said quietly. "Achmed." Then he repeated their names more loudly to get their attention. "Come, my pretty urchins, it is time to dress your master. Come at once or by the beard of the Prophet I will chastise your soft bottoms."

Chagrined by the interruption but without the slightest sign of embarrassment, the boys stopped and looked at their lord. Noting his state of arousal, their bright eyes lighted with sensuous invitation as lascivious grins spread over their handsome faces, but they quickly realized it was useless at the moment. First dressing themselves as he bade them, they then proceeded to clothe their tutor in delight. He did not let them touch him intimately. All the while they worked he was thinking of the clash of wills that must shortly take place, of the orders that forbade dispute to avoid alerting Dracula to the imminence of his peril.

"Go thou, Mustapha, and spread honey upon him," the sultan had said. "Soothe him with the balm of our love as you would your wives or catamites, and instruct any member of your entourage whom he questions to be mild. Allah applauds duplicity when practiced against infidels. While we show him the face of our friendship on the left we will wear another countenance on the right, and prepare to unleash the hounds of war."

"Pray don't release them too early, O Enlightened One," Inonu muttered now. "My bowels will not take well to the stake."

Then he smiled a little crookedly. Every Osmanli in Turkey knew the Wallachian's sobriquet today. Kazîglu Bey—the Lord Impaler. They said it in respect for the man's ferocity, for Turks understood this. But he, Inonu Pasha, did not respect him. Let him first be tried in battle against the armed hosts of the empire, not other Wallachians or helpless civilians. Let him show his mettle against the veteran Turkish battalions, the squadrons of *spahis*, the janissaries so zealous in war. *Then* let men speak of respect. Until that day of judgment he was no more than a mangy cur fit to show his fangs to women and children. What man of courage or integrity could admire indiscriminate murder?

Although a considerable interval passed, it seemed to Inonu's distracted mind that only moments later he stood with the others in the throne room of the palace, making his formal obeisance to the creature who sat that throne. Dracula seemed all affability. He had just returned from his hunting lodge at Cîmpulung where, so his courtiers said, he'd had excellent luck with his falcons, the very fast breed called peregrines. He boasted that tonight they would all dine on partridge or quail or pheasant as they chose, for his hawks had downed all three. He chatted convivially. Even when dinner was served in the elegant dining room he was still playing the gracious host. If at times he seemed to stare at the heads of Inonu and the other Turks, the ambassador noted it only casually, setting it down to a trick of his own overactive imagination. The man was peculiar, that's all. No one ever knew what he was thinking they said, and none could trust him, least of all his own fear-ridden subjects. The sooner the army moved against him, the better.

As the evening wore on the conversation turned to politics. Dracula was very well informed, Inonu noted, even for a prince, but assumed that much of this was due to Turkish education as a boy. Suddenly, he found the man addressing him directly for one of the very few times that evening. In Turkish.

"Perhaps Your Excellency can enlighten us. It is rumored that Iskander Bey will sign a peace with the Porte soon. Is that true?"

Gazing at the large-eyed despot where he sat at the end of the table, Inonu considered. "Your Highness, the question is well taken," he said, then reverted to Romanian in deference to the others. "Scanderbeg is in a strong position. His Albanian fortresses stand like islands of rock in a sea of Muslim strength. He slowly bleeds us."

Dracula spread his hands on the edge of the table. Dressed in black and silver, he gave an impression of extraordinary elegance, the hard severity of his face heightened by an incredibly wide mustache that was stiffly waxed.

"Like a running sore," he said simply.

"Yes, Your Highness. The comparison is apt."

The ambassador was thinking of the tales he had heard; of Dracula's Transylvanian wife, a boyar's daughter, of how he had rescued her from the death march to Poenari he had ordered three years ago only to ravish her, then marry her in a sort of meaningless gesture; of one of his mistresses who told him she was pregnant to try to please him, of how he opened her belly with his sword to prove she was lying, then watched her slowly die in agony; of women he impaled for unfaithfulness to their husbands, Christian priests for "lying" about the Gospel, merchants for "cheating" their custom, peasants for stealing a few coppers. There was even a story that he held a great feast and invited all the poor to attend, that he fed them bountifully, then burned them alive as earlier he had done with the Saxon youths.

Yes, the man could make even a warrior son of Islam uncomfortable.

"Then the rumor is true," came the voice again. "The sultan will offer the olive branch."

Inonu nodded. "In all probability, Your Highness. We are all growing weary of war."

Toward at least two of his own courtiers Dracula cast meaningful glances. Though Inonu could not be sure, he thought that one was Grigore Panaitescu, the *postelnic*, or foreign minister. The other was Vasili Luca, *spatar*, or commander of the army. Because of the angles of their heads he could tell nothing of their responses. He cleared his throat and waited. Dracula changed the subject and time slipped by. When the repast was over, all of them adjourned to the throne room where Dracula mounted the throne as though granting a formal audience. Inonu thought *this* peculiar, too. Looking around, he was surprised to see the large number of armed men in the place.

Once again, Dracula seemed to resume his former thoughts. He gestured for silence and got it. "Your Excellency," he said, and his eyes now appeared to glow in the torchlight. "A short while ago you spoke of peace. You implied it was a universal desire, the wish of Turks, Albanians, everybody. Did I take you correctly?"

Inonu sensed a crisis approaching. He looked at Ismet Bayar, his chief advisor, believing that he and the others were thinking the same as himself. This prince could turn hostile in a moment. They were surrounded by his troops. Eleven unarmed men alone in a nest of vipers.

"Yes, Your Highness. Quite so. Peace was favored by Mohammed."

"Yet he was a warrior."

"When occasion suited. Only a fool would let the scimitar grow dull."

Dracula's laugh was as mirthless as the tearing of silk. "So? Then, perhaps, only a fool would talk of peace in a world endlessly devoted to war. Don't you think?"

Inonu bowed slightly to concede the point. "*Inshallah*," he said in Arabic. "As God wills. We mortals can but strive for enlightenment, lord, not guarantee it. The question of peace or war does not rest with us."

"It rests with Allah?"

"Exactly, Your Highness."

There was a long pause. Then Inonu felt a sensation he had never experienced before. The hair had risen on the back of his neck.

"Then Allah is aggressive indeed," said Dracula at last. "Perhaps you can tell me why the sultan mobilizes on the Danube."

There it was. Inonu squared his shoulders and drew himself to his full height. "The Danubian fortresses have been Turkish for a considerable time," he replied, "as Your Highness is aware. When garrisons are periodically relieved, the arriving replacements may perhaps look like mobilization. Some come in. Others go out. A more or less endless process."

"Replacements."

"Precisely, Your Highness."

"And you expect me to believe that?"

"Your Highness is a man of shrewd discernment. Doubtlessly, it has occurred to you that as unarmed plenipotentiaries we Turks are in a poor position to lie."

"You have seen the stakes in the courtyard then?"

"Oh yes, and in various other strategic locations. Very impressive, my lord."

"And you would not lie."

"Surely, Your Highness jests. Why should the Turkish army mobilize on the Danube? Greece is ours. Constantinople and the Straits. Most of the Black Sea. What more can we need?"

"There is the rest of the Balkans."

"A paltry conquest, Highness. Had we wanted the rest of the Balkans we could have taken them long ago."

"Romania included, of course."

"I'd rather not talk about Romania, Highness."

"János Hunyadi thought you wanted Hungary."

"Yes?"

"He thought you wanted all Europe, given the time to swallow it."

"Yes?"

From the throne he sat on Dracula leaned far forward. The flaming brands on the wall cast his shadow over the assemblage. The long black locks met beneath his chin. His beringed fingers glittered.

"So do I, Inonu Pasha. You may return to Constantinople. You may tell the sultan that I recognize preparations for war when I see them—and am ready for his assault. And say you this when you appear before him. He will not find Prince Vlad and the Wallachians the easy prey the Byzantines were. Constantinople was only a city and a few walls but we are a mighty people. We will defeat you. Tell him that. United under my leadership our strength will increase tenfold. We will smite the heathen Turk hip and thigh!"

Dracula had knocked over his wine glass and its contents was spreading like bright blood. He was on his feet. "And tell him *this!* I will cut his army to pieces! Those who die will be the lucky ones! You fear my stakes? They will spread out from Tirgoviste like the spokes of a wheel, thousands of them! On every pale a Turk will hang—generals, emirs, *pashas*—the sultan himself if I take him! Do you understand me? Tell Mehmed I'll spit his dirty carcass on the highest stake of all! He lays claim to high position? Tell him I support his claim! I'll raise him above my army for the ravens to pick at—but first I'll sew him in the skin of a pig!"

There was a stunned silence. Inonu thought he could hear Dracula's heavy breathing but nothing else. It was quite simply a declaration of war. This madman seemed intent on letting him deliver it to Constantinople. But would he change his mind in a trice and slay them all? The ambassador knew it was time to leave.

"Your Highness has made himself clear," he said quietly, "and there is merit in candor. We will depart immediately, my lord. I'll convey your message to the sultan."

Dracula's lips were parted in a faint smile. "You may do that," he said, "but not until we've settled a point of protocol."

"Protocol, Your Highness?"

Dracula straightened his bent body. "Why yes. It is something that has troubled me since your arrival at my court, a matter of seeming discourtesy."

"Discourtesy, my lord? I was not aware—"

"Why do you not remove your turbans in my presence? Do you seek to offer insult? Why do you do this toward a great ruler?"

Now Inonu was sure of it. This demented offal of a sick camel had found his excuse and they would never leave here alive. Again he glanced at Bayar, then riveted his gaze on the Wallachian, almost *feeling* the pressure of the surrounding soldiery.

"This is our custom, my lord, which is that of our country." He knew that Dracula was aware of this but dared not antagonize him. "'Tis a practice ennobled by Koranic law."

The madman gave an abrupt jerk of his head. He said, "I too wish to strengthen your law so that you may be firm. General Luca's troops will assist you. Luca, it is time. That's it. Ah, Inonu, your turbans will fit the tighter for the addition of a few nails, will they not? Yes. Take them, general! *Take* them, I say! They who spit on our sovereignty will feel our wrath!"

It was over quickly. Knowing resistance was useless, Inonu made no move nor did his cohort. The nails were short he discovered. They would penetrate the skull but he doubted they would pierce the brain. They bore themselves well. Not one of them cried out in his agony. When they stood with their blood flowing down their necks and dripping on their kaftans he glanced at their tormentor impassively, heedless now of the risk of enraging him.

"We accept your hospitality," he said, searching for words in the burning pain. "And hope—to repay it."

Surprisingly, Dracula remained calm, having apparently already determined on an unwavering course of action. He spoke without visible emotion. "Go and tell your master that he is accustomed to endure such shame from you but we are not accustomed. Let him not impose his customs on other rulers who do not wish them, but let him keep them in his land."

And that was all. A short time later the Turks found themselves on the road leading out of Tirgoviste, on horses escorted by Wallachian cavalry. The road back was long. The enemy commander allowed them to stop and dress their wounds. Abdullah Midhat, an old man, lost more than the others because his blood was thin, and fainted twice.

Although most historians believe this event occurred in 1462, a few think it happened earlier, claiming that the sultan of Turkey simply ignored it.

Perhaps they should read again *History of Mehmed the Conqueror* by Kritovoulos of Imbros. It was not something the proud and savage Mehmed would have ignored, for no more heinous insult could have been flung at him. Dracula knew the Muslim army was poised and ready, knew that war was inevitable. When he nailed the turbans to the heads of the Turkish emissaries he simply anticipated his enemy. The act was insufferable. He was aware of this. It was a coldly calculated gage of battle thrown down at the foe's feet. It triggered the great invasion.

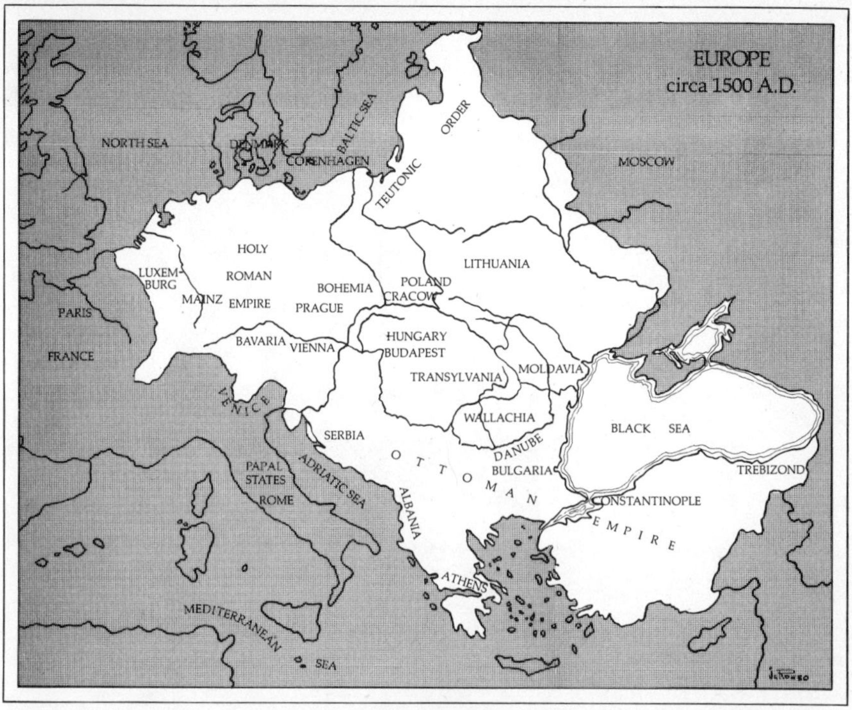

Above: A map of central Europe in the late fifteenth century.

Right: The house in Sighisoara, Transylvania, where Dracula was born.

Right: János Hunyadi's Hunedoara Castle, where Dracula may have spent some of his youth.

Below: The chapel at Balteni in which Dracula's father was assassinated.

Castle Bran, where Dracula probably stayed as a guest of János Hunyadi. With its high battlements and vast halls, secret passageways and hidden cells, Castle Bran conveys the spirit of Dracula's time.

The now ruined walls of Castle Dracula, overlooking the Arges River.

Mountainous terrain near Castle Dracula.

Solomon's Tower at Vísegràd, where King Matei kept Dracula prisoner from 1462 to 1474.

A page from an illustrated pamphlet about Dracula published in 1499, showing an impalement scene.

6

The Great Danubian Campaign against the Turks

"I will not fight with a river at my back! *That* is why I didn't cross the Dambovita to engage them before they reached it!"

In the hot confines of the command tent Dracula's strident voice was like the crack of a whip. His officers fell silent. Through the tied-back flap of the entrance tiny points of light could be seen, floating motes of sunlit dust stirred up by the just-returned horse with its empty saddle.

"And no more mounted scouts will be sent out, look you. In this heat with the land as dry as parchment the dirt they throw in the air is enough to alert Constantinople, to say nothing of an enemy at our door. Our rider is raven bait by now. The Turks may dally with him for days before they kill him. They've learned my trick of dismemberment by four horses tied to the victim's limbs but they won't use that. I abandoned it because it killed at once and they will have dropped it, too. Mehmed is more subtle."

He paused. "Fortunately, their captive knows little of our dispositions."

He picked up his pointer. About 18 inches long, it was shaped like a miniature stake and had become famous with the general staff. He knew this and was amused by it. Turning to the large makeshift table, he dropped its point on the map spread before them.

"Where are they?" he asked quietly. "We've known their route and their whereabouts every moment until now, and fought them and slowed them repeatedly these six months. Upriver on the Danube to Nicopolis. Disembarkation. The march north up the east bank of the Olt. From Turnu to Slatina all the way to Pitesti, then eastward. Straight at us. They want Tirgoviste badly. You'll pardon my smile, dear friends, but I think they want me even worse. It is said the sultan doesn't like me."

He began to laugh and everyone laughed with him.

"General Matusa," he said suddenly, the smile turned sour. Lopsided. "You say you think they crossed the Dambovita last night under cover of darkness and are hiding in the forest on the high ground to the northwest of us. Why do you believe this?"

The tall, spare general rubbed his chin, his lips compressed into a thin line. "Because otherwise we would have seen them by now, Your Highness. The country is too flat for concealment to the west and southwest, too open—"

"Why haven't we seen the glare from their cooking fires after sunset?"

"Light rations they consume raw, my lord. Cereal grains, dried fish, dried fruit. That abominable coffee of theirs—"

"Is being drunk cold, say you, or not at all. Yes. The dainty janissaries won't stomach it, you know. God's faith, they'll depose Mehmed in favor of an *houri*, a queen of the harem with bangles on her arms and kohl on her eyelids. At least a dancing girl can satisfy their other chief appetite."

Once more the laughter was general. "All right," Dracula continued. "Let's suppose that my tactic of burning every town, village, and crop along their advance has made them hungry enough to eat such doubtful provender. Take my pointer, Matusa, and show us their whereabouts."

The general did so. "I think about here, my lord."

"You are pointing to a wooded area exactly halfway between two rivers, the Dambovita and the Ialomita. *Between* the rivers, mark you, not *on* one of them. Where is their drinking water?"

"Lord, they are close to the headwaters of still another river, the Ilfov. It should provide them—"

"Hah!" Dracula's broad grin displayed his white teeth. "Your observation is shrewd but for one thing. We know there are three squadrons of *spahi* cavalry with the vanguard of their army. Three squadrons. Yet your designated area is very difficult mountain country. These are horses, not goats. What are they going to do with horses up there? Maybe, like the steed of Perseus their mounts are winged, eh? Every one a Pegasus? Nonsense. They are not in the forest. Give me back my little stake and I'll show you where they are." He took it and pointed. "They are *here*, my masters of war. You were nearly right, Matusa. They do get their water from the Ilfov. But they're not in the mountains or hidden by forest. They're on level ground. You forgot this gorge, did you not? It cuts deep and its walls are high. *That* is why we haven't seen them. On the west side of the river the banks are broad and long, almost brush-free, like a sandy parade ground flanked by cliffs. On the east side, look you, a narrower wooded strip. It's a cul-de-sac out of which Mehmed intends to pour his army in a torrent against Tirgoviste, his queen's gambit in our little chess game. I might also point out that it has but one exit. Here—to the south."

Again all were silent. They seemed amazed by the revelation.

"Your pardon, Highness," said Matusa, "but may I ask how you can be so sure of their bivouac's location?"

Dracula placed his pointer on the general's chest and slowly tapped with it, beating time to his words. "Because—I am a ruler—of very—unusual—sagacity." He turned his head and shouted over his shoulder. "Sentry! Bring to me my jar of preserved mementos."

The sentry entered with a salute and handed it to him. In what appeared to be clear fermented spirits, three human tongues lay at the bottom of the glass.

"Perhaps I should call them *memento mori*," said Dracula, "since they stand for death heads in a way. To be brief, they belong to Turkish prisoners taken late last night by General Gales's men but interrogated in his absence. They were Muslims of the best type. They spat at me and called down Allah's curses on my head. My threat to render them speechless and sew them in swine skins did not move them. They told me nothing—yet it was from them that I learned all."

Matusa, always more bold with him than the others, seemed incredulous. "My lord speaks in riddles," he complained.

Dracula nodded. "And you, General Luca, do you think I speak in riddles, too?"

The little man half-shrugged. "The mind of Your Highness is always too deep for the rest of us," he observed in his sycophant's way. "They spake not yet they revealed their army's whereabouts. Perhaps they pointed?"

"They did not point. General Gales, have you solved this riddle? Or is it too much like the one posed to the Philistines by Samson?"

Gales, one of the new breed of boyars created by Dracula since the destruction of the old, shook his head. He said, "Unfortunately, I am only a cavalry commander, my lord, not a magician. I have heard it said Your Highness has the power to speak with bats and wolves, the power of a warlock. Maybe, with such an all-seeing eye—"

"Dost doubt my power, knave? Dost mock?"

For a moment prince and general stared at each other coldly, but it was the general's gaze that dropped first. "Never, Your Highness. I only meant to say—I only—"

Dracula was toying with the tiny stake again. "Understood!" he snapped. From his doublet he drew a small leather purse, opened the drawstring, and emptied its contents on the map table. "Look at them, all of you. They are sand grains I took from the boots of the captives. Note their unusual size and coarseness. That is Ilfov River sand. I'd know it anywhere. Did not I and my brother Mircea hunt there with falcons in boyhood? The Dambovita's sand is more fine, the Ialomita's much darker. True, they had to cross the Dambovita to get where they are now but the more lately acquired grains will have displaced the earlier ones. They are on the Ilfov. They cannot be seen. There is only one location where this would be possible."

No one spoke. Everyone waited.

"I was testing you," he said. "As generals in my army you're supposed to be able to *think*, aren't you?" His burning glance seemed to shrivel them. "We will attack them where they stand. I don't intend to wait here and be hit. We'll steal a march on them. Tonight we'll move at sundown and be in our assault positions three hours later. You're surprised? You think the men can't make a march like that and fight a battle at the end of it? Then I'll tell you this. These are *Wallachians*. They can march *three days* and fight without a rest! And *win!* I know these men. I have 31,000 of them. If I had five times that number I could smash the Turks flat and raise our standard in Constantinople! Multiply the figure by ten and I could conquer all of Europe from the Black Sea to the channel of the English! Speak not to me, therefore, of the difficult."

They waited. In the cramped quarters of the tent Dracula began to pace, then stopped abruptly and swung to confront them. "You, Gales, will march with me. You aren't as well tried in battle as some others but you understand cavalry tactics. We'll have 9000 men with us, not a large force, but enough if we achieve surprise. Anything more would be unwieldy."

He paused as his gaze shifted from face to face. "Luca, as *spatar* you command the garrison of Tirgoviste, 22,000 of the best including our flanking units in the hills. They're Matusa's responsibility. Your second in command will be General Radului, remembered as having distinguished himself at Varna. You and he are old cocampaigners and should do well together. So? A joy to contemplate, is it not? The day is young. We have work to do."

He made a sign of dismissal, but Gales lifted an arresting hand. "Your Highness, may I ask what size force you expect to encounter in this attack?"

Dracula blinked. A dragonfly entered the tent and landed on the map. With a single stroke of his pointer he cut it neatly in half. "At least a quarter of their army will be there by now, 30 to 40,000 men."

"And we will attack them?"

"We will. The longer we wait the more they'll reinforce. Why do you think they haven't struck us yet? Time is on their side, not ours."

There was a murmur of half-concealed dissent which Dracula caught at once. Reaching down with both hands he took the two halves of the dragonfly and fitted them precisely together, staring at the spotted wings that still twitched spasmodically. Then he looked up at them.

"As a battle stratagem it is simple. Have you heard of Alexander the Great? Alexander of Macedon? His title was well deserved. He invaded the Persian Empire with 35,000 Greeks and moved against King Darius who had a million soldiers. You'll find it in Plutarch if you care to read it. How could this Macedonian king dare to accept such odds? For one thing, he intended to cut them up before they could concentrate, as I intend to do tonight. For another, he knew the Persian nature as I know the Turk, their crippling superstitions. If he killed Darius they would take it as an evil omen, a sign from their chief god Ahura-Mazda. Their morale would break. Their retreat might easily become a rout. This is what happened at the battle of Issus when Darius fled the field. His cowardice was even more of a blow than his death would have been."

Again his glance ranged from face to face. They were watching him intently, spellbound.

"Well, don't you see it?" he asked.

General Radului pulled at his beard. He said, "My lord, we will kill the sultan."

"At all costs."

Matusa was studying the nails of his right hand. Then his glance crossed Dracula's. "And suppose it costs us our entire attack force, Your Highness? Suppose your own life be forfeit?"

Dracula straightened his body. His face was covered with sweat. Some of it even dripped from the ends of his incredibly wide mustache. "I said *at all costs!* This Turkish muckrake is on my soil with his thrice-accursed host. My domain. *Mine!*" He jerked a thumb to his rear. "That city back there is mine, too, and he wants it. Dost think I'll suffer this outrage while there is breath in my body? Now by the Eternal God I swear this to you all. Tonight Dracula attacks. If my death be the price fate demands in return for the blood of Mehmed, so be it. If I fall among their lance points, *still* will I reach him and take his head with my sword! Aye, though I be holed like a fish net! Generals of Wallachia's army, mark me. Mehmed II, Sultan of Turkey, Defender of the Faith and the Chosen of Allah, has met his certain nemesis. After tonight only the worms will know him. I will expose him for the pitiful sham he is. The imams of Islam will honor him not nor any mosque be built for him. His name—his name—damn his soul to hell—shall be writ on water!"

The moon was nearly full. As he lay in the great thicket, tortured, as were his men, by biting insects, Dracula was glad of this. The soft light fell like the glow of a million burning candles on the river Ilfov, lighting the water they would have to cross, shallow at this point but turbulent, lighting also the Turkish camp beyond it, a place of many thousands but one where no fires burned.

He slapped frequently at the ticks and chiggers that tormented him and his men did the same, yet he knew this could not be heard by the enemy. It was the horses that worried him, Wallachian stallions grown restless because the light breeze was toward them and they caught the scent of the Turkish mares. He feared the wind would shift. If it did it would carry their neighing cries of need to the Turks. He could not control them. Blinders would not settle them down nor would tightened bits in their mouths quell the mating urge. Now his nerves were on the stretch and he fell prey to acute impatience. *Why* had the scouts not returned?

He rolled on his side and scratched madly at his groin. Damn all crawling and flying things! *Damn* them! It was like the battle of Crasna all over again, like the mite-infested forest where he and Stéfan had waited with Bogdan's army for the Poles—he and Stéfan. That dram was one of the bitterest he had ever swallowed and now it rose like bile in his throat. Cousins they were, close companions in their youths, comrades in arms in action after bloody action. He, Dracula, had kept the oath they had sworn and put Stéfan on his throne with Wallachian troops. And now? First the man ignored his pleas for military assistance. Then, in a treacherous blow worthy of Judas himself, he threw in his lot with the Turks. According to the reports of spies, even now Stéfan was marching against the port of Chilia on the Danube, a Dracula fortress to which he intended to lay siege. *That* was the measure of his gratitude. Even the venal Vlad the Monk was no worse than that—even the hated Radu who now rode with Mehmed as a Turkish general pledged to kill his brother.

"Stéfan," he said aloud and the green eyes glistened wetly. "One friend. Once."

As he sweated in this agony of waiting his troubled mind worked ceaselessly. This was 1462, a signal year in the history of Europe. On this night, June 17, he might achieve what six months of ferocious campaigning had failed to accomplish, the halting of the Turkish offensive and the turning back of their forces. It was not beyond reason. Already he had done the impossible and they knew it. The Spaniards called his way of fighting "the little war," *guerrilla*, but no one had ever fought it as he had done; outnumbered five to one; facing an enemy who always until now had been victorious; fighting without allies; burning his own ground black—waste—devastation—pillage to forestall pillage. Yet always coming against them again to attack and attack and attack. At long last he'd abandoned the line of the Danube. He'd been on the offensive for half a year, but now he was in retreat. All of Christendom *knew* he was in retreat, driven against his own capital, his back to the wall. Yet *still* he fought on. *Still* he clawed at them—as he would tonight—in a few minutes—as the beats of Mehmed's craven heart drew toward their ending.

Again he could hear the sounds from the Turkish camp across the river; occasional shouting and laughter; then a kind of musical titillation that might have come from the very numerous female camp followers; all the dissonances of an army cautious enough not to light fires but sufficiently sure of its impregnable position to impose no order of silence. Now there *were* flames. He could see them. Surely, they must be for cooking. Yes. Why should the Muslims worry about it? They were well hidden here with no reason to believe they'd been found. Soon the odor of braised lamb turning on the spits would come to him, the sound of slaves chanting as they performed the many tasks required by so large a force.

He got to one knee, then to his feet. The ticks were making his skin crawl, infesting him like body lice. Why should he stay on his belly when they would eat him either way? He thought of the Muslim prayers. Five times daily they prayed, the last shortly after sunset. He'd heard that last prayer. The Wallachians preparing their attack had listened to it as the Turkish holy men lifted their voices in the ageless wailing minor. At Egrigöz he'd learned some Old Persian, even studied Khayyam's *Rubaiyat*. Now, inexplicably, the lines came back to him, causing his lips to move silently.

"Alike for those who for today prepare, and those that after some tomorrow stare, a *muezzin* from the Tower of Darkness cries, 'Fools! Your reward is neither here nor there!'"

Reward? Yes, search for it in vain. All life was an illusion, glory an ever-receding, unattainable chimera. Aware of the thousands of men crouched down to his right and left, he made his way through the dense foliage to his horse. Far blacker than the night was this animal, darker even than the soul of Mehmed.

"Strigoi," he said softly.

The great charger turned slightly, his nostrils distending as he scented the air, ears pricked to catch the sounds of the mares. Lovingly he nuzzled his master's hand, accepting sugar.

"Ah Strigoi, tonight you carry me to death or victory. Half Arab you are and fleet, and fear is unknown to you. Do you know what your name means?" He stroked the slick hide of the shoulder, finding it slightly damp. "It is 'feathered demon of the darkness.' How perfect for my warhorse when already the peasants call me *Moroi*, the Undead. And *Vampir*, the Drinker of Blood. Great men always love their horses. Do you know that? Alexander and his Bucephalus. Caligula and his Incitatus. Dracula—and Strigoi."

He mounted, then sat very still in the saddle. Some of the men would notice it, he knew, but none would mount their own horses until the command was given, for Wallachian discipline was rigid. Memories came crowding, scenes out of the recent past. Caligula. The name made him think of his wife, the Princess Drusilla. How vainglorious the claim of her boyar father, he who with her mother had died beneath the walls of

Poenari. Not only of Dacian lineage were they but of *Roman*. Was that why they'd given her such a name? Long ago in Rome there was another Drusilla, Caligula's sister and paramour. But *that* Drusilla loved the emperor, was worthy to be his consort. And this one? Although she accepted her slave status and groveled in sexual ecstasy, moaned and writhed and was insatiable, this one did not adore her husband and prince. She hated and feared him.

An officer approached him. Catching the glint of moonlight on helmet and breastplate, Dracula leaned from his saddle to listen.

"The Muslim pickets are all dead, Your Highness, silently strangled or killed by arrows. Our scouts are all back. They report a condition of quiet in the enemy camp. The Turks show no sign of unease. The sultan's tent is where it always is, exactly in the center."

Dracula slapped at an insect as his mount stamped his hoof to dislodge them. "And looking as always?"

"Embroidered in gold, my lord, with the crescent and star at its peak. Unmistakable."

"The janissaries?"

"They mount the usual guard there. Maybe 300 strong."

"Available reinforcements?"

"Some thousands more on the north and west sides. They'll sleep with their weapons as usual, Your Highness. Unless taken by complete surprise—"

"They could defend formidably."

"Yes, my lord."

Dracula considered. "We will give them a little more time to settle down, then hit them and ride out of this pestilential hell. Are the torches ready?"

"Yes, Your Highness."

"My compliments to General Gales. When he gets the signal, tell him to ford the river exactly where I indicated. Anywhere else could be disastrous."

"Yes, Your Highness."

"Carry on."

As he watched the man's diminishing back in the lunar glow he knew the precaution he had taken, putting Gales upriver from himself, was useless. If the general failed to press the attack or was routed he could not head him off. He himself would be too deeply engaged for that. Could he trust these new boyars any more than the old? Gales had done well on the Danube, fought brilliantly and earned his generalship. He *had* to trust him. It was now much too late to replace him.

An hour later, with little sign of activity in the foe's camp, he gave the order all had awaited. At once an owl hooted on the left and was answered on the right. Dracula drew his sword, unslinging the shield at his back and slipping his left hand and forearm through the leather straps.

"Now!" he rasped at the nearest horsemen. "This is the moment history demands! *Our* moment! Attack! Attack! For God and Wallachia!"

He did not wear spurs. He would never use pain-giving rowels on Strigoi. He tugged lightly at the rein and eased his weight forward, lowering his helmeted head.

"Strigoi, my comrade. My steed. My avenger. We're for them, Strigoi. We're for them now. *Like Zeus' thunderbolts, Strigoi!*"

At a canter they moved toward the river, straight toward it, never wavering. Dracula felt himself exhilarated, racked by a fast-mounting frenzy of longed-for violence and seething hatred. Around him the thousands advanced at the pace he had set, but he was scarcely aware of them. Sand. So much of it. Then water. Water everywhere. Strigoi's hooves ricocheted off wet rock and he slipped once but recovered. He was fetlock deep, then in it to the belly as white spray dashed across his withers and his powerful neck plunged up and down in breasting the current. Dracula howled. He *howled* deep inside himself, uplifted by a sense of burgeoning freedom such as he had never known. He would not fight with a river at his back? Why had he changed his mind? Was he so sure of himself against these odds? Was he? *Was* he?

The river gurgled in the shimmering moonglow. It foamed and threw itself from side to side. It was *alive.* Dracula laughed as he felt its chill clutch. He had always known that. Now the primitive pagan in him, never far beneath the surface, surged madly upward.

"Oh river god," he crooned softly, "betray not thine own. It is Wallachia who crosses thy domain now, a blade against the heathen. War with us not. Drown us not. Bear us on thy bosom to victory!"

He glanced to both sides. Torches on the river, the fiery brands of picked men who would burn the Turkish camp. But on his right they held back. Gales *held back!*

"Attack!" he shrieked at them. "Attack! Attack! Attack!"

He saw lights on the other shore. They were coming awake now. Some Muslims had caught up branches from the smoldering fires and were waving them into brightness, shouting and gesticulating. He hurled a curse at them. He was pushing ahead. Urging Strigoi. Driving on. Then he was on the far bank... climbing... Strigoi finding foothold in the sand and rock... and open, level ground bathed in moonlight... galloping now ... the charge. The *charge!* A group of Muslim soldiery came at them like a surging sea and were met by Wallachians in the full brunt of the battle shock. Cut... thrust... parry. Steel against steel. All amid curses and shouting, the wheeling of wild-eyed horses, foam flecking their flanks and flaring nostrils. The onslaught of 9000 men against the surprised, sleepy-eyed Turks was nightmarish. Hellish.

"Die!" shouted Dracula and struck. "Die! Die! Die!"

The janissary kettledrums sounded the alarm. Louder and louder they reverberated, throbbing in the dust-choked heat of the night. Out of the melee a face suddenly rose; a hawk nose above a black beard; a spiked Saracenic helmet over a white turban. Mounted. A lightning-fast white Arab. He caught the flash of descending steel and raised his shield to deflect the scimitar.

"Have at thee!" he roared in Turkish, thrusting and hacking wildly to get around the protecting buckler.

"Dog of an infidel!" shouted the Turk. "May Allah curse thee!"

Then the man was decapitated by a horseman at his rear. The antique Seljuk casque fell to the ground, the head still in it, the blood gushing in spurts from arteries fed by the still beating heart. And strike. No quarter given or asked. And strike. The rising clamor of clashing arms, shouts, oaths, screams of mortal anguish was deafening, deafening, *deafening!*

Dracula rose stiff-legged in his stirrups and slashed straight down, severing the arm and shoulder of a *spahi.* Where was the royal tent? Where? *Where?* A janissary clung to his saddlecloth and thrust madly. He leaned low, struck below the greaves, and hamstrung him. A *spahi's* horse smashed against him and bit Strigoi on the neck. They locked. Clashed. Cut. Parry. Counterstroke. Run through the unprotected armpit and dead in the saddle, the Muslim's corpse kept the seat of its plunging mount for several seconds before being hurled to the dust like a sack of oats, the spiked shield driven into the ground.

"Kill the heathen swine!" a Wallachian officer shouted, waving his sword. "The sultan's tent is to your right front! Kill him! Kill him!"

Then the officer was dead, beheaded by a scimitar. And tents were burning, the torchbearers igniting them as the battle raged. And death.

Death everywhere as the dirt-fouled atmosphere grew thicker and thicker. Dracula stared. His horse had stopped dead in its tracks, snorting loudly, his highbred flanks quivering, steel-shod front hooves pawing the ground. He could not see the royal pavilion. But suddenly the star and crescent appeared before him as though floating in air, disembodied above a pall of swirling dust. *That* was it. Was the cur cowering inside? Had he thrown down his turban before his generals and begged them to defend it? Mehmed. Conqueror of Constantinople. Pariah. Swine begotten of swine. Swine above all. Swine to the very guts!

"Thrice-accursed heathen pig!" The words poured out of him as he pointed with his blade. "*There* is his tent! Break through to it, Wallachians! Cut him down! The best of you brings me his gargoyle's head! Forward, Strigoi! Forward!"

The gallop was straight and hard. A spear sang past his face. Then another and another. But when the pavilion was reached it was empty.

"Fire this dung mound!" he commanded a mounted torchbearer. "Burn it! Burn it, I tell you! If you find the pig who belongs in it, burn him, too!"

The order was obeyed. The horseman rode straight through the tent, ripping his way out at the far side, igniting it immediately. It burned with great speed. Pausing an instant to watch, Dracula saw the forward center pole that bore the crescent standing alone and afire, the cloth all consumed; and suddenly it seemed that this emblem of Islam again hung suspended, like a phantasm created by evil *jinn* in the days of Al-ad-din. He looked about wildly.

"Mehmed!" he screamed in the enemy's tongue. "Mehmed! Thou filth! Thou hell-spawned son of perdition! Thou gutter-bred swine! Come to me! Come to me! Come to me! Art Shaitan with thy conjurer's tricks? Nay, the devil art thou not, but only a man!"

He found himself reaching down to help one of his soldiers—uselessly. The Wallachian had been gutted and unhorsed. He had staggered to his feet, taken a few steps, reeling, in his already glazing eyes a look of utter stupefaction. In his hands he held his dripping intestines. He dropped to his knees, then pitched forward on his face.

Dracula watched him with a feeling he'd never known, a kind of inner woe. Then instantly he was involved again in furious melee and found himself fighting for his life. The janissaries had regrouped, were concentrating at the battle standard. Shouting his war cry he broke through a body of them, taking three heads with the most murderous backstroke the Balkans had ever seen. But there were too many. *Too many.* He was quickly surrounded. Again he cut his way out. Eyes blazing, his appearance frightful beyond description, he fought like a fiend possessed, helmet and breastplate and greaves covered with the blood of his enemies. And fought. And fought. A sword stroke cut through his reins and he grasped the saddle-pommel. Then the pommel was slashed away and he fripped Strigoi's mane, cracking a Turk's skull with the sharp edge of his shield.

And the Wallachians reformed and renewed the attack. And an hour passed. Clouds drifting across the moon darkened the night. Hundreds died, then thousands; and always it was the sight of Dracula that inspired the attackers; the remembered image when none could see him; the terrible demoniac aspect; the dread among many of his followers that he was really not human but a god. Son of the Devil. The Lord Impaler, Kazîglu Bey. Moroi of the burning soul that is damned. *Moroi!*

It was a night to remember. In Romanian history it came to be called, quite simply, "the Night of Terror."

Although the fighting continued until four in the morning in a desperate see-saw battle of half-blind confusion, Dracula failed in his purpose. Mehmed II was neither killed nor captured, nor was the Turkish army beaten. It was, however, very seriously bloodied before the Wallachians disengaged and retired. Estimates as to its losses vary. The highest was given by Balbi, envoy of the Republic of Venice to the Porte, whose letter to the Doge put the Muslim casualties at 15,000 against a third of that for the Wallachians. It is perhaps unfortunate that he signed his documents using only his last name, as did some other witnesses. Unfortunate, also, is the fact that the Romanian archives are silent on the fate of the reluctant General Gales. A significant point: after this date his name ceases to appear on documents dealing with the boyars. But let us go back.

As has been indicated, by the close of the reign of Dracula's grandfather Prince Mircea, in 1418, Wallachia had been reduced to the status of a vassal state of the Turkish Empire, paying annual tribute. Not quite a *pashalik*, or province, but with its sovereignty much reduced and its independence seriously compromised. To a man of Dracula's imperious and haughty nature this was unbearable, as indeed it would have been to many a less tyrannical ruler who nonetheless possessed pride and self-respect. That the Danubian ports and fortresses were in Turkish hands was another source of extreme irritation, for the strategist in the Wallachian prince clearly perceived the danger. By militarily dominating the line of the Danube the ever-aggressive Ottomans had permanently extended their frontier, consolidated their entrenchment in southeastern Europe, and created a deadly staging area for the further penetration of the European continent after overrunning what remained of the Balkans.

Faced with the magnitude of such a threat, even a totally sane man might well have become desperate. But Dracula, the manic-depressive, was not sane. During those times when the depressive phase was dominant he could just barely tolerate the situation, while brooding over it with all the potential menace of a cornered tiger licking his wounds. But in the manic phase? That was another matter. Cross him when that was on him and a madman awakened, a maniac made all the more dangerous through the retention of tactical knowledge and strategic insight.

It was this phenomenon the sultan faced when he mobilized on the Danube. The Turks, used to confronting Christian armies that fought them toe to toe, were wearied and half-demoralized by this paladin of guerrilla warfare; this *shadow general* who struck and disappeared only to strike again from another vantage point; who favored the night attack when darkness promoted great confusion in an army the size of the Turkish; whose troops lived off the land; whose ruthless policy of attrition left only smoldering ashes in the path of the Ottoman advance; whose almost unbelievable savagery and cruelty were fast becoming legend.

It was the same *scorched earth* policy General Kutuzov used against Napoleon when the 500,000-strong French *Grande Armée* invaded Russia in June of 1812; the same the Russians employed again when 2,700,000 German troops crossed their frontier in June, 1941. And in the Hundred Years' War, how did the French at last defeat the English even though the latter won all the major battles? Again it was the slow process of wearing the enemy down. In that lengthy and grueling conflict the French general, Bertrand du Guesclin, proved to be one of the fourteenth-century's veritable masters of attrition warfare.

As a strategic and tactical recourse of determined and brave men a guerrilla defense can work miracles—if there are enough of them. Not only can it result in the cutting of vital communications in the enemy's rear, but the strategic retreat (sometimes called the *phased withdrawal* because it depends on predetermined successive lines of defense) offers another crucial advantage. As the invader pursues the retreating army, the former's *lines of communication* grow steadily longer and more vulnerable to enemy action as those of the defender grow shorter and hence more secure. Ultimately, unless it is beaten and overrun during one of the initial phases of invasion, this process results in the defending force being able to fight on what are called *interior lines*, a very distinct tactical edge. But sheer armed might will tell in a war that lasts long enough. In the end the disparity of numbers made Wallachia's defeat a certainty.

Actually, the inevitability of war between Dracula and Mehmed would have been obvious to an astute observer as early as 1459 when the Wallachian prince began to flagrantly violate the so-called capitulation treaties. Although he cynically reaffirmed them in 1460, he no longer did anything to honor them. Simply stated, they required the same annual tribute (*haratch* in the Turkish) of 3000 gold ducats that had been paid in Mircea's day. (In his scholarly work *Southeastern Europe under Ottoman Rule*, Peter F. Sugar states that this sum was not raised until 1503 and then only to 8000.) Further, they stipulated an annual visit by the Wallachian ruler to the Porte to swear vassalage to the sultan and kiss the hem of his robe. It is not easy to imagine Dracula doing this. One can almost *feel* his inner rage. By 1461, also, the Turks were demanding the yearly child quota for the janissaries. His flat refusal to grant it (on grounds of sovereignty, not humane ones) was entirely in character.

If not specifically mentioned by treaty, there was much more that was *implied* by these acts, at least in Turkish minds. They signified total submission militarily, politically, and personally. If in theory the subject state retained a measure of sovereignty in the persons of its prince and boyar council, the reality was something else. The principality could make war and peace, but let it *try* to do so in a manner contrary to Turkish wishes. Its foreign policy was in pawn to the Porte. Than that single fact there was no surer sign of Ottoman dominance.

In Dracula's mind, apart from border skirmishes in the south with Turkish-held Bulgaria which were relatively frequent, all-out war between Wallachia and the mighty Turkish Empire was inevitable. There were two factors of chief consideration. The first was to secure his throne by the elimination of the old disloyal boyar families and the pacification of his western frontier, meaning the Saxon "enclaves" in Transylvania. He pursued that aim with the results already noted. The second and equally important purpose was to gather allies.

From the beginning it seemed obvious that only two powers could be expected to lend him material aid: Hungary out of self-interest as much as anything, for a Turkish army on the Danube was assuredly a threat to Buda; and Moldavia, not only because this principality was clearly a

Turkish target but also, Dracula hoped, because the pledge of alliance sworn mutually with his cousin Stéfan would prove mutually binding.

As to the first, King Matei—although he practiced the usual royal duplicity and loaned him troops to help defend Chilia—clearly hated him. There was the little matter of the savage terror raids into Transylvania, a territory claimed by Hungary. There were the duchies of Amlas and Fagaras, also Hungarian in Matei's view, a sovereignty bitterly disputed by Dracula. And there was the memory of János Hunyadi, Matei's late father, a man who had precious little use for any of the Draculesti and had proved it by the part he had played in the deaths of Dracul and Mircea. Matei may well have believed that an alliance with Dracula would be a betrayal of his father's principles. When the Wallachian emissary Radu Farma arrived in Buda, Matei read Dracula's letter. It was polite and respectful but urgent, very personal as between Christian rulers. "Gather your whole army," it said, "...accept to fight with us here." It is not difficult to imagine the monarch's thoughts as he perused it. Already he had his excuse for denial, his embroilment with the Germanies, with the Holy Roman Emperor Friedrich III. In part, the letter continued as follows:

> If Your Majesty does not wish to give your army, then only send as many as you wish, the Transylvanians and the Székelys. And if Your Highness is willing to lend help, then be good enough not to delay and let us truly know your mind. Please this time, do not delay our emissary who is bringing this letter to you. Send him back to me immediately and swiftly. Let us in no way leave unfinished what we have begun, let us push this affair to a conclusion. For if the Almighty will listen to the prayers and wishes of Christianity, if he will favorably listen to the prayers of his unworthy subjects, he will give us victory over the Infidel, the enemies of the Cross of Christ.

Ironically, without Dracula's knowledge there *had* been some help sent him, a large quantity of gold direct from the Vatican's treasury. Pope Pius II had been devious. Knowing the Danube to be in the hands of the Turks, he'd sent it by a circuitous route to Buda, charging Matei with the responsibility for its reaching its destination. Dracula never laid eyes on it. Some of the papal bullion may still be in Buda today.

As for the behavior of Prince Stéfan in this crisis, historical opinion is divided. Romanian scholars in particular tend to excuse his treachery against Dracula on grounds of survival, pointing out that the Danubian fortress of Chilia was essential to Moldavia's defense against the Ottomans, that Dracula's Wallachian-Hungarian garrison lacked the strength to hold it, that Stéfan therefore acted under extreme duress of circumstance. Possibly. On the other hand, Dracula's mental aberration must have been well known to the shrewd and opportunistic Stéfan, as was the Wallachian's overweening ambition. If you couple madness with the lust for power, then add to that heady brew resounding military victories over no less a force than the Ottoman army, what is the sum of the parts? Wallachian expansionism? Almost certainly. Dracula's ultimate invasion of Moldavia in the interests of what Germans of a later century would call *realpolitik?* A distinct possibility. When Professor Karl Haushofer, "the Sage of Munich," devised his geopolitical doctrine for the use of Hitler and the Nazi party he might almost have had Dracula in mind. So might Niccolò Machiavelli when, only fifty-nine years after Dracula's death, the Florentine intellectual published his most famous work, *The Prince.* True, the actual model for the book was Cesare Borgia, the most ruthless conqueror and infamous despot of the Italian Renaissance. But Borgia resembled Dracula to an almost uncanny degree, as will be seen.

There is a curious footnote to Stéfan's treacherous move. He did indeed invest the stronghold of Chilia, maintaining the siege from the eighteenth to the twenty-fifth of June, 1462. On June 22, however, he was wounded in the ankle by Hungarian fire from the walls and withdrew from the action with the redoubt still untaken. He never completely recovered from this injury. Apparently a case of recurrent and latently systemic blood poisoning, it plagued him for the rest of his life. Although he was to live another forty-two years, dying on July 2, 1504, according to a report left by his chirurgeon, this never completely healed injury was a factor in the prince's death. Thus he followed in the preordained path of Achilles.

There is still another thing which stamps Dracula for what he was at the time and colors many of his actions, the fact that he was basically a medieval survival, a historical anachronism. The High Middle Ages had passed, however, and like it or not he was forced into the role of a man of the Renaissance. There were very few in Europe who could still be stirred by the age-old call to crusade. János Hunyadi had been one. Pope Pius II was another. But these were rare exceptions. For the most part, the crusading zeal in the West had died with Louis IX of France (Saint

Louis) when in 1270 his second expedition against the Muslims, at Tunis, resulted in his dying of the plague. Yet Dracula's *purpose* remained unchanged. There is evidence he thought of himself as a ruler who had inherited the laurel wreath of Hunyadi, that he deeply resented the action of the late Pope Calixtus III in conferring that honor on Scanderbeg. Dracula yearned for European recognition and military fame, yet by a strange combination of circumstances his name was to be all but blotted from history.

Interestingly enough, with his second assumption of the throne in the fall of 1456 he went so far as to confide his hatred and distrust of the Turks to a document bearing his signature. He had just reaffirmed his vassalage to Constantinople with what sincerity we already know. Now, deciding to test the water in Hungary's province of Transylvania, on 10 September he wrote to the elders of the city of Brasov. Informing them of his reception in Tirgoviste of a Turkish embassy, and claiming only peaceful intent toward the Brasovians, he made clear his opinion that the Ottomans sought to end Romanian internal calm by sowing political and religious discord.

> The time and the hour has now come, concerning what I have previously spoken of. They (the Turks) are seeking a way to loot your country passing through ours.... Our wish is to do no evil against you, not to abandon you, as I have told you and sworn. I trust I will remain your brother and faithful friend.

Other than to exchange polite amenities, Brasov showed no interest in him. Doubtless, the ferocious raid of April 2, 1459, was partially provoked by this slight.

As concerned possible allies against the Porte then, by the autumn of 1461 Dracula's options were already shrinking rapidly. He wrote more than one letter to Buda. He also contacted his cousin Stéfan and was met with ill-concealed prevarication. What of the Republic of Venice, the great sea power which stood to lose so much in the Mediterranean? Would *they* act in time? Although Pietro Tommasi, its ambassador at Buda, urgently advised the Doge and the Venetian senate to place the maritime city-state on a war footing, nothing was done. Eventually, in 1463, a thoroughly awakened Venice would confront Turkey, but by then the situation in Wallachia had already been decided.

Was there anyone left? Russia, under its grand duke, Ivan III—

Poland, under its king, Casimir IV—Bohemia, under its king, George of Podebrad—the Holy Roman Empire under its emperor, Friedrich III—all were far from the scene of impending conflict, their rulers more concerned with internecine strife than a possible foreign invasion. The Balkans had been largely overrun by the Turks. Other than Romania itself, only Albania and Montenegro still resisted, and the former would fall with the death of Scanderbeg in 1468. Montenegro alone—Serbian, Orthodox, and unconquerable—was destined to retain its independence.

It must have been with a feeling of bitter frustration and a sense of inevitable doom that Dracula pushed events to a conclusion in the winter of 1461. Because his Danubian campaign is so well documented there are figures available for the strength of the opposing forces. Depending on which chronicler one consults, the Turkish strength is given as anywhere from 60,000 to 300,000 men, a curiously large disparity. Tommasi is responsible for the former estimate, the Turkish historian Tursun Bey for the latter. Although the truth is difficult to ascertain, it is perhaps unreasonable to assume the sultan would employ a lesser host against an army in the field (and especially one commanded by Dracula) than he did to lay siege to Constantinople in 1453. Unfortunately, the size of the latter force is also in dispute. Kritovoulos of Imbros, a contemporary, claimed the Ottoman army investing the city numbered 150,000. In the author's opinion, that which invaded Wallachia could scarcely have been less.

Actually, there were *two* Turkish armies at the opening of the campaign. (Possibly Tommasi was aware of only one.) The main contingent was commanded by Mehmed. The fact that his Byzantine chronicler Chalkokondyles states that it took 25 *triremes* (war galleys with three banks of oars) and 150 transport vessels to carry it up the Danube will give some idea of its size. This force burned the river port of Braila to deny its use to the enemy. From the southern Bulgarian city of Philippolis (today called Plovdiv) it was planned that the second army would move northward to join the first. This it did without serious opposition, probably arriving at the rendezvous port of Vidin (site of the Roman Bononia) in early June. But the Ottomans found no place to disembark. Everywhere Dracula had been before them he left smoking ruins. Opposed by very accurate Wallachian archers at Vidin, the vast Muslim array withdrew many miles downriver, eventually going ashore at Nicopolis.

That then is how it began. Dracula attacked them on the Danube. For six desperate months he fought the invaders as no man had done since the Tartar conqueror Tamerlane. Yet inevitably he was driven back and back, withdrawing his mauled and bleeding force up the Olt River toward his capital of Tirgoviste. There, as has been noted, he regrouped his army and launched his famous night attack, almost achieving his primary goal of finding and killing the sultan. Failing in this, believing the defense of the city against the combined Ottoman might would probably cost him his entire force, he retired to the northeast, determined to engage his cousin Stéfan and the Moldavian-Turkish contingent he believed was besieging Chilia, the key to the defense of eastern Wallachia.

Before departing he left something behind for Mehmed. A suicide detachment of cannoneers and incendiaries remained in Tirgoviste. When the Turkish army appeared at dawn following the Night of Terror, they fired on the Turks, behind them a rising pall of smoke, for the city was in flames. Then they too disappeared.

The Muslims entered the gutted, half-ruined capital. They found it stripped of its treasures even to the richly ornamented chalices in the churches, and inevitably all the wells had been poisoned. And they found something else. In the course of the long campaign Dracula had taken a great many prisoners, more than 20,000 altogether. They'd been concentrated here. They were *still* here. On the infamous killing ground where the older boyars and their wives had died, the mile-long gorge outside the city, the corpses of all of them hung on stakes. A few thousand, more recently taken, were still in the process of decomposing and the nauseating stench of putrescence was nearly overpowering. But time, the elements, and the region's voracious ravens had reduced countless others to mere skeletons in rags. Among those still vaguely recognizable from shreds of clothes were Hamza Pasha, governor of Nicopolis, whose prehostilities mission had been to lure Dracula to that city on a pretext and there take him alive; and Toma Catavolinos, his Greek subordinate, assigned by Mehmed to the sharing of this task. Both had been beheaded by Dracula at Giurgiu, then taken to Tirgoviste for impalement, heads and all. The sultan's reaction to this fearsome sight revealed a surprising weakness. He asked: "What can we do against a man like this?"

Concerning this event, Chalkokondyles commented as follows: "Even the emperor, overcome by amazement, admitted that he could not win the land, from a man who does such great things, and above all knows how to exploit his rule and that of his subjects in this way."

Although the slaughter of this pitiful multitude (as always, it included many women and children) was clearly sickening to the Muslim leader, it was not the only factor to influence him. By this time the first cases of plague had appeared in the Turkish army, always a great blow to morale. We are reminded of Napoleon at Jaffa, finding plague among the Turkish prisoners, seeing it begin to infect the French, finally abandoning his intended conquest of Egypt after losing his fleet to Nelson and being repelled at Acre. Ancient history also provides comparisons, perhaps the most memorable of which was Attila, king of the Huns. This vicious tyrant, fratricide, and military genius nearly took Rome itself, but despite a popular legend it was not the eloquence of Pope Leo I that turned him back in 452 A.D., it was plague spreading in his army.

Characteristically, seeing the agony of his men and the bubonic swellings in their groins and armpits, noting the dark-colored corpses symptomatic of the dreaded Black Death, Mehmed decided to save himself, to retire from the battlefront and withdraw from the country. The forces that were to pursue Dracula he placed under the command of the Impaler's treacherous half-brother, Prince Radu, and the pasha of Silistria. With the rest of the army, sick in his heart and for all practical purposes a beaten man, he returned to the waiting transports at Nicopolis and sailed down the Danube. By 29 June he was in the burned-out river port of Braila where an actual commission bearing Radu's name was written and affixed with the imperial seal. By 11 July he was once more in his staging area at Adrianople where he had chosen to rest before returning to his capital.

It was a pattern of cowardice that sorted well with the sultan's previous behavior on the Night of Terror. Of that weird battle in the moonlight a veteran in Dracula's army—one of the very few who could write—left a personal though anonymous account which has survived. Bearing the date 1464, sent to Pius II by his legate, Nicolas Modrussa, it had this to say on the subject of Mehmed's character.

> Dracula provoked an incredible massacre without losing many men in such a major encounter, though there were many wounded; he abandoned the enemy camp before daybreak and returned to the same mountain whence he had come, without anyone daring to follow him, since he had caused so much terror and trouble among all. I learnt by questioning those who had participated in this battle that the Sultan lost all confidence regarding the situation. During that night he secretly abandoned

> the camp and fled in a shameful way. And he would have continued in this way had he not been reprimanded by friends and brought back, almost against his will.

According to the various accounts, at the opening of the Danubian campaign Dracula had anywhere from 22,000 to 30,900 men, again depending on which historical source one chooses to believe. That the author selects the latter figure is due to the fact that Wallachian armies in the days of Dracula's predecessors very seldom numbered less than 30,000 effectives. Moreover, despite his avowed military genius, it is difficult to conceive of him accomplishing the things he did with materially less than that. In the six months of fighting that occurred between December of 1461 and June of 1462 how many men did he lose? There are no precise figures available. Nonetheless, judging from the primitive state of medicine at the time and the tendency of wounds to fatally infect, there is little reason to believe the Wallachian soldiers fared better than the Turkish.

He also made a serious mistake. Enraged by the failure of his night attack to accomplish its objective, he ordered the impalement of every man who had been wounded in the back, accusing such unfortunates of cowardice in the face of the enemy. ("You are not a man but a woman!") The numbers who died so are unknown. What is certain is that it caused an additional lowering of morale, a very ruinous one, and contributed perhaps more than anything else to the mass desertions that followed. So that it must have been with a much reduced force that on 18 June, 1462 (the day after the Night of Terror), he began the long march eastward to attack the lesser of his separated enemies, avenge himself against Stéfan, and raise the Moldavian-Turkish siege of Chilia.

He never got there. We know that repeatedly his army was intercepted, that Radu's 4000 Wallachian cuirassiers attacked him, the detached Turkish forces, and Stéfan's Moldavians who surely must have realized they were warring against their own interests. In battle after battle he outmaneuvered and outfought them all, driving them toward the Dobrogea, the marshes of the Danube's lower reaches, the deadly swamps of the river's broad delta. But he was losing men rapidly and could not replace them. And gradually the enemy grew stronger, consolidating his front, throwing in reserves hastily brought up from storied Varna in the south.

Until a day came between 25 and 29 June when a decisive action was fought. It was in relatively flat country called the Baraganul (Baragan

Steppe) about 45 miles south-southwest of Braila in the vicinity of the ancient Roman town of Vasilium, modern Vizirul. Dracula was beaten. His losses weren't documented. All we know positively is that from this moment began the long and bitter retreat to the west—about 175 miles as the crow flies—a retreat subject to more desertions, days and nights of intense suffering for his exhausted men that were to end with his taking sanctuary in his lofty castle on the Arges River, the restored Castle of Agrish.

Curiously enough, Mehmed did not destroy what was left of Tirgoviste, a fact attributed by some historians to the night attack which so unnerved him. Whether that was actually the case or whether he planned to rebuild the capital city to serve as the royal seat of his puppet Radu may never be known. There was only one outstanding fact from the Turkish viewpoint. Dracula had been defeated but had escaped. He was mad, he was undoubtedly still full of fight, and the fortified eyrie he had selected for his retreat was virtually impregnable. Just how the Turks discovered he was there is a matter of conjecture, that Mehmed gave immediate orders for his destruction a certainty.

Very simple. He had plenty of food and an unlimited water supply, was high on a mountain crag behind walls which in places were 10 feet thick. All they had to do was to take him, torture him (that for the sheer satisfaction of it), cut off his head and send it pickled to Constantinople. Many a veteran emir must have felt misgivings at the magnitude of such a task, for already superstition was having its demoralizing effect. Capture this lunatic under such conditions? The mission could be costly, too costly. Had they known the truth they might have spared themselves the worry, even taken the time to celebrate. His army had dissolved like the mists of the morning. He could no longer fight. He was almost alone.

7
The Castle on the River

The severely austere stone room called The Monk's Rest was the uppermost chamber in the highest tower of the Castle of Agrish and had but one window, a portal flanked by fluted columns that overlooked the Arges River far below. It was a lonely place, never more so than on this strange and melancholy night. A narrow, hard, and uncomfortable pallet served as a bed; a rough-hewn oaken table and chair as furniture; an ivory crucifix in one shadowy corner as divine protection.

It was to this retreat that Drusilla had come as to a sanctuary, fleeing the citadel's lower regions with the first of the Turkish round shot the day before; and on this dark, nearly moonless night it seemed to her to be the only refuge she had in all the world.

Just now she lay on the pallet on her back, a pillow of straw for her head, her stays loosened for easier breathing, and gazed steadily at the flame of the candle burning on the table. Her brow was furrowed with care and woe, her dark eyes deeply troubled. How much longer could it go on, she wondered? Her vicious husband had always been dangerous and unpredictable, even in victory. Now in defeat he was more subject to wild, unreasoning moods than ever; more quick to anger, to lash out, to show the few retainers he had left that he was still a force to reckon with, a man to respect and fear.

She sighed deeply. He was mad into the bargain. She knew that now. Long had she suspected it—ever since he'd caused her parents' death on the terrible march to Poenari—but now she knew. She saw that madness in many things. Sometimes it was in a look, an indescribable expression in those glittering green eyes. At others she saw it in his deeds or his words, actions and pronouncements that froze the blood of those who still served him. And what would be the final outcome of all this now that the Turks and Radu's men were here at last? Just across the river they were, their guns already emplaced on the ruined battlements of Poenari, a fortress as high as Agrish itself. All day yesterday they had fired. In her mind she heard Dracula's voice.

"Don't fear them, Drusilla. All they have are cherrywood cannon. Small bores and lightweight shot. What fools they are. They have men enough to haul both gun-carriages and bronze barrels to the summit of Poenari but not the foresight to so arm themselves. Cherrywood, can you believe it? That is all they've ever had on this campaign, all they brought with them. Hah! They will never breech my walls!"

Don't fear them. But she *did* fear them. She feared them terribly. What would they do to her if she were captured? She was not a brave woman, had never been that, and now her increasing dread drove her toward the edge of hysteria. The Muslims were cruel and savage, barbarians from another world who did not even know the meaning of mercy. They took women in *coitus per anum*. She knew that already, for many were the tales rife in Christendom of what happened to captive females in Turkish seraglios. She was not a virgin to this act thanks to her husband's perverted desires. But to be taken thus by twenty or thirty or a *hundred* men; to be used and abused like the lowest whore in the brothels of Constantinople—she couldn't bear it. She *knew* she couldn't bear what others of her sex had borne ever since the Crusades and the terrible Seljuks. It was unthinkable!

In a highly distressed state she flung from her bed and moved toward the window, trembling in every limb. God help her, she was *aroused!* What was the matter with her that she could feel this burning desire at the mere thought of being foully ravished by so many? She could not define her malady. She knew only that her tyrannical master's brutalizing of her helpless white body excited her in ways she had never dreamed, instilling in her a sick longing for him even while she dreaded him. To admit it to herself made her deeply and wretchedly ashamed. She felt used and dirty, utterly and hopelessly debauched. Yet it seemed she *must* be mistreated like this or go out of her mind with frustration, her unfulfilled and sinful desires.

At the casement she gazed out into the starless night, feeling chilled and weak. Suicide? Her hand moved to her breast where a dagger was concealed in the stays of her corselet. Had she the courage to do it? Oh dear God, had she the courage to *live?* There were fates worse than death, the nameless fates so often suffered by women in this bitter world. She had only one consolation. There was no child to share her coming doom nor did she carry one within her.

"'Tis small solace, Drusilla," she whispered to herself, "but it is all you have."

At that moment she heard an explosion, saw the bright flash from across the river, and seconds later felt the slight concussion. Desultory firing at night was the Turkish way, she knew, done for its *nuisance value* as Dracula put it, just a single gun banging away. Yet she feared that, too, for always it reminded her of what might come at any moment. Could Dracula defend this place against a determined assault? He had no army anymore, nobody at all but a handful of gunners and a few horsemen. "We'll cozen them," he had said with a sly grin. "When I return their fire with ball for ball from the ramparts, look you, how can they know my strength? They think I have half my army here. That is why they hesitate."

But she knew better. The Turks were awaiting reinforcements just as they had done at Tirgoviste, but this time with masonry-shattering mangonels and rams. For the moment they amused themselves by hurling shot at the castle. But soon, very soon, they would find *another* amusement within its battlements. Again she felt the insistent vaginal tingling, the undeniable burning excitement that inflamed her to the bone marrow, and she breathed a prayer for forgiveness and salvation. She had long been secretly a Catholic. She crossed herself from left to right in the Catholic manner, disdaining the way of the Orthodox as always when alone.

"*In nomine Patri, et Filii, et Espiritu Sancti*," she whispered in the Latin she had used for matins since childhood. "*Quo vadis, Domine? Pietà, Domine. Mea culpa. Mea culpa.*"

But in the empty charnel house of her desolation it seemed to her that from all the great vastness of the universe there came no answer.

* * *

The overwhelming sensation he had of the river in the darkness was one of cold. As he swam in its chill embrace the janissary, Celal Hamid, knew the current was strong enough to carry him well downstream before he could complete the crossing. He had allowed for this. It was why he had entered the water much higher up where the Arges was even wilder than here, why he had slunk like a stalking wolf at the very base of the hill bearing Dracula's castle after slipping silently out of the Turkish camp unobserved.

He fought the cold. He wore no armor, boots, or turban to weigh him down and was only in kaftan and pantaloons. But across his back was the great reflex bow he had been trained to use so well, made in the Mongol fashion, and a quiver of barbed arrows. And in his mouth were two pieces of tightly folded parchment bearing duplicate messages written by him. He was glad he was one of the few soldiers in the army who could write; glad, too, that he could breathe through his nose alone, keeping his lips sealed against the water. His saliva would not penetrate the vellum and smear the ink. He would strike a blow for Romania this night, though no minstrel would sing of it nor saga record it. Yes, the Turks had enslaved him long ago. Yes, he served in their army, bowing down with the rest when the *muezzins* in the minarets called the faithful to prayer. But he was still a Christian in his heart, distantly related to Dracula, and a Transylvanian. Celal Hamid they had called him these many years, and when he was at last killed in battle they would bury him under that Turkish *nom de guerre*. But he remembered another name, one of which he had been proud. He was Nicolae Anghel.

When the current at last swept him against the bank he caught an overhanging branch and hung on. Suddenly he needed more air and had to take the parchment from his mouth to gulp great lungsful of it. He was shaking even more now. He wondered if the chill would last until the ague struck him. Then he remembered that he and the others had crossed the river already the night before and he had survived *that*.

He looked straight up, trying to see in the dim light of the pale crescent moon. Higher than heaven it seemed in imagination. The Bluff of Poenari they called it. Terrifying. Deadly. Maybe unclimbable. Yet, surveying it from across the Arges during the day, he thought he had seen irregularities offering possible handholds and footholds—if a man were agile enough. And what appeared to be an almost flat shelf of rock two-thirds of the way up. If he could reach that—

He hauled himself out of the water and lay on the bank, gasping. Was it some madness that had overtaken him that he would attempt this? What was this rage in the blood that *forced* him to do it? He did not know Prince Dracula. He had never laid eyes on him. Did he hate the Turks so much then? Yes, he hated them. He hated them for enslaving him; for *every* Christian who had been enslaved; for their arrogance in thinking they could conquer Europe; their penchant for sex with young boys; their bigotry that made all religions save their own a foulness in their eyes; their remorseless Asiatic cruelty; their racial prejudice and their pretensions to the ultimate mastery of the world. Most of all, he hated them for something far more personal, for the wife who was lost to him on his capture and her unknown fate, her miserable, altered destiny. It was enough, wasn't it? It would justify the risk, wouldn't it? If he were caught it would be better if he fell from the cliff. Much better. His commander, the half-crazed Moorish general Abdu-l-Khalid, would have him buried in an anthill or slowly roasted alive.

He raised his head. Yes, the cliff was high—but not so high as the paradise he would never reach if he failed in this self-appointed mission. He got to his feet. He knew at thirty-eight he was too old for this impossible ascent in darkness, that even a superbly conditioned athlete might never make it. But Sultan Mehmed had fled the battlefield at Tirgoviste and with his flight had vanished the myth of Turkish invincibility; vanished, also, much of Anghel's respect for them. He was only a soldier, not a sultan; only a simple Christian, not a Muslim seer. But he would climb the Bluff of Poenari.

In the great hall of the castle, to all outward appearances Dracula sat at his ease. He sipped wine, legs outstretched, staring with eyes that had seen too much of life into the blazing fire on the hearth. He was remembering. He was just short of thirty-two years of age, yet there was much to remember. At the moment his mind was on his generals and what had happened to them. Only Vasili Luca was left of that rank. Gales had deserted during the night battle near Tirgoviste and his remained a debt unpaid. Matusa and Radului were killed fighting to the last in the blood and fury of the Dobrogea. General Baleanu was captured by Radu, and may God Almighty help him.

He glanced over his shoulder. General Grecu lay in a room in the keep, seriously wounded during the retreat and slowly dying. God help him as well. He drained the glass and got to his feet. There was no longer an army in being, only a handful of loyal troops and a few attendants. No longer an army. He approached the fireplace, laid a hand on the mantel, and smiled grimly to himself. They were here at last. He had long expected it and now it had happened. Just across the river at Poenari, occupying the ruins and firing their guns. Radu would drink his blood as a cat would lap milk. So would Ismet Kuprili, the Turkish commanding general. They had already cut off the major alpine passes. He could count on that. But if he decided to imitate a goat and *climb straight over them*, could he reach King Matei in Brasov—or would they take him as he emerged from the farther foothills? By the eternal it was worth a try, wasn't it? The assault must come soon. He had spread some soothing pap before Drusilla to calm her but he knew the truth well enough. He must find his way out of this trap or die. It was the simplest of calculations. Somehow he must create a diversion to distract their attention just long enough—

He heard a slight noise and glanced in its direction. Sometimes it was hard to believe the eleven-year-old boy approaching him was his son. The stripling would be taller than he some day. He had something of Radu's good looks but he didn't hold that against him. Indeed he loved him for the very traits that he himself lacked: his charm, his grace, his boyish courtliness tempered with warmth and affection, a tendency to value honor. What a pity he was a bastard, that his mother was dead, that Princess Drusilla disdained him as the son of a mere mistress when he would so have welcomed her love. As it was, he always came to his father, unashamedly offering his heart.

He spoke to the lad fondly. "Gherghina. It is late for you to be up, isn't it? Does Alexandru know of it?"

Characteristically, the boy came quickly to the defense of his middle-aged guardian. "No, father, he thinks I've gone to bed. He is asleep himself, I believe. But I came down here to—to—"

"To see me, is it not so?"

Gherghina was in his arms at once, rising on his tiptoes to kiss him on the neck. "Yes, father. Oh yes. Yes. I get so lonely—sometimes."

Dracula held him close. "I know you do, son. But you are a royal prince and must guard against displaying emotion to others lest they take advantage of you. Remember, to sit on a throne is to be at the summit—and that *is* a lonely place. Loneliness is the fate of princes."

His curly head on his father's chest, Gherghina seemed content. "But I will never reign, my lord. I am not—I am not—"

"Legitimate?"

"Yes, father."

Dracula smiled faintly. "You attach too much importance to it. If I sire no more sons *you* would be the heir presumptive. Anyway, legitimacy is no guarantee of virtue. My father, Dracul, was born on the wrong side of the blanket. And bethink you of what the illegitimate have accomplished in history. Take the Normans. Four centuries ago they had a prince named Robert the Devil, one of whose loves was a milkmaid. She gave birth to William the Bastard but it was a proud title. After he defeated King Harold at Hastings he made all Britain his domain. He who had been Duke of Normandy was then called William the Conqueror, King of England."

Gherghina looked up at him with large brown eyes. "But I am happy now, my lord. I don't want a throne."

Dracula nodded, reflecting on the blood-drenched past. "Perhaps it is as well," he said. "When you possess a throne you must needs defend it, a task that may lead you into the dark ways of the devil. I defended mine, my son, and ever and anon Satan was at my shoulder, whispering in my ear, tempting me, often—often taking my light away so that I could not see. Sometimes I searched for it, that lost light, but never found it again. Methinks—methinks 'tis a wonderment."

He felt a catch in his throat and paused, releasing his grip on his son. "I mean, my little Gherghi, where does our light go when it leaves us—and we see it no more? Do you know?"

"No, father."

"Do you know, my love child?"

"No, father. I—I don't know about the light."

"Ah. Quite so."

He was thinking of her now, Gherghina's beautiful mother, Faustina, seeing her as clearly as on the day she died. Of a fever they said. But was it that—or did Drusilla have her poisoned? So warm his sweet Faustina. From his first taking of her when a youthful exile in Suceava to their last fond embrace she had loved him. Had she fared better with him than she would have done with her former master, the treacherous Petru Aron who had abandoned her? Yes, for a while. But win or lose it was her he should have married, not Drusilla, for what did lineage matter at the final accounting? It was Faustina who had been truly regal, not his present consort.

He gazed at the stone staircase now that led to Drusilla, a woman thus far barren, giving him no son when an heir was of vital importance. But to what would his son be heir now? What would be his heritage? A defeated ruler had nothing to give, no legacy to bestow save that of flight and eventual destruction. The Turks or Radu's accursed men would kill such a child if he now existed, as they always slaughtered the progeny of beaten monarchs. Then they would rape Drusilla to death on the spot or turn her into a harem concubine, a plaything for Mehmed and his debauched favorites. What sort of fate was that for the wife of Dracula and a princess? Could he save her from it? Better his sword than the degrading phalli of the enemy. His steel that would be more merciful than their unchaste and conscienceless flesh. His steel—

As he stared at the steps she had ascended he wondered how much time was left to them. Then at a slight noise he turned suddenly. General Luca had entered the room, halting and bowing, a dwarf who had proved himself a giant at the disastrous action near Vasilium. He was grateful to Luca, grateful for his valor and steadfastness even though he had done no more than his duty. He spoke to him as a friend.

"Vasili?"

"My lord," said the officer, "I come only now from General Grecu's bedside. I do not think he will last the night."

"Is he so far gone?"

"Yes, Your Highness."

"And Theodoru Panu's healing arts cannot save him."

Luca shook his head. "Panu is only an army chirurgeon, lord. He would need the magic of a sorcerer to—"

"I see. Well, generals die, too. And princes, kings, and emperors. Even sultans, by the rood, is it not so, Vasili?"

"Quite so, Highness."

"I would have to kill him anyway—when the Turks cross the river. If he goes this way I am spared that melancholy task. For which I thank God."

"Yes, Highness."

"I will see him presently—before he departs."

Luca only nodded. Dracula looked at Gherghina.

"Go to bed now, my son. The general and I need to talk."

Obediently, the boy walked to his father and kissed him on the cheek, grasping his sleeve with eager affection. "Good night, my lord."

"Good night, Gherghi. May the angels bring you sweet dreams. The sweetest in all the world."

As he watched his son retire, Dracula nodded Luca toward a chair but remained on his feet. "What do you estimate our chances of reaching Brasov?"

Luca shook his head. "Not good, Your Highness. I see no way of getting out of here without their knowing of it. We might stay ahead of our pursuers but what of our enemies to the north? How do we get through the mountains with their troops holding the passes?"

"Are we sure they hold them?" He was probing and testing. "Are we *sure* of that?"

"They are not fools, my lord. Just before it was annihilated, Baleanu's scouting force was the last in contact with the enemy cavalry in their vanguard. They reported them across both the Arges and the Olt. A major force. *Spahi* horse, *azapi* infantry, janissaries. They close in from all sides. Damn his heathen guts, the Emir Ismet is as wily a veteran as we are likely to see."

"Ismet Kuprili? He fears me."

Luca cleared his throat nervously. "When you had your army, my lord."

"No, it's a superstitious fear. Our spies say he's had it from the beginning. He fears me as *moroi* and *vampir* more than prince or general. It's these swine across the river who concern me. It's that bloody-minded son of a Moroccan camel, Abdu-l-Khalid, now in possession of the heights of Poenari. True, his cannon are a joke. But he's mad and you cannot trust a madman, particularly a mad Moor. He is cunning, you see, like one of our Carpathian wolves. What is he *thinking?* He cannot take Agrish from where he is now and he knows it. Does he hammer us with shot to create a diversion? If so, from whence comes the main stroke and at what hour? I tell you, Luca, without a scouting force I am blind in this place. Khalid can get at us before we know it."

"And your orders, Your Highness?"

Dracula began to pace, but stopped and turned to face the other. "Think you we can trust the report that Matei is in Brasov?" he asked suddenly.

Luca considered. "I don't know, my lord. With the Turks now in Wallachia, the king of Hungary would logically look to his eastern border, to Transylvania. Field headquarters in Brasov is indicated. However, Giskra commands there and seems competent enough."

"Jan Giskra is a Bohemian and a mercenary. Matei may not fully trust such an ambitious foreigner. But how would this monarch receive me?"

"He has been no ally of ours, lord. Other than a few Hungarian troops at Chilia he sent us nothing. Nothing for six months on the Danube. Nothing in the Dobrogea when all depended on it. Nothing here when fate finds you in dire straits. I think he's still full of spite for your Transylvanian raids, and for Amlas and Fagaras. I wouldn't trust him as far as—"

"You think he'll betray me to Radu?"

"Or to the Turks, Highness. There's precious little to choose between them."

"Yes. Well put, Vasili." In the reflected firelight Dracula's eyes gleamed like polished emeralds. "Well, we have no choice it seems. 'Tis a gamble against a certainty. It is clear to me we must abandon this castle tomorrow night and head for the Fagaras range. We'll make our preparations at once. Alert the blacksmiths. I want all mounts reshod with the horseshoes on backward. We'll let the Turks find only incoming tracks, not an outward trail they can follow. Fortunately, we've still a few cannoneers. At dawn you will order them to stand to their guns and await the enemy as they did at Tirgoviste. That's all, I think. Tartu and Lurie will see to our provisioning."

"Do all standing orders still apply, my lord?"

"Yes. Summon the chosen mountaineers from Arefu and tell them to meet me here within the hour. Make sure they include only the most experienced alpinists."

Luca bowed. "As Your Highness commands."

Nicolae Anghel had reached the shelf of rock at last. As he hauled himself up to lie flat upon it in the fearful darkness, he was gasping heavily while his mind spoke the prayers for the accomplishment of a great miracle. He had done the impossible. Of that he was certain. He might not make it down alive but at least he had reached this point, this godsent granite projection, and from here he should be able to send his warning to the castle, to alert the prince before it was too late.

His exertions had been enormous and he was dizzy from weakness, trembling with fear and cold. Suicide or not, he wasn't going to take *unnecessary* chances. He would conserve his energy. He would lie prone and quiet in his soaking clothes, fight off the chill and exhaustion, and get back his strength. Then—then the mighty janissary bow was still secure at his back, still waiting for the greatest use to which it would ever be put. He thought of how he had trained with it for years, and trained and trained, of how he had fought with it in battle after battle; yes, even against the very men whose chieftain's life he would now try to save. Many a heart he had stopped with its lethal arrows, many a soul released from its mortal flesh. But now? Now its errand would be to *prevent* further slaughter, a mission he prayed would be accounted good in the eyes of God, something to weigh against his many sins.

He heard his own heavy breathing but no longer did he gasp like a landed fish. He was settling down now, becoming calm, steady enough to hear the turbulent waters of the Arges far below in the cloaking dark of the night. Very carefully and slowly he turned on his side to look for the castle across the river. At first he saw nothing but a small rectangle of light at about his own level. Then, very gradually, the lofty outlines of the Castle of Agrish impressed themselves on his senses, the loom of a blacker prominence within the universal blackness. The light was the flame of a candle showing through a window. It could be nothing else. Surely it was sent by heaven itself, for how else but through such a portal could his shaft penetrate the walls and his message be read? He heard a cannon go off above him and knew they were firing aimlessly on Poenari heights.

With a ponderous effort, shaking again from the fear of falling and with every nerve and tendon taut, he got to his feet, shrinking against the wall of rock as though he would melt together with it and become one, fighting dizziness and panic. He dared not look down into that clutching void. Slowly, with infinite pains to keep his precarious balance, he unslung the bow at his back, selected an arrow by touch, took one of his two messages and fastened it behind the broad head. Was the distance too great? He had never shot under these conditions nor anything remotely like it. Was it even *possible* to judge such a thing? He'd given himself two chances. He had brains enough for that. But could he draw and release without pitching headlong over the edge? He shuddered at the unnerving thought, sweating again now.

"Oh dear God!" he murmured and drew the bow. "Destroy not thy servant, Lord, for I am Christian and a Muslim never. End not my days on this forlorn rock, I beg thee."

Three fingers on the string, the nock of the arrow between forefinger and middle, his nails pressing his jaw and the first joint of his thumb under his earlobe. He felt the ligaments of his back draw tight with the strain. Sixty-five pounds of pull, the tested strength of a Turkish war bow. He could draw it but how could he aim it? What elevation did he need at this range? How far was that window with its target of light? Was there loose shale beneath him? Would his foot slip at the last moment and plunge him into stygian space to crushing death?

"Steady, Nicolae," he heard himself mutter. "Steady now. Soft as you release. So soft you know not the moment. Soft you now. So soft..."

When the string sprang forward the arrow soared through the night with a high-pitched whirring of rapidly displaced air. His eyes glued to the distant light, he saw nothing. Could it pass through the window without his knowing it? No, his sight was far too keen for that. Where had it struck the wall of the tower, low or high? There was pitchblende in the Ottoman camp. He could have stolen some of it, ignited it, used it on the arrowhead to blaze a telltale trail. But then the Turks would have seen it and traced its path to his vantage point on the cliff. How long would he be alive then? He must have shot low, not high. Errors at long range were usually so, the distance underestimated, true of a night shot especially, he reckoned. There was still the duplicate message. He had one more chance.

Again he fitted parchment to arrow. What a terrible irony if he peradventure struck the prince, he thought, or his wife as she sat beneath the window. How frightful if he, Nicolae Anghel, did the janissaries' work for them. God forbid it.

"Almighty God, *forbid* it!"

He drew for the second time. His last chance. His judgment was blind, without precedent of experience, his calculations instinctive now, something to be felt rather than reasoned. Yes. Yes, that *had* to be it. An angle not far from maximum elevation. He thought of every long-range shot he had ever made. Damn the night and the darkness. One had a *feeling* for distance or one had nothing. A great archer would know the right angle in his bones. *He would know it absolutely*. In the end it was a matter of talent.

Again he released. Again his ears were assailed by the short-lived vibratory whine of the shaft's curving flight. He held his breath. It must strike home. It *must* or all was lost! Then he saw the light go out. Yes, by God, it was extinguished! He had seen the shaft enter the window. In that split second he had seen it. Had they snuffed the candle in the usual way? No, by the saints, his shot had done it! He sighed deeply. It *was* a miracle, something beyond the power of the will, beyond any human power. Somewhere deep in the soul of him he knew this one single arrow could change the course of history.

She faced Dracula like one of the Furies from the pit, disheveled, frightfully distraught, in her hand what looked like a piece of vellum still in a state of curl. She stared at him. She had come down the stone steps from her lofty asylum and now stood at the bottom of the staircase, visibly shaking. In the center of the great room he remained very still and regarded her quietly.

"Drusilla? You look unwell. I take it something has disturbed your sleep."

She made no reply. The parchment dangled from fingers that appeared nerveless, as though they hadn't the strength to hold it. She was deathly white.

"What is it, my dame?" He sensed her barely suppressed panic and was disturbed by it. "Have you taken some foul humor that you appear thus before me? I warned you against mandrake root in your tea, remember? It will not promote conception. That is medieval nonsense, the idle superstition of ignorant midwives. The only thing that will get you with child is what lies concealed behind my codpiece."

Still she did not speak.

"What have you in your hand?" he asked. "Is it the contents of that missive that brings you here as pallid as wax? Let me see it."

She took a hesitant step forward, then stopped, extending her slender hand with the vellum in it. "This came through my window," she said tonelessly. "On an arrow from out of nowhere—a few minutes ago. It put out the candle. Can you imagine my unearthly calmness, my liege? I, Drusilla, Princess of Wallachia, took flint, tinder, and steel, and relighted it. Like one of those Spartan princesses you admire so much, wasn't it? And now I am here and I hold it in my hand—and you have brought us to this. This is the result of all your warlike deeds, your endless plans for conquest, your heartless rapine and eternal bloodletting. Bitter fruit, my lord. Your head beneath the axe. My chastity violated. For you, a nameless and unhonored grave. For me, endless shame in a Muslim harem without even the Cross of Christ to assuage my pain. I foresee no limit to my miserable degradation—nor to my suffering."

He walked to where she stood and held out his hand. "Give it to me."

She made no move to obey. "You are fond of Roman legend, my

lord. You once told me that under your tutelage I would become a true daughter of the Horatii, as resigned to my fate and meeting it as bravely as the Sabine women. But it is not like that. *I* am not like that. I will not serve both God and mammon—in a Muslim brothel."

"Give it to me," he said again, this time more sternly. "Fool! You defy me at your peril!"

She handed him the parchment. He spread it in his hands. Then, because the light was poor, he strode to the nearest burning candelabra and read the roughly scrawled Transylvanian script.

> To His Royal Highness Prince Vlad III of the House of Basarab, greeting.
>
> Know you, my liege lord, that janissary and *azapi* units of the army of the Emir Ismet Kuprili are even now on your side of the river. This force under the Emir Abdu-l-Khalid and Wallachian rebels under Prince Radu, about 5000 in all, is bivouacked in the forest not more than a league north of the castle, and is planning to attack you on the morrow with siege towers, battering rams, and heavy arbalests. There is no question they will make a breech.
>
> In the name of God, Your Royal Highness, and for the sake of the Wallachian people, make your escape while yet there is time, I beg you. I am a janissary slave but a Transylvanian, and in my heart still a Christian. May God grant you peace and protection, my lord, and may He confound your enemies always. I beg His blessing for you, my Prince.
>
> A Son of the True Cross

Dracula laid the unsigned vellum on the table. "Arrows in the night," he muttered to himself. "Possibly a Turkish trick to get me outside the walls. But no. No, it has the look of sincerity. I *feel* it in my bones with the strength of truth itself. The enemy on *this* side of the river—and I with no presentiment of it. Verily, it passes strange that my senses should be so dulled."

He turned to Drusilla triumphantly, raising his voice. "Do you know what this means? The janissary would not dare shoot his bow from among his comrades. He would have to get away from them and isolate himself.

In God's sooth, the arrow could have come only from high on the cliff above the river. He climbed it, don't you see? For me, for *me*, mark you, he climbed the Bluff of Poenari *in the dark!* Can you even conceive of such devotion? And they say I am finished. We would have left tomorrow night. Now it will be tonight, that's all. A slight change of plan."

She shook her beautiful head. "You *are* finished, my liege," she said. Her voice was high-pitched, vibrant with strain. "You may struggle a while longer like a fish in a net—but your day is nearly done. Would I might be here to see its sunset."

Some instinct warned him of her intention. "Drusilla," he said, pleading for the first time in his life. "It needn't be like this between us. I am not as remorseless as you think, not an Attila or a Tamerlane. I have no wish to harm you. I regret the passing of your parents. Yes, even though I know they conspired against me. I was unduly harsh, crazed with suspicion and hatred. Were it all to do over again—"

"You would love me."

He groped clumsily for words. "I—I have not been indifferent to you."

"Haven't you, my prince?"

"We—we could start again, Drusilla—make a new beginning."

"With what, lord? Are there pieces still to be found—of us?"

"Drusilla—"

Suddenly she swung about and shot up the steps. He followed her, running all-out, but nothing was as fast as she.

"Come back!" he shouted as he climbed. "Come back, Drusilla! I will not hurt you! Come back! Come back!"

He was appalled and amazed at his terrible sense of urgency, astounded by the power of the fear that gripped him. Once he nearly had her by an ankle but slipped and fell, abrading the flesh of his left hand on a granite step. After that there was no overtaking her. She reached the Monk's Rest and was through the door. In a trice she was at the window, turning to confront him, one pale hand on the casement, poised, ready to leap. At the threshold he stopped dead in his tracks. He felt weak and sick, monstrously, irretrievably defeated. His face as ashen as hers now, he heard his own words as though spoken by someone else.

"One more crime to lay to my account—and this the blackest of all."

She was gazing at him with something almost of pity in her eyes, her dark hair glinting softly in the candlelight.

"Goodbye, Dracula."

He made a feeble move to stop her. "Drusilla, for the love of God! Don't! *Don't!*"

Too late. Like a disappearing moonbeam that had never had any reality she was through the window and out of it. She did not scream in her long fall. Stricken dumb, physically paralyzed, he stood rooted to the spot, his eyes on the awesome, unfathomable emptiness which was all she left behind. He tried desperately to cross himself but could not raise his hand. He felt nauseated. He was very weak. After a long time, finding he was able to move his legs, he staggered toward the window and stood there shaking, gazing blindly into the darkness of the pitiless night.

"Forgiveness," he whispered soundlessly. "O Man of Nazareth—forgiveness."

But the only sound that came back was the moaning of a light wind.

Of all the periods of his strange life Dracula's campaign on the Danube has received the most attention from historians. However, as with the more obscure happenings, the coverage was often misleadingly subjective and at times not at all reliable. This is perhaps to be expected. Most of the chroniclers were either Turkish, and therefore naturally biased, or Byzantine observers traveling with the Ottoman forces, men badly positioned to maintain a strict neutrality. The Greek Chalkokondyles clearly favored the Porte, so obviously that the accuracy of much of his narrative is more than a little suspect. So, glaringly, did Kritovoulos of Imbros, the only one of the lot who witnessed the fall of Constantinople in 1453. Their fellow Byzantine, Michel Doukas, on the other hand, was capable of a certain objectivity.

Interestingly enough, of the narratives dealing with the Turkish invasion of Wallachia, the one that was the most detailed (and curiously unbiased) was left to posterity by an anonymous Serbian soldier fighting for the Muslims, a man known to historical researchers only as "the Janissary of Ostrovita." He appears not to have been an officer and his account dealt mainly with the opening months of hostilities. Nonetheless, it seems to have been more soundly based than those of such Ottoman historians as Enveri and Tursun Bey.

A German of considerable literary influence, one who played a strangely unorthodox role, was Michel Beheim, meistersinger in Vienna to Emperor Friedrich III and the House of Habsburg. Resident with his sovereign at the famous Austrian spa of Weiner Neustadt in the winter of 1463, he wrote a long narrative poem on the subject of the Turkish invasion in which he threw light on both Dracula's bravery and his many crimes. His sources of information are not precisely known. However, under the circumstances it was easy for him to catch the ear of the Holy Roman Emperor. In their eagerness to get at Dracula, the Ottomans had violated the neutrality of two provinces under Austrian protection, Bosnia and Herzegovina.

As one traces the course of events from June 1462, when the Danubian campaign came to an end, through the night attack near Tirgoviste, the defeat of Dracula in the Dobrogea and his retreat to the west, the documentation becomes more and more scanty until by the time he reaches the Castle of Agrish it disappears entirely. The chroniclers had gone home. Prince Radu seems to have retained no historian at the time. Dracula himself, preoccupied day and night with the threat of imminent death, probably overlooked the need. What can the historian do when the archives are silent? He has but one option. He turns once again to Romanian folklore, the ballads sung even today in Arefu and other villages still existing in the area of Castle Dracula, the peasant tales still passed down from father to son and preserved by word of mouth.

The only things we know about what transpired at the castle after Dracula and his few remaining followers occupied it are of folkloric origin. They tell of his first wife and how she died a suicide, frightened to the point of despair by the message shot by arrow through the castle window. Did it really happen as described? Was it more than mere legend? Very probably. Even today, the locality on the Arges where her battered body is said to have come to rest is still called *Riul Doamnei*, "the River of the Princess." We are not told where she was buried. Neither do we know if the janissary who shot the arrow survived his desperate gamble. Did he fall on his way down in the darkness? One slip is all it would have taken. Perhaps a day will come when a fisherman's hook will retrieve a bone or skull, or even some scrap from a once-powerful reflex bow such as a piece of curved wood with a horn tip. Could such an artifact be distinguished from those of other invaders on the river, the Tatars who came a century earlier, for example? Probably not. Yet if it were found close to the Bluff of Poenari—earthquakes often shift large masses of concealing silt, even the accumulation of centuries, and this is a region known for its earthquakes.

What of the Turks? Did they really fire their cherrywood cannon from the heights of dismantled Poenari? It seems likely. The local peasants will point out a small plateau on the forlorn, windswept summit, a ground ideal for hurling shot at the now overgrown and nearly invisible ruin across the river. Does this place have a name? If you ask them they will nod in the affirmative. It is called *Tunuri*, "the Field of Cannon." One is forcibly reminded that history may forget—but the people never do.

What about Dracula's son? Was he really at the castle with him? The folktales say that *some* royal offspring was there. We know it could not have been Mihnea (later known as Mihnea the Evil) because this prince, one of two legitimate sons of the second wife, was born not earlier than 1466. It could not have been Vlad Tepelus (the Little Impaler) either, nor Prince Mircea, for both were born of future mistresses and sired too late. Then who was this boy? The lore of the castle tells us much without naming him. He was probably eleven or twelve years of age at the time. He started out with Dracula on his escape. However, an unexpected occurrence thwarted all efforts and the lad never made it. Let us fill in the details.

As anyone who has visited European castles will know, secret staircases and corridors are to be found in plenty among them; a natural precaution taken by rulers who were not always popular and whose regimes could be (and often were) overthrown by some bloody *coup d'état*. The Castle of Agrish was no exception. It had a spiral staircase, very long and steep, that was apparently built inside a tunnel leading to a natural cavern. This cave fronted on the riverbank. When on the night of his escape Dracula reached it with his son, some twelve of his followers, and the five mountaineers chosen as guides, they found the horses previously tethered there and waiting for them, mounts with their shoes reversed to deceive the enemy.

As he had done at Tirgoviste, so here, also, Dracula had commanded his gunners to keep up a sporadic fire as a *ruse de guerre* to cover his escape. The scene then develops. It was a dark night. The trail leading up from the river was steep and narrow, and high above them the castle's guns were firing. No one knows just where it occurred. Apparently frightened by the detonations, the horse carrying Dracula's son shied and reared up, throwing the boy out of the saddle. What happened? The various tales are largely obscure. Some modern interpretations would have it that Dracula abandoned the little prince without a second thought, but this would be to deny the pride of blood of such a man, a love we may suppose was concentrated all the stronger in his only son at a time when his dynasty was so close to utter destruction.

Far from immediate abandonment it is more likely that an intense search was made, the father risking everything by the protracted delay. The boy was not found. Why did he not call out to the searchers? Logic would indicate he was unable to do so, probably because of serious injury or unconsciousness. It is not difficult to imagine the emotional condition of the father in this crisis that followed only hours after his wife's death. An only son lost, no assurance of ever siring another, his own death probably imminent, and with it the final extinction of his line. We may be sure it was with a mixture of heartbreak and rage that he gave up the search that night. We can almost hear it in his voice and see it in his eyes as he gave the order. Another man so tried might have stood his ground and fought to the death. History affords numerous examples of such filial devotion. But suicidal tendencies were not part of Dracula's makeup, at least not then. More characteristic was the fatalist's acceptance of his losses while still harboring the fading hope of a frightful revenge.

According to folklore there's a fascinating ending to this story, something almost like a fairytale of the brothers Grimm. We are told the boy survived after all, that a shepherd saved his life, became his protector, and raised him in the village of Arefu as though he were his own son. Twelve years passed while the youth grew to manhood and Dracula remained far away in Hungarian custody. Then, with the release of the father and his coming to the throne of Wallachia for the third time, the two were reunited. The shepherd knew who it was he had befriended. When he took him to the father, Dracula, delighted and at times capable of great generosity, made his son's benefactor a rich man through the granting of certain crown lands.

There is a curious addendum. After Dracula's flight across the alps the Ottomans occupied the castle and partly destroyed it. Prince Radu seems to have shunned it, hating all things that reminded him of his half-brother. However, at a later time, during the reign in Wallachia of Dracula's cousin, Radu cel Mare (Radu the Great), the archives mention a certain boyar of "princely lineage" who served for years as the castle's governor, staying on, it would appear, even into middle age. The end of the tenure of this man marks a turning point in the castle's history, for after his death it lay deserted, open to the elements and the ravages of decay. His name was Gherghina.

While folklore may not always mirror historic fact, more often than not it is fairly close to the truth, as painstaking research has frequently substantiated. An example lies in the intriguing tale of "the rabbit skins." The saga tells us that Dracula and the others climbed northward into the rugged, ice-choked Fagaras range, their goal the fortified city of Brasov (today called Orȁsul Stalin) where reports had it that King Matei was headquartered. From a high elevation they witnessed at a distance the Muslim attack on the castle, then the repeated explosions as the Ottomans or Radu's men ignited gunpowder to partially demolish it. They then pressed on. Near the headwaters of the Arges, they seem to have emerged onto a plateau between parallel escarpments (about 33 miles northwest of the medieval city of Câmpulung), an area called "the Sheep Plain" or *Plaiul Oilor* in Romanian. Here they rested. They were now at a point almost due west of Brasov, and could reach the city of Fagaras and its venerable castle by following the Olt River.

Before they went any farther, Dracula decided on a rare move for a prince in his situation, the rewarding of the five mountain guides who had served him so well. Mindful of the fact that part of his treasury lay in the baggage train, he asked them what they would have. They replied they had done no more than other loyal subjects. He then insisted. "Choose between money or land," he told them. To men of the soil in any country the choice would have been the same. They chose the land at once. On the skins of recently snared rabbits, using a granite slab still identified as the Table of the Prince, Dracula's moving quill deeded extensive lands to these men and their heirs in perpetuity. Where are these deeds now? Historians may only speculate. In the village of Arefu, hard by the ruins of Castle Dracula, even today the mere mention of them may still bring knowing smiles. Is this where they have been hidden down the centuries, the most prized possessions of the original legatee's descendants? The question must ever appeal to the romantic imagination.

The subsequent scene opens with the arrival of Dracula and his party in Brasov. It was winter now. With a considerable force of Hungarian infantry and cavalry (the latter to be deployed to watch his border with Turkish-occupied Wallachia), King Matei had established his headquarters in the city on 3 November. We can imagine the battlements of the fortress covered with snow, the initial meeting between king and prince, the false display of cordiality on both sides. History is with us again, folklore left behind with the final descent of the fugitives down the north slope of the Fagaras range. Dracula, we may be sure, asked for troops. Matei, we may be equally certain, hedged adroitly, indulging in his own well-practiced brand of deceit and prevarication. There are indications that he hoped to get more gold for pretended crusading purposes from Pope Pius II, that he feared papal repercussions if he alienated Dracula before that goal had been achieved. Meanwhile, finding the still ambitious and ever-warlike Wallachian an embarrassment, he offered him the use of the Romanian castle of Piatra Craiului (Königstein in the German) 6 miles across the frontier in a part of Wallachia not yet under Turkish occupation. Without an army, knowing he was helpless to defend the place, Dracula had no choice but to comply.

For the man still spoken of in whispers in Constantinople as Kazîglu Bey, the Lord Impaler, there followed a period of what must have been almost unendurable frustration and simmering rage. He had no troops, no court worthy of the name, not even a wife in whose womb he might with good fortune implant a legitimate heir. Concubines he must have had in plenty, for surely Matei would have supplied them as a simple courtesy from one ruler to another. The real master of Königstein, however, was not Dracula but Matei's aggressive chief of staff, the Bohemian military adventurer Jan Giskra, a man who *was* supplied by the king with a large body of soldiery. That Dracula had no way of controlling Giskra is obvious; that Giskra was strategically placed at the castle as a royal spy to report the Wallachian's movements is equally so. It was a situation that could not long endure. The Impaler had been in residence only a matter of weeks when Giskra, acting on Matei's orders, arrested him and placed him in close confinement. Pietro Tommasi, envoy of Venice at Buda, later wrote to the doge that Dracula had been taken into custody on 26 November.

Historians are not certain of what prompted Matei to act when he did. It may have been word from Rome that the horn of plenty had ceased to give of its substance, or a suspicion that his royal guest was conspiring with disaffected Hungarian officers to murder him in a bold *coup d'état*. It may even have been the so-called Rothel letters written on 7 November 1462, two odd missives intercepted on their way to the Ottomans and Prince Stéfan, purportedly bearing Dracula's signature. These letters are distinctly out of character. In them the writer not only admits his wrongdoing and implores his foes to forgive him as an abject repentant, but even offers to join a Turko-Moldavian alliance against Hungary and to connive in any attempt to capture Matei. They are almost certainly forgeries, as most Romanian historians have branded them. There was no town of Rothel in Transylvania, so the geographical source of the letters is untraceable. Dracula would scarcely have committed such a plot to writing while under the king's control. And, even further removed from reality, was a Dracula who would offer an alliance to the Turks *under any conditions whatever*.

Who then wrote these letters? They were perhaps dictated by Matei himself. He was a man in need of self-justification. The papal gold he'd been sent had never reached Dracula. He had failed to join that prince in his stupendous efforts to contain the Ottoman offensive in the south. Having acted thus as a traitor to Christendom itself, what is more logical than to hurl the odium of treason at the only unwavering crusader still living except Scanderbeg?

Are the accusations of certain historians concerning Matei true then? Was it by his order that the ruinous Saxon atrocity tales concerning Dracula were spread throughout Eastern Europe? Again, the motive was there. Even stronger was it there for the Germans, who may themselves have forged the letters, subsequently circulating those copies, one of which found its way to Pope Pius II. Be the truth what it may, regardless of the role played by the king, when his command was given Dracula and his entourage were without hope of flight or defense. He was seized at Königstein and put in chains, then taken to Brasov and locked in a dungeon under guard, the opportunity to confront Matei and to hear the charges denied him. It was the beginning of a great change in his life and one that would radically affect his destiny.

On 6 December, still a fettered prisoner, he was on his way to the Hungarian capital city of Buda, there to await the pleasure of the Magyar diet whose justice he knew to be harsh. The land was locked in the grip of a rigorous winter. The year 1463 was close at hand. He must have felt much as his father did when fleeing to certain death in the marshes of Balteni. Dracul had at least had a sword at his side. Dracula had only shackles. By any reckoning whatever his chances of lengthy survival were poor. As the carriage in which he was held drove through the bitter cold, he must have felt the chains of fate tighten, perhaps, in imagination, even the sharp bite of razor-edged steel as it sliced through his neck. But who knew better than he the slenderness of the thread of life? Who better than he the unfathomable nature of human fate?

8

The Prisoner of Vísegràd

The day was cold and dreary, the sky clouded over, the sun invisible. In the highest cell of Solomon's Tower, his isolated room these last years, Dracula stood at the double-arched window with its carved central pier and gazed on the rolling Hungarian countryside spread out below him. He was dressed all in gray, a color he seldom displayed; and through that quiet valley ran the gray ribbon of the Danube; and his soul was gray within him.

Four years had come and gone since his arrest. He was nearly thirty-six now and the world was passing him by. He was Prince of Wallachia, ruler by divine right, but Radu occupied his throne. Radu the accursed, the treacherous running dog who had first blamed his brother for allowing him to be sodomized in Egrigöz (as though he could have prevented it), then had reveled in it. Radu the traitor, the Turkish puppet, disloyal to his own people but claiming to lead them, taking his orders from the Porte. Well, Radu was prince in fact and he, the elder and rightful claimant, was only voivod now, warlord; yet Voivod of Wallachia, as proud a title as anything royal and far more lasting. Had not the great Hunyadi been Voivod of Transylvania? And would the White Knight's people not remember that beyond his siring of a king? Dracula the voivod. Vlad Tepes, the Lord Impaler. The terrible Kazîglu Bey. Ah how they blackened his name from Buda to Rome to Constantinople, from the borders of Russia to the Mediterranean. How they reviled and mocked him behind his back when safe from his reach and his wrath.

He heaved a sigh and felt his breath catch in his throat. Whatever it was, this *thing* inside him, it was betimes almost more than he could bear. Memories haunted him, vile, sickening memories. Horror racked him. Yet had he been given a choice? If you are born amidst a nest of ravenous, blood-sucking vampires and fighting for your life from the very cradle, are there *options?* Nay, by the eternal God, it was dog eat dog and the devil take the hindmost! It had always been that since the cave and blessed was the man with enough sense to realize it. Still . . . still . . .

Unbidden, Khayyám's meaningful lines came to his mind and hung upon his lips. "Oh Thou, who Man of baser earth didst make, and ev'n with Paradise devise the Snake: for all the sin wherewith the face of Man is blacken'd—Man's forgiveness give—and take!"

There came a light knock at the door. It was not the pike butt of one of his well-bribed guards, but the delicately applied rapping of human knuckles. He thought of how he "owned" all his jailers through the mere dispensation of gold, how he'd always done so from the beginning of his detention here, his *house arrest* as they called it. It had not been so in the first year. Buried in the grim river fortress of Vàcz he'd been truly a prisoner in those days, deprived of everything and badly treated. Then Matei had changed his policy, restoring his confiscated wealth, bringing him here to Vísegràd on the Danube's bend as his "honored guest." It had meant a shift in the political wind, of course. This was the year 1466. Matei could not stomach Radu much longer and would soon move against him openly. Matei—

The knock came again.

"Enter," said Dracula.

The door opened. Through it stepped a very little man in saffron and violet taffeta, a graying, middle-aged dwarf scarcely two and a half cubits in height. Closing the door the diminutive one bowed deeply, making a graceful flourish with his plumed hat. When he straightened, his broad smile sparkled with two gold teeth. His rapid breathing and flushed face betrayed his haste. He spoke in indifferent Romanian.

"I bring the best of news, Your Highness," he said with extreme affability.

Dracula nodded. "Indeed, Zundi? Sit you down. You look winded."

The dwarf took the proffered chair and smiled again. "'Tis a long way up the steps, my lord, but my desire to please you made me hurry. I'll be brief. His Majesty, King Matei, Light of the Magyars and Defender of Christendom, accepts with extreme pleasure the offer of Your Royal Highness to become a Catholic. He said it was most gracious of you, my liege, and can only result in a much closer bond between your two houses."

Dracula nodded again. "Very diplomatic. Since he threatened to keep me a prisoner for life unless I did so, he made his point most adequately. Of course, I doubt that the Metropolitan at Curtea de Arges would agree with him, Orthodox churchmen being what they are. Nonetheless, we will score a victory for the pope. Spake the king of a possible marriage?"

Zundi raised a bushy eyebrow. "He did, my lord. Uh—I believe some mention was made of His Majesty's beauteous niece, the Viscountess Helena Corvinus. She—"

"The rank is correct but not the name." Dracula frowned. "Do not trifle with me, little man. You know I would press my suit for another. Indeed, it was you who arranged to have her visit me here on three occasions."

Zundi's smile still survived but had lost its winning bravura. "Your Highness refers to the Lady Valeria, of course, the king's ward."

"Yes, the Viscountess Valeria Szilagy."

"Your meetings with her were always very correct, Highness, very—uh—discreet."

Dracula laughed. "They were more than discreet, they were sterile. But I wish to change that. She, too, is related to the king; therefore, suitable to his purpose and mine. And she pleases me. Can you think of any reason he might refuse me her hand?"

Zundi considered. "If His Majesty seeks a different match, my lord, it is clearly for reasons of state. Perhaps—forgive me, Highness, perhaps he envisages the Corvinus crest worked into the escutcheon of Wallachia."

"So? Yes, perhaps. Regardless of that, the Szilagys are as prominent, are they not? Their line as old?"

"Indeed, my lord. Older."

"But Matei would dictate to me in this?"

"He might, my lord. That is—"

Dracula felt his choler rising. "He had two requirements, look you, satisfaction of which would again make me a candidate for Wallachia's throne with full Hungarian support. First, that I turn Catholic. He and

I are now agreed on that. Aye, though they brand me apostate in Wallachia forever. Second, that I marry into his family to establish an alliance based on blood. The Szilagys are his kin. What objection can he have?"

"I do not pretend to know the royal mind, my lord."

"Nor do I, forsooth, but mark you this. If he contemplates the renewal of war with the Porte, if he wants me to lead the fight against Radu and the Turks, he must needs accommodate me. By God, Zundi, I'll brook no opposition in this matter and you may tell him so! I *want* that woman!"

The dwarf shook his grizzled head. "Your Highness, I fear that events have gone beyond your present reckoning. The Turks are not a factor at this point—nor is your brother Radu."

"What do you mean?"

"Highness, I keep my eyes and ears open in Buda, and especially at the court. I am very good at it. That is why you employ me as your *unofficial* plenipotentiary. Now I've ridden again this considerable distance to bring you intelligence."

"Yes?"

"My lord, it is a secret still known only to a few. Count Faludi. Count Szilagy. General Karolyi. Possibly other members of the general staff. Rome has broken off relations with Prague and recalled its legate. Pope Paul II has excommunicated the king of Bohemia, George of Podebrad, as an unregenerate Utraquist, a forsworn Hussite heretic. The situation is grave."

"And Matei?"

"Papal pressure has forced him to join a coalition with the Emperor Friedrich III against George. The fact that the Bohemian king is Matei's father-in-law is irrelevant."

Dracula pondered this turn of events. It was amazing how a heresy endured when its opponents were stupid enough to make a martyr of its founder. They had burned the reformer Jan Huss at the stake in 1415. That was fifty-one years ago. Now George of Podebrad espoused the dead man's cause more staunchly than ever. The Holy Roman Empire and Hungary feared him for it. The pope feared him. All Catholics feared heresy like the plague and Matei must now prove the steadfastness of his Catholicism. Clear enough. For the moment at least, Turkey was a secondary enemy in Magyar eyes and Radu of little account. He spoke his thoughts aloud.

"Then Hungary is on the eve of war with Bohemia."

"Very nearly, Your Highness. In two weeks, three at the most, Buda will likely begin massing its levees."

"And the people know nothing of this?"

"Not to my knowledge, my lord."

"It seems an odd time for Matei to concern himself with my religion. Or my marriage, for that matter."

"He guards his rear, Your Highness. When he goes into battle he wants no enemies at his back, not even one nominally in his custody."

"Shrewdly put, Zundi. I chose well when I made you my aide." Dracula began to pace the length of the small room, then stopped suddenly and walked to the farther window. "All right, I'll let Matei pursue his aims and I'll pursue mine. I want Valeria Szilagy and you will help me get her. She is a virgin, is she not?"

"So it is said, my lord."

"I am gazing up yon hill now. High it is, with Matei's summer palace at its summit, the Danube and the city of Vísegràd at its base, and everywhere within that palace the signs of Magyar power and opulence. He is a renowned patron of the arts is Matei, the father of the Hungarian Renaissance. He spends a fortune on his collections. But I tell you this, Zundi. Nothing he ever collected is as satisfying as his bevy of voluptuous women, the peers of all that I saw in the sultan's harem."

"His queen does not approve of them, Your Highness."

Dracula laughed at the jape. "I dare say. Nonetheless, Valeria Szilagy is a finer bit of fluff than any of them and yet intact. Is there still to be a masked ball at the palace?"

"In a fortnight, my lord, on the Thursday after next. Uh—barring the unforeseen."

"Good. I feared war preparations would have canceled their pretty masquerade. Am I still invited?"

The dwarf smiled. "His Majesty mentioned that, my lord. It seems he fears his enemies will make capital of the free rein he has recently given you, your occasional public appearances at his side and all that. You are still invited to attend the ball, but—"

"Yes?"

"But when the guests remove their masks at the stroke of midnight—"

"I am to quietly disappear."

"Exactly, Your Highness. His Majesty's words were—uh—to fade from sight. After you've been baptized in the cathedral and the people know of your conversion—"

"I will be more acceptable in court circles."

"Something like that, my lord."

"Very well. Now attend me, Zundi. I have a flare for the dramatic. On my recent sojourn with him I agreed to assist Matei with his entertainment on the night in question. You will help me with this and 'tis all arranged, look you. We will go to the palace today and rehearse it as planned. We may indeed have to rehearse it on every day that remains."

"We will join the mummers, Your Highness?"

"After a fashion, but as an entity unto ourselves. Did you bring the preparation I asked you to get?"

The dwarf handed him a small glass vial. "Genuine cantharides, my lord. As you predicted, it was very dear. Yet you have two dinars in change."

"You have done handsomely to track this elixir down. Keep them."

"My profound thanks, Highness."

Dracula held the vial up to the light, studying it. "Yes, it is the right color." He shook it and looked again. "The right consistency, too. Observe it, small one. Tincture of cantharides, the most potent love philter known. Guaranteed to thaw a hundred virgins be they ever so inclined to chastity. Know you of this?"

"I have heard of it, my lord, but I know it not."

"They make it from the powdered wings of certain green beetles, a very special insect. It was not unknown in ancient Rome, I believe, but the name of the powder would imply it was developed by the Greeks. Indeed, I think it was used in Troy itself, though Homer spake of it not. Perhaps Paris seduced Helen with it."

"May I ask the secret of it, Your Highness?"

"The secret? Oh that is simple enough. 'Tis a blister beetle. It causes an itch the woman cannot scratch, a persistent, burning, genital itch. Really quite maddening, they say. The vagina actually swells. All that is required is that the seducer be at the wench's side when the fit to copulate is upon her. The cantharides does the rest."

"Remarkable, my lord."

"Isn't it? To take any difficult objective, Zundi, one must employ the proper tactics. An old and tested military axiom."

"My lord is very wise," said the dwarf.

"And very battle-hardened. A seasoned campaigner. Actually, I prefer a certain amount of resistance in a woman, for it adds spice to the game. Yes. Oh yes."

Concealing the potion in his doublet, Dracula smiled with inner satisfaction. He proceeded to explain the plan he hoped would first give him the girl he desired, then, ultimately, restore the throne of his fathers. That the little viscountess would lose her precious maidenhead in the process he considered a foregone conclusion. But hymens were *made* to be broken, were they not? That, too, was axiomatic.

The hilltop palace of Vísegràd, summer residence of the kings of Hungary, was stunningly beautiful. Never had it been more so than on this bright evening when a thousand burning candles lighted its glittering interior, throwing into startling splendor the imported Greek statuary, the Etruscan vases, the Nilotic bas-relief sculptures from Lower Egypt, the Ming porcelain from far Cathay, the incredible crystal butterflies from Hither Asia. There was much marble about the place, some of it the exquisite Carrara variety of northern Italy, as white and semitranslucent as a maiden's breasts. The magnificent Persian rugs from fabled Isfahan were much remarked upon. There were mounted Turkish scimitars from mysterious Damascus; Hellenistic pikes from the Trebizond; even, in a special room of their own, a collection of fabulous *katanas*, the samurai fighting sword of the forbidden empire of Dai Nippon, reputedly smuggled out of that mystic land by heretical Shinto priests. With either the damascene or Nipponese blade it was said a man could shave himself with the facility of a razor. In all of Europe only the Spaniards had such weapons, the famed swords of Toledo, and they had stolen the secret of the steel long ago from the invading Muslims.

On this special occasion of the great masked ball, gypsy musicians had been hired. They played on lutes, tambourines, and castanets. The noble guests danced the Hungarian *czardas* and the Romanian *hora*. Ultimately, to the surprise and delight of many, Turkish belly dancers appeared during one of the rest intervals, a reflection of the uneasy peace of the moment, and danced very sensuously to their own music as they would have done in Constantinople. King Matei was amused by his court's reaction to this, for female seminudity was rare in Europe, at least in public. As he and his queen sat surrounded by their subjects, the monarch smiled and applauded, encouraging his courtiers to relax and do likewise. The endlessly flowing wine made it easier. As it circulated through the ranks of the notables, the romantically inclined among the men began to make their presence felt, a circumstance to which the more promiscuous women quickly responded.

One of the latter was Countess Militsa Faludi, wife to Count Michael, one of the king's advisors. A woman of forty, her marriage had become a sham long ago. Now, knowing herself to be still attractive, very much inclined to amorous dalliance, she sat apart from her husband (himself a notorious rake) and conversed lightly with a friend of hers of equally easy virtue, the widowed and still youthful Countess Ilona Kossuth. For increased privacy the pair talked behind their raised fans.

"My dear, there is something *different* about this gathering," said Militsa. "Have you noticed?"

Ilona nodded. "If you mean that His Majesty has outdone himself in magnificence—"

"No, I refer to the members of this august assemblage. Their masks do not really conceal their identity any more than ours do. Do you think?"

"Certainly not with some of them." Ilona's smile displayed her unusually good teeth. "I'd know Anna Harsanyi anywhere. She has a figure like a cow. I mean, that bosom—"

"It is not their appearance to which I refer, dear. It is the curious absence of people who should be here. Follow my gaze around the room from left to right, will you? There is Feodor Kurytsin, the Russian envoy. So barbaric he is, as befits the representative of Ivan III, Grand Duke of Moscow. Do you mark him?"

"In the vermillion and mauve. Yes."

"He speaks with the Venetian envoy, Pietro Tommasi."

"In the satyr's costume with the golden mask."

"All right. Next is Count János Kodály and his countess. Then the Italian, Antonio Bonfini, His Majesty's court historian. Do you recognize them, Ilona?"

"Oh yes."

"The notorious Bianca Malipiero. Dear merciful Christ, what stories she could tell with those full, red lips! And how appropriate in scarlet."

They stared together intently at this comely woman. Said once to have been the mistress of Francesco Sforza, Duke of Milan, she was now an influential courtesan in Buda.

"An attentive swain on either side of her," observed Ilona, "and the lowest décolletage at the ball. How typical."

"It is that hot southern blood, my dear. I am so glad we Magyars are free of it."

They both laughed at this.

"Niccolo Modrussiense," Militsa continued, "the papal legate from the Holy See. Ah Roma the Eternal. What I would give to be in his city in the spring. If nothing else, that gaudy pendant crucifix would give him away. The carbuncle in it is worth a king's ransom."

"Yes, I follow you."

"Their Majesties, of course. Count Ferenc Szilagy, the king's advisor. The Viscountess Eva Kormendi. The Viscountess Helena Corvinus and her handsome captain of horse, Erno Zapolya. Poor Zapolya. They say she is carefully chaperoned. Are you still with me?"

"I think so. Dear God, Militsa, you have a rare eye for identifying a man's body, I vow, no matter how well his face is masked. How are you always so sure?"

"Oh most of them wear the same costume year after year and I've memorized them, that's all. But where are the others?"

"What others?"

"The military elite who should flank the king and queen, and are conspicuous by their absence. Where is the general staff, Ilona?"

"The gen—"

"General Bela Karolyi is always at the king's side. Where is he tonight? Where is General Balassa? General Horthy? General Jaszi? General Kosary? Even their aides are not here."

"You can identify *them* as well?"

"I should think so. I've slept with at least five of them."

"What do you think it means?" asked Ilona.

"I don't know. Military maneuvers, perhaps. A frontier threat with the staff called into special session because of it. Possibly a—"

"The Turks!" Ilona exclaimed, growing suddenly pale. "Oh Militsa, the Turks!"

"Don't fret, my dear. If an invasion had started, look you, the king would not be here either. Neither would this ball have been held. I merely remark the oddity of this martial eclipse, that's all. 'Tis a curious thing." She leaned closer to the other woman. "And I've noticed something else. Where is our little virgin this evening?"

"Our virgin? Oh you mean Valeria."

"Yes. The Viscountess Valeria Szilagy is His Majesty's ward. At a court function of such distinction she should certainly be with him."

"Maybe she is indisposed. Virgins are more subject to cramps than we are. Remember?"

Militsa, ever mischievous, lowered her lashes in mock modesty. "Ancient history, my dear. Other than the incredible Valeria, for whom there is no accounting, there are perhaps six virgins in Buda. But I cannot imagine who they would be."

While she spoke, an audible murmur rippled through the hundreds of revelers like the spread of concentric waves when a stone is dropped in a pond. Seeking the source of this, both women quickly found it. A late comer had arrived, a man dressed entirely in silver-trimmed black and wearing an ebony horned mask of Satan. Every eye was riveted on him. He stopped before the King and Queen, made a slight bow, then walked to one side of the great hall beyond the press of the multitude and seated himself casually. Aloof. Seemingly seeking no further attention. Alone.

"Who is *that?*" asked Ilona nervously.

Melitsa smiled. She said, "A man who knows how to judge the effect he has on others, I should say. Oh bless me, to judge it to a nicety—like the greatest of strolling players."

"But who *is* he?"

"You mean you don't know?"

"Melitsa, for the love of heaven tell me his name!"

"Prince Dracula."

"Dracula!"

"None other."

Ilona seemed appalled. "But he is wearing a poniard. How can they allow—?"

"He could wear a sword if he wished. Haven't you heard, my dear? He accepts the Faith and is to be rebaptized. The king has given him his parole."

"But the king barely acknowledged his presence."

"A little charade for the benefit of others. They play at ducks and drakes."

"To squander time, do you mean?"

"To dissipate rumors. Dracula is Matei's prince in reserve, look you. Hungary needs him. Who else can fight the Turks as well as he? Do you know what they say? They say he cut them to pieces on the Danube. Yes, I mean it. The sultan jumped into one of his boats and fled down the river like a frightened hare. Fled for his life, mark you, and with an army five times the size of Dracula's. Fancy that."

"But why then—?"

"Why was the prince beaten, you mean? He was betrayed by his own brother, so the story goes. The Dobrogea and all those dead men. Defeat and slaughter. A terrible business. That he is filled with hatred for many in this world is a matter of general knowledge. That he is also filled with the most delightful sperm is equally a fact."

Ilona's concentration redoubled instantly. "He has women? I mean, at Solomon's Tower?"

"Women?" Melitsa's pert nose wrinkled charmingly. "Only enough to exhaust a squadron of horse, I think. They come and go like moths round a flame, uh—with the king's approval, of course. As for Dracula, I'm surprised he can even walk. And there is another thing about him still more fascinating."

"Oh tell me. Tell me."

"You've never heard the tales? Why do you think they call him the Prince of Hell? There is a rumor about fiendish, diabolical rites at his Castle of Agrish, that he performed the Black Mass there with naked virgins spread-eagled on the infernal altar. Oh God, can you imagine what he *did* to them?" She was mouth to ear with her listener, enclosing them both with her fan. "But here is the question all Buda is asking. Is he truly the devil's chief disciple, His Satanic Majesty's chosen one for supreme power on earth? Or is he—Satan himself?"

The Countess Ilona Kossuth shuddered as though taken with a chill. She made the sign of the cross and blanched visibly. "I—I had heard these things," she said guardedly. "But—do you think they are true?"

At that moment, Melitsa's reply was drowned by a roll of drums and servants with snuffers began extinguishing the candles, turning the great ballroom darker and darker. Stepping within a small circle of still remaining light, the white-haired royal chamberlain made an announcement.

"My most gracious lords and ladies, honored guests and distinguished personages, kindly attend me."

At once the huge audience grew hushed. Not even a feminine twitter was heard nor the nervous clearing of a throat as the majordomo continued. Melitsa noticed that Dracula had disappeared.

"By the gracious will of Their Majesties you are tonight vouchsafed the rarest of privileges. But tremble for your souls when you witness this. Call upon Almighty God through His divine mercy to protect and save you from the scorching fires of hell. For here among us at this moment, appearing out of nowhere as though this were indeed Walpurgisnacht itself, is no other than Mephistopheles, Prince of Darkness!"

The chamberlain withdrew. The room was darkened still further. Yet where he had stood there was concentrated a vertical shaft of light, an effusion so brilliant that only a sorcerer or necromancer familiar with the use of multiple mirrors could have explained its origin. The light seemed to undulate, to grow alternately dimmer and brighter. Then it actually shimmered as minute flecks of sparkling phosphorescence drifted very slowly through it from top to bottom, repeating and repeating. This eerie manifestation was known in Hungary and Romania. From palace to manor house to peasant hut they knew of it. Such a drifting mist shot through with infernal light heralded the coming of a vampire.

"*Ordög!*" came the dreaded shout from some horrified viewer, the male voice high-pitched with superstitious awe. "Devil!" Then it was repeated over and over as others took it up.

"*Ordög!* The saints preserve us! *Ordög! Ordög!*"

If there were women on the verge of hysteria, the tendency was momentarily curbed as a figure appeared, the now sinister figure of a man in black and silver wearing the mask of Satan. While the onlookers held their breath this phantomlike being stood silently in the light, a chilling specter. Then his arms were lifted palms out and very slowly spread. It was as though by this gesture he blessed them from another world, gathering them unto himself with some diabolical benediction, some secret rite of the damned. Then he faded from view, passed from light into darkness, and appearing in his place out of nowhere a naked girl hung suspended on her back in midair.

The watchers gasped. The girl was motionless, her white body beautiful in the unearthly radiance, incredibly, shockingly alluring. Her long black hair hung down. She wore a small black mask. Militsa Faludi was quick to notice that her pubic hair had been removed.

"I think she's a Turk," she whispered to Ilona excitedly, "or an Egyptian. They often shave their women. Oh how delicious!"

Seemingly awestruck, her companion made no reply.

"Enough to give one sapphic dreams," muttered Melitsa, a lewd tremor in her voice. "We must think on it, dear, you and I. Sappho was more than a great poetess, you know. The rites at the Castle of Agrish. Remember?"

The wide-eyed Ilona found her speech. "You mean Drac—"

"Of course."

Suddenly, small rectangular sections of wood appeared and before the spectators realized what was happening the floating girl was surrounded by them, boxed in, only her head still visible at one end and her bare feet at the other. Again there was the figure in black, in one hand a sword whose long blade flashed blindingly in the glowing illumination. He seemed to speak without moving his lips.

"You have all seen the power of God. But read what it says in holy writ. Everything in heaven has its counterpart in hell. Read the Book of Revelation. Standing against Father, Son, and Holy Ghost are Satan, Antichrist, and False Prophet, the Unholy Trinity. Against the Light is the Darkness. Against the Way is the Other Path. I am one who has trod the Path. The power of administering death is mine—and of restoring life. Look you then upon the secrets of the ages. Enter the realm of Hades ye who dare and cross the River Styx with the infernal boatman Charon. You who do not believe in the power of hell—behold!"

Very slowly, while the spectators held their breath in the grip of some unnamed dread, the black-sleeved arm of the speaker moved, the hand gripping the sword moved with it, and the gleaming blade passed through the box and emerged at the other side.

"He's *killed* her!" a woman screamed. "Oh my God, he's run her through the chest!"

Pandemonium seemed about to ensue, but as though in the grip of a warlock under a spell of enchantment the audience was paralyzed, helpless. No other sound came from them. Now a muffled drumbeat began, and while the devilish tattoo rolled on the man in black, as though continuously armed from some unseen source, pushed sword after sword through the fragile housing concealing the girl's body. Time seemed to stop. Life on earth itself appeared to drift in a nebulous limbo as the onlookers, shocked beyond speech, sat dumbly like so many wooden puppets, overwhelmed by their own outraged senses. Even the king and queen were mute. There was the girl, obviously lifeless now, a dozen pitiless blades plunged through her vitals. Her murderer threw an ebony cape over girl and box. He had become invisible. His voice, as though emanating from the very bowels of the earth, resounded with a hollow ring.

"Master of Death I told you, did I not? Ah but Master of Life, also. Do you still *doubt?* Are there still scoffers among you? Then attend me—and witness the evidence of your own unbelieving eyes!"

The victim's head and feet were no longer to be seen. The cape concealed all like a shroud. Suddenly, it was snatched aside and straight up from the box there rose the shape of a very small man. The sides fell away. The dwarf smiled in the light and bowed three times, turning on his heels as he did so. Stunned, those who beheld him appeared to heave a vast collective sigh. The girl was nowhere to be seen.

"It's Zundi!" came a shout of recognition. "We know you, Zundi! Some other might cozen us but not you!"

The little man bowed again. "To be sure, it is I," he said. "And now, while the servants rekindle the candles, Your Majesties, my lords and fair ladies, any of you who wish may come to where I am standing and inspect the floor for the girl's blood. You will not find a drop, I promise you, nor will you discover her body. As the great sorcerer in black told you, he has trod the Path and can restore life. The girl is therefore alive and well, uh—but momentarily indisposed."

King Matei began to applaud. Automatically the others followed. The applause swelled, growing unexpectedly enthusiastic, then gradually died away.

"Who was the girl?" asked an officer of foot. "Tell us her name."

Zundi shook his gray head. "I am sorry, sir. This is a name known only to him who has the power to reveal it. It would in any case be a flagrant indiscretion that would do the lady harm."

"Just tell us if she is of the court," said another. "'Tis being bandied about that she's a Turkish dancing girl but I think she is Hungarian, someone we all know. Can you deny that? Can you—?"

The speaker stopped short. With a slowness that made the change only gradually apparent, as the room had grown lighter, the area where the dwarf was standing had become dimmer and dimmer. Now it was quite dark. Only an errant gleam of light flickered here and there. Like a creature without material existence, a gnome from the land of limitless, unimagined dreams, the little fellow had vanished.

In the small bedchamber lighted by a single flambeau Dracula stood looking down on the girl. She still seemed in a daze. Although he'd covered her nakedness with a blanket, he had done so only because her nurse Calga was still in the room, because he would not share her unclothed beauty with anyone, even visually. His mind was racing. Oh dear merciful Christ, she was lovely! He had never seen anything like her in his life, and now he intended to make her his at all costs. *At all costs!* He turned to the stout middle-aged woman who hovered nervously in the shadows.

"You have done well, nurse. She was like so much clay in my hands both before and during the performance. 'Twas the *imsak* that made it possible. She never really possessed complete awareness."

Calga seemed to whimper softly. "I'm so afraid, Your Highness. They would give me the rack if they knew of this. They'd give me to the tormentors. Oh my God, suppose this drug kills her!"

"It does not kill," he said, scrutinizing her narrowly. "You do not intend to betray me, do you, woman?"

"Oh no, Your Highness. Never."

"I would become nervous if I thought that, and my nervousness could undo you. *Imsak* is a weaver of dreams, that's all, distilled out of a magic lamp from the moist breath of a thousand *jinn* in the long ago. The Persians call it *hashish* and have used it since remote antiquity. Do you suppose she would have cooperated without it? Gone out there and performed in the nude? Do you think I could have shaved her? I did it for her sake, you know, the best possible disguise. They will never believe her Hungarian with a shaved pubis. They think they saw a Turkish belly dancer. You must understand that I intend to protect you both. You do understand that, don't you?"

"Oh yes, Your Highness. I—I believe you."

"Good. How long ago did you give her the cantharides?"

"About twenty minutes ago, my lord."

"In the wine as I told you?"

"Yes, Your Highness."

"It did not make her sick?"

"No, my lord."

"I thought it would not. I have seen these two combined before, always with the desired result. Now I need some time to be alone with her. You say this room is seldom used?"

"Very seldom, Your Highness. It is only for visiting clergy of the lower orders and there are none in the palace now. None are expected."

"Excellent. If all goes well you will be rewarded. You will take your post in the chair outside the door and feign sleep, warning me instantly of anyone's approach. Two short knocks, three long. Do you understand?"

"Yes, Your Highness."

"Very well, Calga, to your place now. And remember, look you, you are procuress in this. Your survival is tied to mine."

"Yes, my lord."

The nurse opened the door and went through it. Dracula drew a long breath. At last the hour was here, almost the very moment. He remembered how she had felt in his arms when he'd carried her blanketed form through the dim, torchlighted corridors and down the several flights of steps. A monk's cell? It was that indeed but so perfect for his purpose, its very existence unknown to most. He could trust the nurse because she feared him greatly, feared him more than anything else. Matei had given him his parole, had he? Matei would choose his wife, would he? Well, he would take the choice out of Matei's hand if he died for it. He would do it *now!* He saw that the girl was looking at him, in her eyes a growing comprehension. She had not known where she was. Perhaps she knew now. He went to the door and shot home the heavy bolt, then returned to the bed and uncovered her nakedness. She gasped and looked down. In a pitiful feverishness of haste one hand covered her groin as she tried to conceal her breasts with her other arm.

"Oh my God!" she groaned in anguish. "What have you done to me?"

"Valeria," he said tenderly, "you are to be mine now."

She was clutching herself in dismay, her tears already flowing. "But what have you *done?* Oh my lord, it is infamous! Infamous!"

"You are very desirable. Intensely so, my dear. It would please me if you called me Vlad."

She snatched at the lowered blanket and tried to cover herself but he easily prevented it. He could see she was rapidly recovering.

"Are you Vlad the seducer or Vlad the rapist?" she asked, her lip quivering. "Oh God help me!"

He shook his head slowly. "You mistake my motives, beloved. I did it to preserve your honor, not besmirch it. *Un dépilage de mon coeur, cheri.* A depilation of my heart. How else could I protect your identity?"

"You mean—?"

"You performed with me tonight, don't you remember?"

"*Naked?*"

"Of course. You wore a mask and no one suspected who you were. We gave them a glimpse of the infernal regions. Clothing has no place there. Valeria, your beauty stunned them. It turned them into fluid and vapor, my little one, and they flowed out of the keyholes. They will never be the same again—after tonight."

The effect of the small dose of *imsak* had nearly dissipated but not the cantharides. He saw she was in its grip, already starting to pant and squirm.

"Neither will I," she said. "Oh Vlad. Vlad, what is wrong with me? I am nude before you and I don't care. Oh my God in heaven, I don't even care! Oh help me! Please help me! I must be losing my mind!"

"Are you a virgin?" he asked.

"Oh yes! Yes! Yes!"

"Then that is what you are about to lose, my Valeria. Your virginity, not your mind. Come to me, my love. Give to me now."

He took her in his arms and felt her surge against him like an irresistible making tide, a woman beside herself with longing and lust. He knew he could lose his head for this. Matei would show no mercy whatever. But it was worth the risk, worth anything. The others were mere indulgences. *Petites divertissements.* Not since Faustina had he felt like this. Nay, it was even deeper than with her, deeper than with all of them together. Never before had he been so smitten, so emotionally involved, so aroused beyond the very powers of arousal. He would have her in the king's own palace, by God, almost under his very nose! *Then* let Matei withhold her from him! How eligible would she be when once deflowered? What princes would seek her then?

He disrobed quickly, fumbling clumsily with his clothing in his frantic haste. He had had very few virgins in the past, only two that he could remember, and neither of them of royal blood. But *this* girl! He would melt into her like flowing wax and she would soothe him, and all the long, dreary years of humiliation, sullied honor, and torn pride would be as nothing, only remembered agony in a vanished dream.

He almost wept as he took her. He was Dracula the deprived, even his throne in the hands of a wretched usurper. But Valeria Szilagy was his. She was *his!*

"Whence came this information?"

In his room in the tower Dracula stood with his back to Zundi, surveying the countryside through the window, trying to determine how this latest intelligence would affect his fortunes. His most valuable jeweled broadsword hung at his left hip, his poniard at his right. He even had freedom of movement now, up to a point. If Matei were to change his mind about things, it was comforting to know he could not again be arrested. This time there would be no surprise. He could at least die fighting.

The dwarf did not prevaricate. Shielding his eyes from an incoming ray of the sun, he said, "Straight from the general staff, Your Highness. They asked me to tell you."

"Then it has truly begun."

"Yes, my lord. Hungarian forces are already deep in Moravia. The Bohemians are in full retreat. Once the army of George of Podebrad has been flanked, I was told, the continuing invasion of Silesia and Lusatia is a certainty."

"And the Turks?"

"Your Highness?"

"If the Emir Ismet and Radu attack from Wallachia, how does Matei propose to stop them?"

Zundi pondered the question. "I would say that His Majesty's confidence in Hungarian might is strong, my lord, especially in alliance with the emperor. King Matei remembers how his father lifted the Ottoman siege of Belgrade only a decade ago. He believes he can repeat the successes of János Hunyadi."

"A lovely sentiment but I fear it will not halt the janissaries. Specifically, look you, what forces can he deploy on his eastern frontier?"

"I know not their number, my lord. The king feels his Transylvanian levees can withstand a possible Turkish thrust. That I know. Hungarians, Transylvanians, Saxons, even the wild Székelys are among them, a very formidable force."

"If it hasn't been bled already to fight George."

Zundi made no rejoinder. There was a long moment of silence as Dracula weighed his position. At length he spoke again.

"War is war, little man, but the securing of a throne by marriage is another matter." He turned to face the dwarf. "How stands the king on my proffered suit? He has been told I would have Valeria and that she is of the same mind. What says he?"

Zundi blinked nervously. "I believe His Majesty is with the army, Your Highness. In any case—"

"In any case—?"

"Forgive me, my lord. It is now almost certain that he reserves your—uh, intended—for someone else. A Milanese noble, it is believed, related to the Sforzas."

"Impossible!"

"My lord?"

"Now I'll prove that I trust you. I trust you because you're like *me*, an outcast. Because you know I will kill you if you betray me. Because you know a single stroke of luck would make me the most powerful man in Romania!"

His face like a flame, Dracula strode to a table, jerked open a drawer and withdrew a folded bedsheet. Partially spreading it, he held it up for the other to see. It was soiled with dark blotches.

"*Look* at it!" he said. "Do you recognize the stains? Blood turns brown with exposure to the air. This is *her* blood, Zundi, the virginal blood of the Viscountess Valeria Szilagy, since Thursday last a virgin no longer. The masquerade gave me my chance and I took it just as I planned. *I* took her maidenhead, not some Sforza duke. She is no longer available for barter. *I* have claimed her, do you understand? You may tell Matei that. Go to the battlefield to find him if you must—or tell them to give me escort there. By God, they will not trifle with me!"

"Your Highness—"

Dracula raised the sheet higher. "Soaked, was it not? Aye, as from flayed and gutted sheep in an *abattoir*. Go to the diet. Give the arrant buffoons my message. Say if they persist in their folly I will hang this sheet in the main square of Buda with my name on it and hers. Say this is Dracula who speaks. Dracula. I will *not* be gainsaid in this. Everything they have taken from me. But not this. Not this, Zundi. Oh dear God, if I only had my army once more, my veterans! How I would make them pay! I say they would *pay!*"

The little man was intimidated by this violence, frightened by what he saw in the other's eyes. He bowed resignedly. "Never fear, Your Highness," he said. "I am sure His Majesty will listen to reason."

Dracula sought to compose himself. He was sweating heavily. The characteristic nervous tic throbbed in his temple. "Tell them, Zundi," he repeated. "Tell them what Constantinople already knows through its astrologers and soothsayers—that Kazîglu Bey is not yet finished. Just tell them. Will you do that?"

As the dwarf looked at the prince, he found that he himself was sweating. "I will," he said, deeply impressed by the speaker's savage vehemence. "Your Highness may count upon it."

"I count on nothing but eventual death. Yet serve me in this and you shall not come to regret it. I think Matei must either laugh or have me beheaded. In his position I would laugh. What would you do?"

Zundi pursed his lips. "I believe—I think I would at least smile, my lord."

Dracula stared at him fixedly. "Upon my faith," he said, "a rare wit was lost when you decided to dabble in statecraft. If I had you in Tirgoviste I would make you the greatest jester of all time."

Thus the meeting ended.

* * *

The writing of history depends to a large extent upon documentation. Unfortunately, of all the periods of Dracula's life, only his brief sojourn at the Castle of Agrish and subsequent flight across the Fagaras Mountains to Brasov is as sparsely documented as that of his capture and long detention by the Hungarians. There are Russian, Slavic, and German narratives, sometimes in agreement, sometimes not. Romanian folklore is silent. It cannot report what was not known. From the time of Dracula's departure from Wallachia until his return to that principality in the final weeks of his life, an interval of more than twelve years, Romanian peasants who had preserved his saga by word of mouth knew nothing of him.

Even the location of his initial imprisonment and subsequent status of house arrest is a matter of historical dispute. Was it at Vàcz (called Vác on modern maps), the fortress prison on the great bend of the Danube's east shore 20 miles north of Buda? Was it at Vísegràd, also on the river but closer to the capital? Or was this length of time divided between the two? Among conflicting accounts one can take one's choice. Interpreting from the Russian narrative, the Romanian scholar, P. P. Panaitescu, believes the imprisonment was entirely at Vàcz, which the Russian chroniclers labeled "Vísegràd" by mistake. The German imperial meistersinger Michel Beheim, on the other hand (as quoted by G. C. Conduratu), identifies the detention site as Iersiu (Wissurd in the German), a clear reference to Vísegràd.

If investigated now, what do the city archives tell us? In Vàcz, today a city of about 21,000 people, neither the municipal records nor those of the cathedral or episcopal palace tell us a thing, and documents pertaining to the prison make no mention of Dracula's name. The same thing is true at Vísegràd. Was he actually held at Solomon's Tower below the palace? A list of the tower's political prisoners of the period exists. He is not on it. Yet the Hungarian Communist government today is very much aware of Dracula's connection with the Vísegràd sites and their value as tourist attractions, so much so that large sums were allocated in recent years to completely restore the tower to its original state and to undertake restoration of Matei's palace.

What does this "blackout" of Dracula's Hungarian detention signify? The Russian narrative is very clear. It reads: "And he was imprisoned at Vísegràd on the Danube above Buda for 12 years." Is this a fabrication? Beheim's poem says it is not. Antonio Bonfini (Bonfinius), Matei's court historian, refers to Dracula at this time, indicating imprisonment at Vísegràd. Niccolo Modrussiense (Nicholas Modrussa), papal legate to the court at Buda, also stands as evidence for Vísegràd. Why? Because he has left us a physical description of Dracula, something he would hardly have obtained except at a court function. The fortress prison at Vàcz was never the site of such functions. Matei's summer palace at Vísegràd was.

Was Dracula's name deleted from the records for political reasons by orders of King Matei? This is perfectly possible, even probable. The Wallachian prince was very important to Hungary, becoming even more so as events made obvious the permanent adherence of both Radu and the Danesti claimant (Basarab Liaota) to the Turkish camp. Dracula was the *only* candidate for Wallachia's throne that Matei could possibly trust, the only one capable of leading an anti-Ottoman crusade. He could hardly be shackled as a common felon, even though he may have been so initially at Vàcz. Far better was it, from Matei's viewpoint, to make an ally of him as Hunyadi had tried to do, but first to tie him to the House of Corvinus through the bonds of religion and marriage.

Who was Dracula's Hungarian wife? History does not name her for us. The Russian narrative says it was a sister of Matei. At least one Romanian researcher, C. Gane, believes she was Helena Corvinus, the monarch's cousin, noting that the Draculesti's use of the Corvinus coat of arms dates from the marriage. However, a large majority of Romanian historians disagree with these choices, contending that his second wife was almost certainly a member of the politically powerful Szilagy clan, also related to Matei, a family with whom Dracula had ingratiated himself in the turbulent post-Hunyadi period. The eminent Romanian scholar George Florescu believes this. So, apparently, do Radu Florescu and Raymond McNally, his equally distinguished American counterparts. The fact that future members of Dracula's family identified themselves with the Corvinus royal line would have been entirely legitimate through the Szilagy connection.

It may be wondered how, in a time of such intense religious feeling, Dracula would dare foresake the Orthodox church and convert to the Catholic. The answer is clearly that even if he had been devoutly denominational, which he was not, he would still have had no choice. Matei did not equivocate. He needed a trustworthy ally on his eastern border; Dracula was highly valued on a battlefield; no other military leader in Christendom had as good a chance as he, given the forces, of stemming the Turkish tide when next it rolled. But neither to the diet in Buda nor to the Hungarian people could Matei justify the release of an Orthodox prince who was a heretic in Catholic eyes. Dracula's conversion must come first, then his marriage to an illustrious Hungarian bride in a Catholic cathedral. After that, the king of Hungary would see what could be done to oust Radu from the throne in Tirgoviste and replace him with his brother.

Needless to say, the actual course of historical events very seldom gratifies expectations. War with Bohemia could not be distantly foreseen. After all, its king, George of Podebrad, was Matei's father-in-law. It meant Hungarian involvement for years, for every Magyar victory required the commitment of troops for extensive occupation duties in the conquered territories of Moravia, Silesia, and Lusatia. By 1469 (with Dracula still in Hungary), the Catholic party in Prague proclaimed the victorious Matei King of Bohemia. But George, a very determined man not as decisively beaten as everyone thought, not only led a counteroffensive that curbed Hungarian power, but fortified his military position by an alliance with Poland's King Casimir IV. Matei was momentarily checked. Frustrated, also, was the plan to restore Dracula to the throne of Wallachia, a move that would have meant the immediate resumption of war with Turkey.

For Dracula it became a question of further patience, agonizing, virtually unbearable patience in a man little blessed with this trait. He had waited for years since his defeat. He would have to wait for years longer, an unknown span of seemingly endless time that could only lacerate his already badly frayed nerves still further, grinding more deeply into his soul the bitter gall of frustration and failure. After his royal wedding at Buda one can almost see him. He is alone. Dressed in his elegant finery but looking worn and tired, he stands in a private chapel by the altar and grasps the cross with his sword hand. It was a Catholic ceremony. He is now a confirmed convert, a hopelessly damned apostate in the eyes of every Orthodox Romanian.

"What boots it how we worship thee, O God?" he asks. "Or by which creed?" Then he quotes from the *Rubáiyát*. "'But helpless pieces of the game He plays upon his chequer-board of nights and days: hither and thither moves, and checks, and slays—and one by one back in the closet lays.'"

He has made his decision. He has no troops of his own. Led by Radu and renegade boyars, a significant number of Wallachia's people are forever alienated from him. If he is again to write history—he must do it with Hungarian lance points.

9
The Exile of Pest

It was the winter of 1468. In the city of Florence, Italy, a sixteen-year-old boy named Leonardo da Vinci was ending his second year of apprenticeship as an artist under the tutelage of Andrea del Verrocchio. In England, another boy of the same age, the hunchback younger brother of King Edward IV, was preparing for the career that would elevate him from the role of Duke of Gloucester into notorious and evil prominence as King Richard III. For the first, there lay ahead a long life and almost unequaled artistic renown; for the second, after a brief period of tyranny, military defeat and death at Bosworth Field in the final battle of the Wars of the Roses.

It was very cold in eastern Europe. In the ancient Hungarian city of Pest on the Danube's west bank, the average citizen was as little concerned with art as with militarism, although many had sons in battle. Victory was prayed for in the war against Bohemia, and the rigors of that struggle, always the worst on civilians, had made life increasingly harsh. Just now, most of these people were concerned with ways and means to keep from freezing to death, with the acquisition of enough food to avoid starvation. For the minority who could read, the broadsheets posted in the city squares said that Hungary was winning. For the majority who could not, the town criers announced the same thing—endlessly. But the casualty lists were posted, too, and they were high. Matei, redoubtable Defender of the Magyars, was gaining his victories at heavy cost.

Along the chill reaches of the Danube the night held no stars to view. There was flying scud in the air, clouds driven by a bitter wind. On occasion it rose to almost gale force, tearing at the heavy signboard of The Robber's Roost, a tavern which bore that name not entirely in jest. Inside, there was a motley and ribald company. Women there were in plenty, most of them slatterns; a handful of nondescript males, most of them unsavory; a liberal garnishing of inebriates; a scattering here and there of military types, men who might or might not have been on legitimate leave from their units. As to that, it would have been hard to say. Uniforms, for example, were still somewhat irregular. The whole concept of a national military establishment was new in Hungary, an experiment credited to its monarch.

Among the officers were two in somewhat threadbare raiment who sat in one corner at a table. The taller, a Hungarian captain, went by the name of Miklos Skorzeny. He had the remains of decided good looks, but for a man of only thirty was already marked by telltale lines of dissipation about the eyes. His companion, a Greek mercenary called Stavros Polyzoides, was older, stouter, the possessor of a florid face ravaged by the pitted scars of smallpox. He, too, showed signs of a drinking habit still only barely within bounds. His speech, however, was yet more or less under control.

"This place stinks," said the Greek. "I've smelled better air in an Athens bordello."

Skorzeny shook his head. "For a man who has experienced campaigning without a woman for months 'tis a strange thing to say," he observed. "Count your blessings, friend. 'Tis the stink of life and love."

The other thought about it. "Dost count thine?" he asked. "Mark you, I am not blind. I've seen it in your face, that look of loathing for this life. It isn't this hostelry, of course. It's Pest itself and all that goes with it." He paused to sip his wine. "But you are not alone, Skorzeny. Take myself. I fought at Constantinople. Yes, it is true. Under the command of the Byzantine Megadux himself—as an officer. And now look at me. It's the place, I tell you."

"It is *not* the place!" Skorzeny's dark bloodshot eyes were snapping. "It is *people!* In my case I made a mistake and I admit it. I violated the oldest rule there is. It says if you sleep with another man's wife make sure you put the cuckold's horns on him without his finding you out. And make certain he is not powerful at court with the influence to do you harm, to—to have you shoved aside like so much manure. Do you know what the garrison at Buda calls us? The forgotten ones across the river."

"Or the lost bastards of Pest," said the Greek. "I have heard that, too. Well, the war won't last much longer. The Bohemians fight like Numidian lions yet lose battle after battle. What do you think is the reason? Magyar generalship?"

Skorzeny shrugged. "Our training and discipline forsooth. The king has built a standing army, maybe the first in Europe since the Roman, but the enemy still relies on peasant levies. Such conscripts of hinds and bumpkins are unreliable. Their battlefield élan is erratic. Now up, now down, and many deserters. Our army will be in Prague soon. And where will you and I be? We'll still be here in this cultural and political backwater, this fetid mire of mediocrity. Buda has one of the most brilliant courts in Europe—but Pest is Pest, a burned-out flame. And what do I do in Pest? I command a pack of grumbling, gutter-bred malingerers fit only to assist the local police to hunt down felons. I tell you, Polyzoides, my military career is in tatters. Ruined."

"Is it really as bad as that, comrade?"

Skorzeny drained his glass and refilled it. "It is worse. For nearly a year I lied to myself. I reasoned we were quartered here for an important purpose, to put down a possible insurrection in the absence of regular troops. Then I realized what nonsense it was. Insurrections occur among the defeated and Hungary is winning the war. In short, we were sent here to rot—like lepers. Do you know there are streets here that were laid down by the Caesars? Cellars and aqueducts, too. Dear God, this place was old before there *was* a Hungary!"

He began to look at the buxom serving wench with an appraising eye. His companion noticed it at once.

"I believe Buda is as ancient," he said. "As for diversion, you may never be a general but you don't need high command to take pleasure of her. I know our lusty Dorottya. She'll wear out ten hardy fighting men in one evening and look around for an eleventh. Nay, doubt me not. As God is my witness I speak sooth."

"A prodigious capacity," said Skorzeny, still remarking the girl's progress as she moved between the tables, her deftness at avoiding the many groping hands.

"The stamina of a brewer's horse," added the Greek, "and with haunches to match. She came from Transylvania. Even the Saxons there praise her merits, I'm told, and *their* women would exhaust a seed bull. Shall I fetch her for you?"

"What is her price?"

Polyzoides laughed. "She comes high enough for most, look you, but I am a friend of hers. Methinks she'll be nice to you for a smile and a goblet of claret."

Skorzeny sat listening to the wind. It was still fitful, still gusting frequently, and blowing as hard as ever. He was about to nod in agreement when the tavern door opened and one of his own men entered accompanied by three stony-faced civil police. They saw him at once and walked quickly over to him. The soldier saluted. He was dripping with new-fallen rain.

"Nagy," said Skorzeny. "A nasty night. What tidings bring you, man, you and your stolid friends here?"

Nagy wiped an arm across his mud-spattered face. "We have been tracking a thief, sir," he said, "a dangerous cutpurse we think may be Donanyi himself."

"Donanyi the highwayman?"

"None other, sir."

"Go on."

"We think he's hiding in Dushan, sir. We've got men there now to prevent his escape. He can't get out. We thought you might want to be in at the finish."

Skorzeny brushed a fly from his cheek. "I do if 'tis truly Donanyi." He turned to Polyzoides. "Dushan District. Ninety percent Serbs. Like entering a foreign country. What think you, friend Stavros? Are you for this sport. *They* are more likely to attack us than the thief."

The Greek shook his head. "I fear no man, Serb or otherwise," he said, "but 'tis your command, not mine. If Dorottya is not to be thine tonight, methinks I'll give her the pleasure of my company." He put out his hand. "Till we meet again. Good hunting."

Skorzeny got to his feet. In his mind was the thought that he could have a tavern wench any time but the chance to capture a man like Imre Donanyi would probably never come again. He, Skorzeny, had been an officer of the Royal Guard, had a distinguished war record, then suffered eclipse. Maybe he could redeem himself at last, be reinstated by his superiors, put an end to this boredom and sense of utter uselessness that was slowly killing him.

"Thank you," he said, and felt his pulses quicken at the enterprise. "Another time with the girl. This could be important to me. You understand?"

The Greek nodded. "Yours the more hazardous game, mine the more satisfying. Fare thee well."

Taking the lead among the men Skorzeny donned his heavy riding cloak and made for the door. His horse was tethered outside. As he left the tavern, the chilling wind and rain struck him full in the face, gripping him like an icy hand that made him shudder. He felt it grasp his mind, too, but shook it off and climbed into the wet saddle. He wondered what was the matter with him. What he felt of course was intuition, the tugging of insistent prescient fingers at his sleeve. He rode down the nearly deserted, cobbled street, seeing it glisten in nebulous moonlight. The others followed. What he didn't consciously realize was that this night was *different*, the shadow cast by the drama to be played out at Dushan longer and darker than any he had known. It would envelop him, that shadow, enmesh him in its smothering folds. Only a miracle could now prevent it from becoming his shroud.

"I'll thank you never to speak of it again."

Amid the sounds of the howling wind and rain outside Dracula's voice was nearly inaudible. "If I provide you and your mistress with a stipend, Vasili, it is for several excellent reasons. One, you are the last of my generals and possibly the best of them. Two, you have served me with devotion and loyalty, never more than now when I am friendless but for you and in self-imposed exile. Three, if I let you starve, who will be my *spatar?* Four, the Hungarians care nothing for either one of us and would reduce me to the status of a serf if I let them. By giving you sustenance I maintain at least a part of my old staff, a very important part. That must gall them exceedingly, and the more they are vexed the greater my satisfaction. So you see, the advantage is not to you alone. I am infinitely better off for having you here in Pest."

In the large, drafty room with its vaulted ceiling and massive oaken beams they sat opposite one another. The three small candles in the semidarkness did little to illuminate. Dracula noted he could not clearly distinguish the features of Luca's face, that he appeared now as he always did on visits made in the evening, a small man in a large chair. Indistinct. Insignificant. But General Vasili Luca, Spatar of Wallachia, was *not* insignificant! How could he be? If *he* bore no distinction neither did the ruler he served. That was why he was in uniform now, because he, Dracula, insisted on it. That fool Matei would *not* reduce them to ciphers. Neither prince nor general would he degrade or defame as long as Vlad Tepes still breathed to stop him. Ah the infamy of the position. The deplorable injustice of it. When he spoke to Luca again it was still in the same quiet tone.

"Do you understand?"

The general opened his hands in fullest acknowledgement. "Of course, Your Highness," he said. "The Magyars have not provided a ducat for me or Marga and I accept that fact. But I will never forget the boon of your largesse."

Suddenly, a brilliant stroke of lightning was followed very quickly by a prolonged and deafening roar.

"That was close," said Dracula. "If you count the seconds between the flash and the thunder that follows, it tells you how many kilometers away the bolt struck. This was less than a kilometer distant."

The crash had straightened Luca in his seat. He said, "Let us hope it struck at Buda across the river, my lord. Nothing would please me more than to see it burn the palace to the ground. I have prayed for that. Once I even prayed the Danube would flood its banks and drown the dirty lot of them. But God failed to hear me. On the contrary, Matei is winning the war."

Dracula got up suddenly. "It isn't his victories that undo me," he said. "It's the losses he sustains on the battlefield." He began to pace the length of the room. "If this goes on much longer, Hungary will be bled white. And where will I be then? Matei *knows* he must finish Radu to secure his frontiers. But he can't do that without provoking immediate war with the Porte. Hungary *had* the power to fight the Turks but this war has changed that. Bah! While the Magyars and Bohemians slaughter one another, the Ottomans stand clear and roar with laughter at them both. When will Europeans learn who their enemies are? Can you answer me that?"

Luca shrugged resignedly. "Your Highness warned them years ago. They did not listen then."

Dracula stopped in midstride and turned to look at him. "And if I had Matei here at this moment I would warn him again. I would tell him to ask Prague for peace. Nay, for more than that—for an alliance against Mehmed. Christians should fight Muslims, not each other. Dear merciful Christ, listen to that rain!"

"A foul night, Highness," said Luca. "I am glad I'm not a mariner. The wind—"

"Ah but 'tis a foul wind indeed that blows no good."

"Your Highness?"

"If you but know where to look for the chink in the armor, Vasili, *every* situation can be turned to advantage. Where is it here? Morion? Corselet? Greaves? Help me find it."

"My lord—"

"Do you know how long I have been in what these varlets call detention? Six years. Six wasted years. You have been in Hungary less than one. And splendid it was of you to come of your own volition from your sanctuary with our peasants; aye, as soon as you discovered my whereabouts. But six years. Precious Savior of the Agonies, I cannot *bear* it much longer! My blade turns in my hand. It rusts. My lance is untrue. Where is the chink in the armor, Vasili?"

"My lord, I know not. I—I am only a soldier."

Dracula went to him and stood looking down on him. He leaned close to him. "Mark you my nether lip, general. The light is faint but methinks you can see it. Can you?"

"Yes, Your Highness."

"The lower lip. Can you see it?"

"Yes, Your Highness."

"Now harken to me. 'Tis true Matei stood silent while I wed a Szilagy but he esteems me not. Nor do his haughty courtiers, may the devil take them off. What do they think? That I am but a petty prince and my dynasty obscure, the royal House of Basarab of small account. But I could tell them this, were I not too proud to bother confronting them. This full nether lip, mark you, is found in only one family in Europe. The Habsburgs." He straightened but remained close to the other. "Yes, by the rood, upon my honor I speak sooth. Every crowned male of the line has had it, this noble lip. Aye, since Rudolf von Habsburg was first elected King of the Romans in Aachen of the Germanies. That was in 1273. How came my family to this? I am not sure. So many royal marriages. But the lip is the proof, is it not? Speak, my friend. Verily, I invite comment."

As always when dealing with him, Luca was circumspect. "'Tis assuredly a noble lip, my lord, right royal indeed. That there were Habsburgs gracing the greatest thrones long before the first Corvinus is common knowledge."

"So? You are wise as always, Vasili."

"Your Royal Highness."

Dracula walked to a small table and took up a flagon. "Absinthe?"

"No. Uh—thank you, my lord."

"Do you fear it?"

"No, my lord."

He filled a goblet to the brim. "Some distrust its emerald-green color. Others decry it because it is distilled from wormwood. They say it rots the guts and the brain, inducing madness." He raised the liqueur to his lips. "But what of that? All things are relative, are they not? Even insanity."

Again the lightning flashed, followed by rolling thunder.

"Listen to the rain, Vasili. It falls on Christian and Muslim alike, sage and lunatic. It knows no distinction. Have you heard of Caligula, sovereign on the Tiber? Never mind. They said he was mad. They branded him insane because he occasionally slept with his horse, Incitatus, and made the great beast a senator of Rome. Mad? Perhaps. But how do we know that such acts were not the physical manifestation of the godhead in man? How can we be sure? Ah, my friend, I tell you there is more to this life than all the sages of history have gleaned from their most studious labors. I know. I have studied the stars and the howling of the wolves—and I know."

"Your Highness—"

"Oh fear me not."

Dracula half-drained the cup and put it down. He grew silent, ceasing to speak for many seconds as though his train of thought were inexplicably broken. Then: "May Asmodeus burn me if it be not sooth," he said, his expression dark and melancholy. "I killed out of self-preservation, that I and my progeny might survive. I killed because God put it in me to kill. I killed..."

His voice trailed off into nothingness. Luca got up and smiled politely. "Your Highness is tired," he said. "With your permission, my lord, I'll be taking my leave of you now. The hour is late. Please believe me, my liege, when I say that I remain your humble servant."

Dracula made no response. He stood as though transfixed. The general left. Many seconds passed before his superior spoke to the closed door.

"We do not occupy the upstairs rooms, my wife and I. They found bats up there once. They will find them again. We—we sleep at this level—in the back of the house. We—we prefer it. Just she and I, and the child in her arms—and the child in her belly. My heirs, look you, good sirs. Mine..."

He turned. Slowly he walked toward the bedchamber. Caligula had been a swine, a murdering, lecherous swine. Why did he praise him? Why did he hold him up for scrutiny and find him good? Because he violated the chastity of his sister Drusilla? Like the Greek gods? But Zeus was a deity, Caligula only a man. Deities could violate their sisters. Drusilla was—*Drusilla!*

He came to the door and opened it. A single candle burned. In its flickering light he saw Valeria and the boy. She slept on her side, Mihail in her arms, expressions of sweet repose on their faces. Like Madonna and Child he thought. Like a painting he had seen in the palace of Vísegràd, the work of the iconoclastic Florentine, Giotto di Bondone. He moved close to the bed. Placing his hand on Valeria's abdomen, he held it firmly, waiting to feel the movement within her. The minutes passed. It seemed a long time. Then it came, a stirring, possibly a faint kick. Nay, it was *vigorous*. Surely a boy. He would name him Mircea after his brother; Mircea, after the lost one whom God should have spared. If he'd had a son by Alceste or Faustina he would have named him that—but the one ran away and the other died.

He removed his hand and straightened his body. He stood there listening to the downpour on the steep slate roof. Elemental. Primeval. Infinitely powerful. He had worshiped power, striven for it, schemed and planned and killed for it, shed his own blood and that of others to create an imperishable dynasty. But what good were sons to a dispossessed prince? Of what use to a man betrayed by fate?

"Fear me not," he said as he had said to Luca, but this time only to himself.

He returned to the parlor and drank more absinthe. From its scabbard hanging on the wall he took his favorite broadsword, sat down, and began toying with it as he harkened to the deluge. It reminded him of the Dobrogea. He remembered how it had rained during the long retreat, and rained and rained, and in his mind's eye he was once again amid the carnage and the clinging mud, amid the twisted bodies, the flowing blood that ran on and on forever. His lips formed the shapes of words, the names of men.

"Baleanu... Matusa... Radului... Grecu... Come you back, my generals... Come you back... Do not mock me as ghosts, phantoms... specters of the Mad Forests of Vlasie. Come you back. Oh God, come you back!"

Scene after scene drifted toward him like fog. His eyes were closed. He twitched spasmodically. Again he was at Agrish, enshrouded by the fearful night and high in the tower of woe, helpless to control events as Drusilla stood poised at the window.

"Don't do it!" he cried aloud. "*Don't do it!*"

When she leaped, unbelievably, he screamed and his eyes snapped open. Where was he? Where—? Had he awakened Valeria and the boy? No, not in such a roaring rainstorm. If they could sleep through this they could sleep through anything. It was then that he heard it even through the fall of rushing water. A pounding on the door. No mistake. A solid, insistent hammering.

He rose shakily, the long sword still in his hand. This was Dushan. The Serbs *owned* this quarter of the city, and hated and distrusted everyone who was not Serbian. They would kill him for a copper. Luca risked his life every time he came here. That was what Matei had wanted, wasn't it? To get him out of Buda and away from the seat of power, expose him to assassination in Pest? Wasn't that why he had sent him to this rat hole to rot? Of course. Of course. Then his death could be blamed on foreigners, the alien denizens of a despised enclave. How typical of Matei.

The pounding came again. With his eye on the door, Dracula noticed he had failed to bolt it. So be it. It was the venture of the unknown intruders, not his. Quickly he moved about the room, blowing out the flames of two candles, leaving only one burning. Dim indeed now was the light, the dark his erstwhile ally, something he could trust. Like a wraith he slipped into the stairwell and stood waiting in the blackness there, the broadsword tightly clutched. They were a group certainly. One man would never come so boldly. They wanted blood. He would give them blood. He would kill their leader beyond a doubt, and maybe some others with him. He was quick. The lightning flashed not quicker than he. He was strong and cared little for his own life. They would pay for this entry. They would pay as they never imagined. He felt the burgeoning rage quicken within him and ground his teeth. This house was all he had in the world, perhaps his final sovereignty. He would defend it to the death.

Abruptly the roar of the rain and the wind seemed to fill the room. They had opened the door and were entering. He pressed himself to the wall, deeper into enveloping darkness, the battle-tested weapon in his hand a faint gleam.

"Search upstairs!" came a shout. "We'll look about down here!"

He saw the leader. The swine was no Serb. He spoke *Hungarian!* No matter, he had violated the sanctuary of a prince. They were spreading out now, a sizable body of them. One or two had climbed the stairs. The Hungarian officer was tall, a moving silhouette against the candlelight. They had closed the door, shut it just in time to ensure the survival of that single flame. But *here* was the man. Right in front of him now. Coming closer, an unsheathed Magyar hanger in his hand.

Dracula struck!

Like a decapitated marionette the officer's head seemed to leap from his shoulders and fall to the floor with a soggy thud. Dark blood gushed. As though suspended by strings the body appeared to hesitate an instant, gore pumping from the neck arteries, before it collapsed.

At first, the men did not notice their leader's silent fall in the semidarkness or see his assailant. Then a soldier gave the alarm.

"He's here! The thief is *here!* God of my life, he has killed the captain!"

Dracula entered the circle of pale light. Behind him he sensed the presence of Valeria and glanced quickly back to see her grasping a small lighted candelabrum. Instantly he stepped between her and the men, holding his right hand low, the blood-smeared blade of the broadsword directed toward them. He spoke in his fluent Magyar.

"Thief?" he snarled. "You have invaded the home of a *prince!* Saw ye not the escutcheon on the lintel? 'Tis the royal coat of arms of Wallachia, *my* coat of arms!" He turned over the hand that held the weapon so the knuckles were up. "Do you see this ring with its royal seal? I am Dracula! I am Prince Vlad III of the House of Basarab and you are intruders in my domain! When your officer entered my house unbidden he committed suicide! Do you understand that? Now take the separate parts of him and get out! If you delay I'll kill you all! On my oath, I'll kill every last mother's son of you! Take that fool's carcass and get thee hence!"

"Your Highness," protested one, "we were looking for a thief."

"And you found death."

"We did not know this was your home, Your Highness."

"Ignorance can be costly. Get out."

Clearly imbued with superstitious dread of the man they faced, not daring to grumble in his presence, they laid the bloody torso and head in a horse blanket and departed. Dracula put the sword on a table. This time he bolted the door, then turned to his white-faced Valeria.

"Is my son all right?"

She nodded quickly. "Yes, my lord, he still sleeps. Oh Vlad, what were they *doing* here? What happened?"

He took her in his arms, holding her very gently because of the child she carried. Outside, the wind howled less. The impact of the rain was subsiding. The storm was blowing itself out.

"Not very much," he said. "Don't be so fearful, princess. A man came to me who was tired of life. I was kind enough to relieve him of it."

She tried to press closer to him. "Oh my husband, will this bloodshed never end?"

"It never has," he said. "Of all the animals on earth, my dear, human beings are the greatest predators, the most savage and merciless, the most cunning and deceitful. Fortunately for us, I am more predatory than any of them and always strike first. It is why we are still alive."

He could smell the fumes of distilled spirits. "You have had more wine?"

"Yes, my lord."

"Good. It will help you sleep."

He heard the rain falling. Down deep inside he felt cold and desperately in need of some unattainable inner warmth. He wanted her badly now, but she was in her eighth month and huge and he dared not take her. Abstention was one of the prices of parenthood in the last stage of pregnancy. He was sweating. He thought he could feel his unquiet blood coursing in his veins. Then he smiled his frigid smile with his wife still in his arms. In his veins, yes, like a fever of unsatisfied lust that flowed in them. But better than the Hungarian. *His* blood was on the floor.

It was three o'clock in the morning. Some miles from where he had fallen, the mutilated remains of Miklos Skorzeny lay on a pallet in the officers' quarters he had once thought of as home and slowly stiffened, a man no longer concerned with barmaids or glory or the war in Bohemia. The storm was rolling away to the west. Occasional streaks of lightning still flashed on the horizon. Distant thunder still reverberated. In the deserted streets of Pest the gutters ran full as before, but here and there no longer inundated cobbles had emerged to glisten grayish-black in the cloud-filtered moonlight.

The streets were not quite abandoned. Through them on the outskirts of Dushan a man wearing boots, cape, and plumed hat all in black strode rapidly through the night. His doublet, hose, and gauntlets were of the same ebony hue. His mustache and long hair had been whitened with powdered chalk. He wore a broadsword and lethal *main-gauche*. His glittering green eyes, ferretlike, constantly darted this way and that as though he expected to be ambushed and was prepared for it. A formidable creature, this man of disguises, and very determined. For Dracula wanted something. He was aroused and in need and wanted it badly. And there was nothing in his background that had ever taught him patience or forbearance, still less self-denial. Anyone who crossed his path was certain to die.

In another ten minutes he was at her door. He stood momentarily and thought about her, the devilishly attractive Hungarian courtesan he had made his mistress long before his marriage. If he had to kill Serbs to reach her side he would kill Serbs; if Hungarians, then Hungarians. Tonight's bloody deed would be reported. They might arrest him on the morrow. But before then he would enjoy Micaela Czabai as never before, forgetting his frustrations in the white-hot cauldron of passion that only she seemed capable of brewing for him this night.

He lifted the heavy bronze knocker, then hesitated once more. Valeria did not know about this woman or the son he had conceived by her, but would inevitably discover her in time. And what would that matter? If he ever came to his throne again he would have a dozen concubines, ten score if he chose. It was only a question of affording them. How many consorts had Solomon, King of Israel? Seven hundred. Nor did the Bible fault him for it.

An errant gust of wind buffeted him, wetting him with residual rain. He knocked lightly with his sword pommel. Then, after a pause, a second time. Then a third, more forcefully. Would she dare leave the house without his permission? He had taken her "out of circulation," hadn't he? He supported her, did he not? Then the door opened. She stood there in her revealing shift, looking surprised, holding a lighted taper. Searchingly he scrutinized her face. Did he see pleasure in her eyes? Yes. Even awakened like this she welcomed him, was open to him, in need of him. He loved Valeria. He knew that and would not deny it. But for the moment Micaela was the pungent, altogether heady wine that spiced his life as none other. She was common as dirt, as plebeian as *cojoc* or *caciula*, the vest and skirts of Romanian peasants. Perhaps her very coarseness was what most intrigued him. He wasn't sure. He knew only that his groin ached for her.

"Micaela," he said, entering and closing the door. "Are you surprised to see me?"

She came into his arms. "Yes, my lord," she said, her breath already quickening. "Oh yes. Is there something wrong? I mean, the hour—"

"There *was* something wrong," he told her. "Now there is not. Tonight I killed a man. It seems to have given me an appetite for other things as well. For you, for instance."

"You were not wounded?"

"Have you ever heard of a man who could wound me?"

"I am always thine, my Vlad."

He kissed her with impetuous, utterly ungoverned desire. "Let it never be otherwise," he muttered as they clung together breathlessly. "I like my women docile and ever-receptive. How is our little Mihail?"

"He was restless because of the wind. Now he sleeps. Oh you always look so old with your hair white."

"Maybe I am. Yes. Ancient beyond your understanding of time." Involuntarily he quoted Caligula from habit. "I've existed from the morning of the world, and I shall exist till the last star falls from the heavens."

She looked at him blankly. He picked her up and carried her toward her bedchamber. As he strode with her softness in his arms he found it exhilarating to be here in her house and about to satisfy himself, indeed to be still alive. He wasn't sure how many had been against him only hours ago. It was perhaps a dozen or more. He believed he could have killed the better part of them—but it might so easily have gone the other way.

"Did you walk?" she asked as they got into bed.

"Yes."

"Has your horse gone lame?"

"My noble Icarus? The gold that paid his price was well spent but the clatter of his hooves would have awakened my wife."

"She would not dare complain. Would she?"

He took her by her bare shoulders and held her at arms' length, gazing into her eyes. "She would have been hurt," he said. "I never hurt Valeria."

"And if she awakens and finds you missing, my liege?"

He fell back on the pillow. "Then that would be fated to happen, wouldn't it? I never quarrel with fate and neither can she. We are all of us subject to it."

"But—"

"Pray ask me nothing more," he said. "Just be generous in your love. The lord of Wallachia craves your generosity."

Micaela Czabai, skilled in the arts of Eros beyond imagining, was more generous that night than ever before.

The existence of the Hungarian mistress is inferred from information given in the Russian narrative. Speaking of a time shortly after Dracula's death, story number 19 reads in part as follows:

> The king (Matei) took his sister (the Russian author takes the minority view that Dracula's second wife was Matei's sister) and the two sons of Dracula to Buda in Hungary. One of these sons still lives with the king's son, the other was with the bishop of Oradea and has died in our time. I saw the third son, the eldest, whose name was Mikhail, in Buda. He fled from the Turkish sultan to the king of Hungary. Dracula had him by a certain woman when he was unmarried.... This was first written on February 13, 1486; later, on January 28, 1490, I have transcribed a second time, I, the sinner Efrosin.

It may be asked why the woman who bore this child could not have been one of Dracula's earlier mistresses in Tirgoviste. This is possible but seemingly improbable. The key lies in the fact that Efrosin saw Mikhail (Mihail in Romanian) in Buda where "he fled from the Turkish sultan." If the boy fled to Buda it was because whoever was his guardian felt he could claim the right of asylum there. His paternity did not guarantee this. Only if he had been born in Hungary, not Wallachia, could he have been assured of it as a subject of the king. That he at first sought refuge with the Turks or their hirelings is incomprehensible and likely untrue. He could not have journeyed alone. Either an adult or adults must have helped him, people who knew his identity. It is extremely doubtful that any sane person would have taken a son of Dracula to the Ottomans unless he did so to sell him for ransom. And with Dracula dead by then, who would have paid it?

If Mihail was truly the eldest of Dracula's three sons born after the campaign in the Dobrogea, he must have been conceived before his father took his Szilagy bride. This would have been easy enough. It is virtually a certainty that Matei allowed Dracula female companionship at Solomon's Tower from the beginning of the Impaler's incarceration there, i.e., prior to his conversion and marriage of state in Buda. Any one of these women could have borne the prince's child or followed him from Vísegràd to Pest.

What about the duplication of the name Mihail? His first son by his second wife certainly bore that name, also. As with much concerning the life of Dracula, the explanation is speculative. Dracul had duplicated the names of sons, as with Vlad (Dracula) and Vlad the Monk. However, in this case it is known that the legitimate Mihail was later called Mihnea, though when the name was changed is uncertain. From 1508 to 1510 he was Prince of Wallachia. He gained an infamous reputation. From what we know of his brief career as a tyrant he thoroughly earned the sobriquet by which history remembers him, that of Mihnea the Evil.

There is something compellingly macabre about Dracula's nocturnal visits to his Magyar paramour, a repeat of what Romanian folktales say he did with an earlier love in Tirgoviste. We can see him passing through the silent and all-but-deserted streets of Pest in the dead of night, heavily armed, ready to strike instantly if accosted, his fixedness of purpose equaled only by his utter disregard for human life. In both fiction and history there were remarkable parallels. Inevitably we are reminded of Robert Louis Stevenson's devil incarnate, Edward Hyde, prowling with grisly homicidal intent in the gloomy gas-lit streets of Victorian London. As the famous novel *Dr. Jekyll and Mr. Hyde* related: "The figure [Hyde] in these two phases haunted the lawyer all night; and if at any time he dozed over, it was but to see it glide more stealthily through sleeping houses, or move the more swiftly and still the more swiftly, even to dizziness, through wider labyrinths of lamp-lighted city, and at every street corner crush a child and leave her screaming."

In the field of historical fact comparisons exist that are even closer. Take, for example, the Renaissance prince Cesare Borgia, the notorious Italo-Spanish conqueror who was born in Italy in the year that Dracula died. While still very young, this man who was ruler, soldier, statesman, and sadist was unfortunate enough to contract syphilis, a disease that eventually ravaged his body and disfigured his face. He was enraged by it, knowing it to be incurable. Some historians believe that much of his brutality was caused by syphilis-induced madness (he may well have developed paresis, or syphilis of the brain) and the self-loathing that made him go masked in deadly after-dark forays in the streets of Rome.

In his book *The Fall of the House of Borgia*, E. R. Chamberlin writes:

> His actions would not, perhaps, have mystified his physician for that summer (the summer of 1503) Cesare's syphilitic rashes were at their most disfiguring. He always affected an element of mystery but, at this period, he seemed almost pathologically reluctant to be seen either unmasked or in daylight. Rome again knew a reign of terror—not now of political assassinations but the fear of a macabre unknown. Rome had always been dangerous at night but now few ventured out after sunset, so terrible was the fear of encountering a gang of veteran killers led by a fantastical masked man who would murder and mutilate with total impunity.

It is fascinating how history repeats itself. Many centuries before Dracula or Borgia lived, their weird propensity for nocturnal prowling was anticipated by an emperor of Rome. He was the homosexual psychopath Heliogabalus, a priest of the sun god at Emesa (Homs in western Syria) who came to the throne of the Caesars in A.D. 218 as Marcus Aurelius Antoninus. He too favored a mask and waded in human blood, performing revolting rites that were normally fatal to most of the participants. Fortunately, the Pretorian Guard of his day were no more able to stomach him than their predecessors could earlier stomach Caligula. The evil genius of Heliogabalus was his mother. In A.D. 222, the officers of this militant organization murdered them both.

The Russian narrative concerning Dracula consists of nineteen stories, of which number 17 deals with his killing of the Hungarian officer. The document (MS 11/1088 at the Saltykov-Schredin Public Library, Leningrad) is fairly explicit. It indicates that the civil authorities with whom the victim's military detachment had been cooperating went to King Matei in Buda to formally make a complaint. Dracula had expected this, of course. When he answered the charge he did so in a way that was typical of him. The narrative quotes him as follows: "I did no evil; the captain is responsible for his own death. Anyone will perish thus who trespasses into the house of a great ruler. If this captain had come to me and had introduced himself, I too would have found the thief and either surrendered him or spared him from death."

It was reported that the king was amused by the incident.

It is fairly safe to assume that at this time Dracula was all but immune from prosecution. He had satisfied Matei's immediate demands, first becoming a Catholic, then marrying within the royal family. Now he was like a cocked hammer, the trigger of which the monarch was waiting to pull. Exonerate him? Matei could hardly have done otherwise. He had taken Dracula out of Buda and away from the seat of power. He had given him his parole. Virtually friendless and unattended in ancient, half-forgotten Pest, the Wallachian prince was in no position to become a political threat. On the other hand he was *available*, a strategist and tactician of much experience and unquestioned military renown, a soldier ready and eager to lead Hungarian forces into battle. To make his position even more clear, Matei went so far as to commission Dracula a captain in the Hungarian army as the Ottomans had once done in the Turkish. Why wasn't he offered the rank of general? It is clear that Buda did not trust him with such power. Time enough for that when war came with Turkey. Then the Wallachian would be too deeply immersed in a death struggle to involve himself in intrigue.

It is one of the ironies of history that Buda went to war against Prague just at the time when the king of Hungary was ready to support Dracula in still another bid for the throne of Wallachia. The matter was all but decided. Matei agreed that Radu must be replaced and was willing to fight the Porte if need be. Even Stéfan of Moldavia, Dracula's cousin, was convinced of the necessity to dethrone Radu. Then the pope took a hand. Paul II, a Venetian named Pietro Barbo, had succeeded the deceased Pius II in 1464. Like his predecessor, he found himself seriously at odds with Louis XI of France. He also inherited the problem of the Hussite heresy in Eastern Europe, a movement doubly dangerous to Catholicism because of the able leadership of George of Poděbrad. To stamp it out became a papal obsession. If Paul II could weld together a powerful enough alliance he could smother Bohemia by its sheer weight. Hungary was to be his "Sword in the East."

His weapon in the west was another matter. Of the Holy Roman Empire it was once said: "It was neither holy nor Roman nor an empire." In point of fact it was German and had always been so, with its power based on the imperial cities of Aachen and Vienna. At its head stood a human contradiction. Emperor Friedrich III, German king and Duke of

Styria, was the author of a famous anagram, AEIOU, and most of his belongings were marked with it. In Latin the letters stood for the following: *Austriae est imperare orbi universo.* (Austria is ruler of the whole world.) In German it sounded equally impressive: *Alles Erdreich ist Österreich untertan.* (All the earth is subject to Austria.)

To make this dream a reality and elevate his own Habsburg dynasty above all others, Friedrich made a practice of contracting influential royal marriages, one of the most successful being that of his son Prince Maximilian to Mary of Burgundy. It had long been in his mind to swallow both Hungary and Bohemia. They had almost been in his grasp. His instrument had been his nephew, Ladislas Posthumus, who for a while had claimed both thrones, the former as László V, the latter as Ladislas I. Then the youth had made the mistake of instigating the assassination of Hunyadi's son, László, and in the resulting tumult had fled to plague-stricken Prague only to die there of that disease.

The hand of Friedrich perceptibly slipped. Without his candidate to manipulate he rapidly lost influence. It was then that he relinquished Bohemia to George of Podebrad and Hungary to Matei Corvinus. He was comparatively unaggressive, even indolent except in matters concerning the aggrandizement of his family. After the fall of Constantinople he refused to join the Christian crusade against Turkey. Considering the haughty tone of the family motto of his own authorship, he was curiously unwilling to unite the loosely confederated Germanies through military action.

Now, in 1466, having failed to establish permanent domination over Buda and Prague, this was the man who joined Hungary against religiously rebellious Bohemia. Yet even at this juncture Friedrich was unwarlike. In large measure he left the Magyars to do the fighting. By this he saved a significant number of German lives but he also sacrificed an important advantage. Whoever proved victorious in the final struggle with Bohemia would, for an uncertain amount of time, control the balance of power in Eastern Europe.

For a while it seemed that King Matei could not be stopped. He was an excellent soldier, apparently having inherited his military ability from his father, János Hunyadi. By 1469, having conquered and occupied most of southern Bohemia, he had himself crowned king of that country, ignoring the Bohemian diet which failed to recognize him. As has been said, the ostensibly vanquished George of Poděbrad fought back successfully but his alliance with Warsaw was expensive. In order to secure Polish aid he'd been forced to agree that the son of Casimir IV be allowed to succeed him on the throne of Bohemia. George died in 1471. As a result, the Polish prince came to the throne in Prague as King Ladislas II.

Meanwhile, two years later, things had finally come to a head in Romania. Stéfan of Moldavia was firmly the ally of Hungary. In the spring of 1473 he went to war against Radu the Handsome and defeated him, failing to capture Dracula's treacherous half-brother but taking most of his family prisoner and occupying Tirgoviste. Radu's wife, Maria Despina, was taken to Suceava as Stéfan's mistress. Radu's daughter, Maria Voichita, was transported there as well, though some historians are uncertain of her status at the time. As much a part of the spoils as any other captured female, it is likely that she too became a royal concubine. However, she must have pleased Stéfan. In 1480, the man history was to call Stéfan cel Mare (Stephen the Great) took this young woman as his fourth wife.

After the fall of Prince Radu in 1473, the Hungarian-Moldavian coalition temporarily enthroned the current Danesti claimant, Basarab Laiota, as prince of Wallachia. In less than six months they were having misgivings about it. Fearing for the security of his eastern provinces, Matei decided to strengthen them, choosing at last as his instrument the bitter exile in Pest. It was a fateful move. The king must have known he gambled dangerously.

The indications are that Dracula was given his captaincy some time in 1474, probably in the spring or summer, and that shortly thereafter he went with his family to Transylvania as commander of the frontier district. Dracul had once held this position in Sighisoara. Now Dracula held it in Sibiu, the very city he had put to the sack in 1457 when some 10,000 Saxons died horribly at his order. How did Matei get them to accept this hated man in their midst? The answer seems to be that very broad economic concessions were offered, profits high enough to make it worthwhile for the surviving citizens to postpone their revenge. That payment in blood remained uppermost in German minds, however, is unquestionable. Dracula was virtually beleaguered in the place, hemmed in by unimagined malice. In that ever-menacing environment it is safe to assume he never went anywhere without a strong bodyguard.

Events then moved rapidly. By November of this year Matei and Stéfan were ready to unseat Laiota, and the Turks, anticipating a resurgence of Magyar militancy, were once again mobilizing their forces. Laiota, lightly regarded as a fighting prince, of reputedly weak character, and suspected of secretly sympathizing with the Ottomans, was scarcely the one to turn on the Muslims now in a war for Balkan independence. There was only one man to do that. Matei and Stéfan had known it all along. However, Hungary's conflict with the Polish-Bohemian armies had intensified and Matei, hoping to avoid a war on two fronts, had sought to escape a clash with Turkey. The mobilization of the Turkish Army left him no choice. He wrote to Stéfan, suggesting that he make the necessary overtures to his deadly kinsman and offer reconciliation. Stéfan complied at once.

We cannot help wonder what Stéfan of Moldavia felt when he agreed to this. He had sold Dracula out long ago, betrayed him to the most implacable of his enemies, the Turk. Did he perhaps remember the days of their youth together? Comrades in arms against the Poles at Crasna? Comrades still when Petru Aron's assassins had murdered Stéfan's father, Prince Bogdan? Did he even spare a thought for the fact that Dracula's sword and Dracula's army had put him on his throne at Suceava? History does not say. Yet Stéfan was highly intelligent. Usually with such intellect goes deep sensitivity, aspects of which are surely the sense of gratitude and the ability to feel remorse. In any case, the essential point had little to do with considerations of morality but only with survival. Moldavia was no match for the Porte. The only Christian general in eastern Europe who might be was a vengeance-ridden, emotionally unstable egomaniac who just happened to be Stéfan's cousin.

But the question remained. Could anyone this side of hell control the Son of the Devil?

From here in the middle of the bridge one could sit on one's horse and survey a winter panorama of utmost grandeur; the snow of the surrounding ranges, already heavier than usual; the lowering sky; the chill water beneath him which flowed already under a thickening layer of ice. Dracula shifted his weight in the saddle and turned to view it all from still another angle. The river ran right through Sibiu with its great cathedral, its fourteenth-century Gothic church, its solid homes of wealthy Saxon burghers who still insisted on calling the place Hermannstadt. It flowed into the Olt which pierced the Transylvanian Alps and plunged southward to the Danube. Sighisoara was not far to the northeast, his well-remembered birthplace on the quiet shore of the Tarnava Mare. And there was Cîmpulung farther south, oldest of Romanian capitals; and Curtea-de-Arges, and Tirgoviste.

He felt Icarus stir beneath him. The big roan was perfectly braced on his four white feet. Now, as he turned his neck and tossed his head to scent the air, his owner saw the white blaze running the full length of his steed's face, beyond it a bank of cloud somewhere over the valley of the Arges. He told himself he was closer to his throne now by hundreds of miles than he had been in Pest. Yet what difference did it make? The coalition had given the Turks reason for concern. One of its partners had defeated their puppet Radu, but had replaced him with Laiota, a knave exchanged for a fool. And the path was long that Wallachia's *true* prince must trod, impossibly long with Hungary locked in a death struggle with the north.

He leaned forward and ran his gloved hand through his horse's mane in a caress. "Ah, Icarus," he said, "you are well named to be owned by me. We flew so high, did we not? So very high. But like most of those who aspire to unlimited greatness—we flew too close to the sun. How empty is life when one's wings are singed. The Greeks understood this." He straightened, watching his breath congeal into mist in the frigid air. "Strigoi was lucky," he murmured. "He was wounded in the Dobrogea and died on the retreat. Noble Strigoi. I shall long remember. Long, long remember."

He glanced toward the bridge's far end. Hungarian cavalry there. Ten troopers strategically placed so that no cutthroat zealot might approach him unaware. At the other end, the direction from whence he had come, were a dozen more. *Hungarian* soldiers, not Romanian. Would he ever get used to them? Yet he was Commandant of the Frontier District just as Dracul had been. His *own* uniform was Hungarian, at least some of the gold in his coffers from King Matei's treasury. These were *his* men. By the word of the king himself they were all pledged to die for him if need be.

He turned Icarus and began to trot toward the south shore, knowing the men to the north would follow him. They did follow. In a few minutes they had overtaken him and now all were ranged in a body, outriders stationed to right and left to protect his flanks. He wasn't popular with the city's inhabitants, he knew, but he was respected. The trouble with the Germans was their peacefulness. Sometimes he wondered what had happened to change them since the days of the mighty Siegfried. Had their blood grown cold? To descend from the heady love of war to the insipid yearning for peace was the saddest degeneration of all. It was also unmanly and shamefully emasculating, un-Spartan. It reminded him of men he had impaled for allowing themselves to be wounded in the back.

By the time they approached his rustic headquarters his mind had taken another turn. For security reasons it was on the city's outskirts rather than within it, for Sibiu itself was considered a nest of vipers. Yet he and Valeria lived neither there nor here. Their house, two miles farther out in the village of Balcaciu, was a quaint domicile for a prince. Matei had chosen ill or well depending on the point of view. The villagers were Transylvanians, not Saxons. They were therefore not thirsting for his blood. On the other hand, its distance from his command post exposed him daily to possible ambush and complicated his administrative problems. Sibiu was where he felt he should be, death trap or not, and on the main road for maximum mobility. He must convince the king of that.

Entering the compound with its extensive barracks and stout wooden stockade, he noted that two horses were tethered at the hitching rail in front. One, the magnificent white Arab, Haiduc, he recognized at once as Luca's mount. The other, a graceful bay wearing the saddle and trappings of a Hungarian general, was unknown to him. There were others about, he saw, the horses of a full squadron of escorting cavalry, their riders apparently already indoors. He dismounted. Flakes of new-fallen snow were already flecking his riding cloak. After standing a moment to watch his guard enter their adjoining quarters, he took the salute of the sentry at the door and went inside, relieved to be out of the deepening chill.

At once all was warmth and cheeriness, the crackling fire his orderly had kindled on the hearth reminding him of days in Tirgoviste when the facilities of an entire palace were at his disposal. Two officers were already on their feet to greet him, one of them General Luca, bowing to him now. Sandor Janosi, a liaison officer detached from the court in Buda, introduced the other.

"This is General Korjus, my lord," he said. "General Erno Korjus of His Majesty's personal staff."

Dracula took off his gauntlet and extended his hand. "General Korjus. You are welcome at this command."

The general was a very tall man and looked down on the prince. He took the proffered hand and shook it briefly. "Your Highness. A brisk day for a bit of campaigning. One needs a good fight to warm the blood."

Dracula nodded. "Or to die like a man instead of rot like a political detainee," he said, watching closely for the other's reaction. "You greet me as a prince should be addressed. This speaks well for your courtliness and sense of dignity."

Korjus arched an eyebrow ever so slightly. "It is only right and just, my lord. It is well known in Buda that your appointment here is only temporary. In His Majesty's eyes you are the rightful ruler of Wallachia. In point of fact, that is why I am here. There is the matter of a certain letter, a very important document of state."

Dracula glanced at Luca, noting simultaneously the quickened interest that Janosi did nothing to conceal. He motioned the others to chairs and took one himself, shifting his sword and resting his scabbard tip on the floor by his left boot.

"A letter, general?"

Korjus smiled faintly. Reaching into his doublet he withdrew a document enclosed in vellum and sealed with wax. Dracula recognized the seal and ribbon at once. It was that of his cousin, Stéfan of Moldavia. The officer handed it to him.

"My profound apology, Your Highness," he said. "I mean, that this missive addressed to you comes to your hand indirectly. Our cavalry pickets on the road, you understand. Military policy in time of war."

"I grasp the need to intercept." Dracula's voice had become distant, impersonal. "I note the seal has not been broken."

"Nor could it be except by His Majesty's order," said Korjus. "The Hungarian army would never willingly violate the dignity of an allied prince."

More and more Dracula approved his respectful tone and demeanor. *Allied prince*. His choice of words was as startling as it was unexpected. "I presume you are acting as more than a mere courier," he said, and looked at Luca again. "King Matei knows the contents of this?"

"He does," said Korjus. "I believe it was written at His Majesty's request."

Dracula sat quietly with the document in his hand. "How fares the war, general?"

"Stalemate, I think. At the moment."

"Do you know what is written here?"

"Only in a general way, my lord. Once you have read it, uh—we can discuss it."

Dracula broke the seal and read the following:

To my Puissant Lord, Most Royal Kinsman, and much loved Comrade in Arms, greeting.

My Vlad, boyhood friend and one-time companion of my bosom, it is doubtlessly the Divine Will of Almighty God that I pen this letter today with the full knowledge and approval of His Majesty, King Matei. As you may know, he and I have long looked upon you as our natural ally, the rightful ruler of Wallachia. Forget our differences of the past, therefore, I entreat you, and believe that what I did was with no intention to injure you personally but was forced on me by political expediency.

If you can accept this claim of mine, dear Vlad, and forgive, then kindly attend my words. This is a time of great change and we stand at last on the threshold of opportunity. As I put ink to parchment Mehmed is mobilizing. Laiota has thrown in his lot with the Turks. Wallachia is therefore without a Christian prince and has only an Ottoman pasha in Christian raiment. Tirgoviste lies open to assault. His Majesty and I are pleased to recognize you as Prince and to support you on the throne with our forces. But first we must fight the Muslims and Wallachian boyar contingents serving Laiota.

The King offers you nothing less than joint command with myself and the Serbian leader in the Roman fashion, proconsul balancing proconsul if you will. There isn't much time to organize on the threatened front, for by the time this reaches your hand the Turks may already be on the march. The appropriate officers will inform you of the details.

This then is the offer, my cousin. That God will guide you in your decision and make us once again as we were at Crasna is the most sincere and fervent wish of

Your ever-devoted and affectionate cousin,

Stéfan of Moldavia

Signed and sealed this ninth day of November, 1474

He read the letter through a second time, then laid it down. "Do I understand it correctly?" he asked. "Matei and Stéfan offer me the throne of Wallachia?"

"If it can be won in battle, Your Highness." The fingers of the general's hand toyed nervously with the tassel on his sword pommel. "Does it say the Turks are even now in motion?"

"It says they may be. I believe you are to supply me with late information."

"That is correct, my lord." Korjus seemed to hesitate. "But only if you accept the command that is offered."

Dracula's lower lip seemed to protrude more than ever. "Accept? Here I command what amounts to a police unit, and wait for a Saxon dagger in the back. No throne is offered me here. Just obscurity, and in the end—oblivion. I am the son of Prince Vlad Dracul, General Korjus, the Son of the Dragon. If you prefer, the Son of the Devil. I have fought the Turks from western Bulgaria to the Black Sea and back again, and lost my realm and my people because of them. Accept? Yes, by God, I accept! Who is the Serbian commander?"

"Vuc Brancovic is our ally."

"Ah. Once Tyrant of Sméderevo. I remember my father speak of George of that family. George Brancovic, the despot who held Hunyadi prisoner after Kósovo Pólje and wanted to kill him. You recall the tale, Vasili."

Luca sat with folded hands. "I remember, Your Highness."

Dracula stood up. "I need information. I thirst for it. If you will come into the map room, gentlemen, we will see if we can pin the Ottomans down. I cannot fight an enemy unless I know where he is."

Moments later, the four of them stood before a large map on the wall. Dracula had long since lost his stakelike pointer. He drew his poniard and handed it to Korjus.

"Locate them for me, general, if you please."

Korjus complied. "In their efforts to flank the Hungarian army the Turks have invaded southern Moldavia by way of the Danube's tributary, the Siret River, and their vanguard is moving north up the Crasna." He traced the route with the dagger blade. "They should now be about here."

"They advance with their whole army?"

"We think—nearly 100,000 men."

"The sultan?"

"He stays with his harem in Constantinople."

"'Tis better suited to him than war. The enemy commander?"

"We are not certain yet, my lord. It may be Kuprili. Possibly the Red Emir, as they call him. Mustapha Sinan."

"Yes. I remember his red beard. His mother must have been invaded by a Saxon." Dracula paused to ponder the situation. "We must delay them as long as possible, then force them to fight for every foot of ground. No quarter, gentlemen. No prisoners. Where stand the Moldavians?"

Korjus pointed again. "Prince Stéfan's last known position was about here. On his native soil he fights a very stubborn holding action. Brancovic is on his right flank—about here. The main Hungarian force under General Karolyi should be in this area now. They are moving eastward by a series of forced marches."

"And the troops to be placed under my command?"

"You and Count Karolyi are to be co-commanders of the Hungarian contingent, about 50,000 men."

"A divided command," said Dracula. "There were times when the Romans found it unwise, even disastrous. But Matei's will be done. I am offered my chance very late and at a disadvantage because of it. The Muslim objective is Suceava, of course. I needn't tell you they must be stopped well south of it, and on ground of *our* choosing, not theirs. It seems I have work to do. I will call my scrivener and dictate my acceptance at once."

"That will not be necessary, my lord. I will deliver it personally."

"Very well. I want battle maps showing the last known positions of all units by name. I want unit strength tables, a list of unit commanders, and casualty estimates when they become available. My immediate question, general, is this. How does His Majesty propose to fight the Turks and Laiota's boyars in the east and still have the strength to hold the Poles and Bohemians in the west?"

Korjus frowned thoughtfully. "It may not be possible, Your Highness," he said. "However, at the moment there is a truce with Warsaw and Prague. 'Tis a patchwork quilt and cannot long endure."

Dracula made no rejoinder. His mind was far away. He gazed out the window and thought of other scenes, other times. Was this really his opportunity at last after all these years? Then where was the berserk blood lust he should feel, the wild exhilaration of the moment to be burned indelibly into memory? Among the men he would fight were Laiota's Wallachians, yet not one Wallachian unit would fight for *him*. It was a bitter thing and unnatural. Perhaps there was augury in it, an omen of bloody defeat and approaching death.

Suddenly he wanted Valeria desperately, to take her in his arms and hang on to her for dear life. He fought against the desire. He felt he must control himself, do all in his power to master this dangerous weakness. What was the matter with him? He knew that Korjus was speaking but he couldn't concentrate his mind at all now. Dear merciful God, was he *afraid* to die? No. No, he had never known fear. This was something else, something down deep in the soul of him that seemed to threaten as though with damnation. *Damnation*.

When he turned back to the business at hand there were tears in his eyes.

10
The Third Reign: A Gathering Darkness

The wind from the north swept down from the steppes of south Russia and froze Moldavia in its deadly grip. The land seemed paralyzed. The rivers were choked with ice. The trees stood like mottled black and white scars against the desolate landscape. No bird sang.

Mounted on Icarus, Dracula rode slowly among the endless slain, heavily muffled in his surcoat and cloak. Beside him rode Luca. To the veteran prince of Wallachia it was a scene many times repeated, but never had he viewed battlefield corpses in such numbers as these, or bodies so starkly displayed, or the faces of war's victims locked in such expressions of rage, horror, and despair. It was because they were frozen, he realized, their final agonized contortions preserved in rigid solidity only hours after death had overtaken them. Here, a Turkish *spahi* lay transfixed by the same flight of arrows that had killed his mount. There, a Hungarian cavalryman had taken a spear between the shoulders, his dark eyes glazed in a look of sudden surprise. Beyond, on the far side of a small hillock, Wallachian and Serbian infantry had slaughtered each other, the bodies slumped in grotesque attitudes like marionettes diabolically arranged by an insane puppeteer. The fallen were spread over nearly two miles of snowy, blood-soaked terrain. He estimated their number at close to 30,000.

"Your Highness," said Luca after a long silence. "I count as many allied dead as I do Turks and Wallachians."

"There are *more*," said Dracula impassively. "We have lost a quarter of our army. When you consider the number of wounded who will die—we have lost a third of it."

Luca's sad acknowledgement bore an overtone of perplexity. "But we won the battle, my lord. The Turks and Laiota's boyars have abandoned the field to us."

"Have they? Will there not be other fields? When a spider catches a fly on the outer edge of its web, look you, it sometimes returns to the center before moving out to feed on it. It simply allows the fly time to enmesh itself further. Flies are stupid, you see. They've been known to tear themselves apart in their efforts to escape."

When Luca made his teeth-chattering rejoinder Dracula was aware of it, but only of the words being spoken, not of their substance. He was looking eastward toward the whitened church spires of Vaslui, a Christian citadel still intact largely because of him. That is what history would call this engagement, he supposed, the Battle of Vaslui. It had been a mighty struggle, an epic, really, yet was ruinously, maddeningly indecisive. His gaze swept the rugged, snowbound landscape. The allied Christian forces, Hungarians, Moldavians, and Serbs, had held the line of the river. In places, the Turks had crossed it on the ice. So had the Wallachians under Laiota. Here and there they had broken through the crust with heavy losses. They had regrouped, spread out, established themselves in strength west of the city, then had their left flank turned by allied cavalry and seen their center at last collapse under relentless pressure.

But *they had retired in good order*, damn them! A huge army caught in a trap, a force that might have been annihilated but for the military genius of one man, Mustapha Sinan. That wily, battle-hardened emir had nearly done the impossible, come within a hair's breadth of turning defeat into victory. It was he who had rallied the invaders, then launched a furious counterattack with what were *supposed* to be beaten troops. And here was the result. Allied dead in the thousands. *Victorious* princes and generals in possession of a battleground choked with more of their own casualties than those of the enemy.

He felt like retching. There was no stench this time. Even the spilled blood was frozen and a frozen field had its compensations. No putrefaction, no bloating, no released gases until the return of the sun's warmth. But he was sick deep inside, gut sick. Instinctively, he felt that his godsent opportunity to break the Ottoman yoke and recoup his fortunes once and for all had come and gone, slipped through his fingers like melted butter. This had been his *last* chance. It would never return. He heard the whine of the wind, felt it penetrate cloak, armor, and the quilted combat singlet beneath his breastplate. He muttered to himself in Latin.

"*Sic transit gloria mundi.*"

Yes, he thought, thus passes worldly glory indeed. On the battle tenacity and inspired leadership of *one man*, be he Muslim or Christian, the fate of thrones may hinge. Damn the Red Emir. Damn him to hell. He heard Luca speak again but ignored him. They *must* get under cover. He remembered a Turkish prisoner once who had been in Mongolia. The Mongols had understood it, the man had said. There were winters on the tundra that could freeze the tongue in the mouth, temperatures so low their herders did their work without talking, fearful to admit the frigid air. And this was the tenth of January, 1475. And the Christians had "won" a great battle. And here rode a Christian prince, the unconquerable voivod of Wallachia, whose chief concern at the moment was to avoid losing his fingers, toes, and tongue to that morbid condition where the blood flow ceased and the flesh turned black.

He glanced to the side in time to see Luca's white Arab defecate. It seemed almost to cheer him. If a horse's bowels could still function in this intense cold, he reasoned, perhaps they could get back to field headquarters before they froze in their saddles. There were more futile goals than that to set one's mind on. He tried to compress his jaws. His teeth were chattering as badly as Luca's now. But in ten more minutes of riding they had reached the outermost line of pickets and were passed through them, and in another ten came in sight of the large, ornate pavilion flanked by its command pennons, themselves flanked by the myriad hastily pitched tents of the army. Already it seemed that a thousand cooking fires were burning among them, chilled and half-exhausted men huddled round them.

He turned in the saddle and looked back. The mounted guard Brancovic had sent to protect him and Luca from possible ambush was still following them. Curious, he thought. When he had lived in Pest's Dushan District, the Serbs had been an ever-present menace to everyone not of their number, an isolated foreign enclave on Hungarian soil. Now a Serbian general detailed his own men to guard him against attack. Did it mean anything? Not much. But once again the bizarre inconsistency of life seemed thoroughly proved, his inveterate cynicism vindicated.

He and Luca dismounted. Before entering the tent they slapped themselves vigorously to restore circulation, ignoring the sentry who stood at rigid attention. Both men took handsful of oats from their saddlebags and fed their mounts. Dracula drew his poniard and carefully removed an ice crystal from his horse's left forefoot. Then they returned the sentry's salute and went inside.

They found a number of generals warming their hands over a brazier of live coals. Count Karolyi was among them. So was Vuc Brancovic. Dracula noted at once that Prince Stéfan was not present, then remembered why. The Moldavian leader and a small cavalry force were the reason that corpse robbers from the city were not at this moment looting the dead. It was vital to Stéfan who had a superstition about it, so vital he had ridden out himself to make sure of things. Dracula considered it a weakness. Authority should always be delegated, the field movements of a sovereign prince restricted to camp, maneuver, and battle line. He returned Karolyi's slight bow. They shook hands.

"You're frozen fish, both of you," said the count, then grinned good-naturedly. "Come and warm yourselves. Kovacs. Lanyi. Make room there for our good Prince Vlad and General Luca. That's it. Nadasdy, you're senior here save only myself. The honor of pouring hot wine for our valiant brothers-in-arms falls to you."

Nadasdy poured. Dracula drank slowly, momentarily ignoring the insult of Karolyi's flippant manner, smiling to himself at the perversity of his own thoughts. What a perfect time for the Magyars to poison the Dragon's son. He had done his work for them. If they had not beaten the Turks and Laiota's boyars today, they would never beat them. Would Matei let him retain his high command permanently? That appeared as unlikely as his restoration to the throne. Almost as though to reassure him, the Hungarian commander laid his hand on the prince's arm.

"You look tired, general," he said. "But fear not. My courier is in the city now arranging for our quartering there. On the morrow a warm bed will be thine." Then he grinned. "And something warm to share it with you if you have need of it."

Dracula said nothing. Inwardly, he was outraged by the other's form of address, always "general," or "prince," never "Your Highness." It was *Karolyi's* courier who had gone to the city, not *their* courier. And Nadasdy? He was a man who could boast one of the oldest escutcheons in Hungary. There was haughty disdain in his every gesture, contempt in his eyes even as he poured the claret. The Nadasdys had been tribal chiefs in the olden time. Doubtlessly, many of them now thought they should be kings.

"As for the major action that is behind us," Karolyi continued, "I have but one comment. A Turkish army 100,000 strong has been beaten by a much inferior force and retreated. A great victory."

Dracula lowered the chalice in his hand. He gazed at the speaker steadily. "Was it, general?"

At the question, there was instant attention from the others and mutterings of disapproval. Karolyi was still smiling.

"You and Luca have just seen it, prince. You've ridden your horses among the Turkish dead. Thousands of them."

Dracula nodded. "And thousands of ours as well. If I may claim your attention I would like to make a few observations."

"By all means."

"We speak of a defeated enemy. Where are their captured battle flags to prove their demoralization? Where are their dead generals who *must* fall in a rout? Where are their troops in the panic of precipitate retreat? A victory say you? Of a sort if you will, but far from anything resembling annihilation. We have mauled the Turks but their army is still intact, still a unified fighting force. If we cannot beat them decisively they will destroy us. They have courage and persistence—and too many men. Their numbers overwhelmed crusading armies before, remember? János Hunyadi would tell you if he were here. He would remember Varna."

He paused. For one of the few times in his life he felt unsure of himself, sensing the growing resentment. Yet he seemed impelled to go on.

"You will forgive me if I fail to share your joy. I have seen more on that field out there than just dead men. I tell you I feel like King Pyrrhus after the Battle of Asculum. Do you know the story?"

"I do." There was not the trace of a smile on Karolyi's face now. "Do you say this was a Pyrrhic victory?"

Dracula raised his goblet and drank. "Yes. And it means we are condemned to fight them again." He was glancing from face to face now, marking each man carefully. "Count your dead, gentlemen, and measure your strength against what must be. 'Tis a crippled eagle that knows not the way of his homing."

"Bravo!" came a voice from his rear. "My cousin is right!"

All turned to gaze at Prince Stéfan, who had apparently entered the tent some minutes before and had been listening. Now he walked toward them with the limp acquired years ago at the siege of Chilia, made a cursory obeisance to Dracula, and took the wine Nadasdy offered him. His strong face was drawn with fatigue and nearly blue with cold. His armored body trembled.

"We have bled the Ottomans," he said. "We have also saved my capital of Suceava, for the time being. But if we had to fight another battle on the morrow or even in a month's time, look you, we would lose." His glance shifted from Karolyi to Dracula to Brancovic, then back again. "Gentlemen, I strongly advise you to quarter our forces in the city at once. Commandeer the homes of civilians as billets if need be but get the men out of this cold!"

Karolyi was looking at him strangely. "Vaslui has not been lucky for us," he said, "a stricken field of ill omen that fills this staff with foreboding." His eyes turned to Brancovic. "What says our stout Serbian ally? Do you share this opinion?"

The Tyrant of Sméderevo smiled wanly. "My men have been decimated," he said with simple honesty. "We need to rest and regroup, general."

"Rest and regroup." Karolyi looked old suddenly and very tired. "A stricken field, as I said. So, they will rob our dead now after all, eh Stéfan? We cannot dig graves in this frozen ground."

Stéfan of Moldavia made a negative gesture. "The cold also protects the fallen," he said. "The thought of freezing to death will deter all ghouls and profaners who might wish to despoil the bodies. I have brought my men in."

Karolyi seemed ready to end the meeting, yet spared a final glance for Dracula. "What said you, prince, about the eagle?"

The Impaler emptied his goblet and set it down. "'Tis a crippled eagle that knows not the way of his homing."

"A Wallachian saying?"

"Wallachian."

"I thought so," said the count. "A philosophical people, these followers of Laiota. What a pity they don't seem to know a Draculesti from a Danesti."

Dracula smiled faintly. "A point well taken," he observed. "Yet 'tis not for lack of my trying to teach them."

At this several of them laughed. As a sudden gust of wind rattled the tent, already stiffening with ice, Karolyi raised his hand for silence. "Prince Stéfan is right," he said. "We must get into the city and seek shelter for the whole army. We may rue this day else. I am reminded of what the Russian envoy Kurytsin said about Muscovy, a land where the birds freeze solid on the branches of the trees. But this is Moldavia. Stéfan, this is your realm. Do you remember a winter like this?"

Stéfan had reached the pavilion exit. Now he turned. "I believe the temperature can go lower still," he said, and glanced at Dracula. "As my cousin Vlad has observed, if we don't crush the Turks it won't make much difference. We have lost too many men. You did say that, Vlad, did you not?"

Dracula was in the act of tightening the lacings of his cloak. Suddenly, in his mind they were young again, two threatened princes in the castle at Suceava faced with the murder of Prince Bogdan. It was all so clear. As though it were yesterday he saw the strained face of his kinsman, the tear-brimmed eyes full of rage and sorrow and desperation, and to his lips came once more the words of long ago.

"Fear not, my cousin Stéfan. We will take their price in blood."

The wind had dropped away. For a moment the tent seemed deathly silent. Then Dracula saw it in the exhausted face. There was something in Stéfan's expression that said he too remembered.

Though Pope Sixtus IV (the successor of Paul II) sent congratulations to Stéfan of Moldavia on the "victory" of Vaslui, two things became quickly apparent to Eastern Europeans. The first, as has been indicated, was that the engagement was indecisive. The other was that Mehmed II, though he had undeniably fled the battlefield during Dracula's famed night attack of years before, was neither basically a coward nor in the least inclined to be a peacemaker. Quite the opposite was true. Indeed, after every setback the sultan appeared only more determined to pursue his course of aggression and conquest. He relished his title of Mehmed the Conqueror. Instinctively, he seemed to know that his taking of the mighty Christian citadel of Constantinople in 1453 would emblazon his name imperishably in history.

After Vaslui, we find him pausing only temporarily to lick his wounds. The Turkish army was reequipped and partially reorganized. Though it had been halted in Europe by Hunyadi at Belgrade and Scanderbeg in Albania, though it was to be halted again at Rhodes by the magnificent defense of Pierre d'Aubusson and his Knights Hospitalers (1480), the fact remained that it had recently won in Asia (Karamania, 1473), and by the time of Sultan Suleiman the Magnificent (1494–1566)

Turkey was to reach its zenith as a world power capable of dominating the Mediterranean and pounding at the gates of Vienna.

Dracula, meanwhile, was once again obliged to wait. Had Vaslui been indeed a victory, there is small doubt that Matei and Stéfan, both of them done for good and all with the Danesti, would have allowed him to oust Basarab Laiota from the throne in Tirgoviste. As it was, he had to content himself with the news that his hated half-brother had made his last mistake even as Vaslui was being fought. In that same month and year of January, 1475, Radu cel Frumos (the Handsome), having taken refuge in the fortress of Bucharest after his defeat at the hands of Stéfan, led his army of Wallachian rebels northwestward against Laiota. The battle was fought outside Dracula's old capital. When it was over, Laiota was still the ruler of Wallachia and Radu was dead.

In the summer of 1475, Matei and Stéfan did something they might have been expected to do earlier. At last, after apparently long and careful deliberation, they not only committed themselves irrevocably to a new crusade against the Muslims but added their signatures to Dracula's on a formal treaty of alliance, an agreement which was given the official blessing of the Vatican. Although few realized it then, the effort they would make would be the last that history would see in generations to break the Turkish grip on the Balkans.

There followed months of war preparations. In Wallachia and southern Moldavia the Turks held strong positions and were content to wait while slowly building their strength. To the north and west of this "farthest advance of the Crescent," the Hungarians and their Slavic allies did the same. It was on 4 August that Dracula despatched a boyar named Cîrstian (a future governor of Tirgoviste) with a letter for the German burgomeister of Sibiu, asking permission to move to that city from its outlying village of Balcaciu. The request was forwarded to Buda. On 21 September Matei wrote to this same official, giving his approval and advancing 200 florins toward the construction of a dwelling. At long last Dracula had status once again, his position officially sponsored by royalty. On 21 January, 1476, the government of Hungary formally declared him to be the rightful ruler of Wallachia. The Porte ignored the provocation. Basarab Laiota, sitting his throne uneasily in Tirgoviste, looked to his defenses and remained silent. The deadly game of watchful waiting continued.

The year 1476 had reached its summer before King Matei thought he saw his opportunity. The war against Poland and Bohemia had dragged on indecisively. Neither side could claim final victory. With the deceased George of Poděbrad Buda might have negotiated in life. But now a Polish prince occupied the throne in Prague, Polish prestige was in the balance, and Matei was aware that only the surrender of all his Bohemian conquests would satisfy Warsaw. Then the unexpected occurred. Faced with widespread revolt in his huge dependency of Lithuania, Poland's Casimir IV met the emergency by disengaging many of his troops on the Hungarian front. Sensing his moment, Matei turned to smite the Turks. He had no way of knowing that within a year he would find himself at war with his erstwhile ally, the Holy Roman Emperor Friedrich III.

Military history affords many examples where an officer nominally in command is forced to rely on a subordinate to do his thinking for him and to court the god of victory. One readily recalls the youthful and daring Clive of India at Arcot; the ingenious Captain Bonaparte at Toulon; the unconquerable Lord Nelson at Copenhagen; and, closer to our own time, the ruthlessly efficient Ludendorff at Tannenberg. So it was to be now with Dracula. Named by the king as commander-in-chief of the expeditionary force organized to engage the Turks and Laiota's boyars was a noble of the old Magyar aristocracy, Stéfan Báthory. Holding the rank of general, he was what a more modern age would call a "political appointee," knowing little of war. He had two notable namesakes. The first had fought as a crusader at Varna and had died on that field. The second, far better known, was that descendant whose youngest son became king of Poland (1575) and whose niece, Elizabeth Báthory, is remembered in history and legend as the notorious "Blood Countess," lesbian murderess of more than 600 virgins, a genuine female vampire.

Dracula's subordination to Báthory can be accounted for in various ways. Some historians have said it was because the Impaler's army was mainly comprised of Hungarians, Transylvanians, and a small contingent of Székelys, that the absence of his own Wallachians in its ranks therefore reduced him to the status of a mercenary. Another and perhaps more cogent reason is seen in the fact that Matei, who had never trusted any of the Draculesti, not only had no intention of giving lasting power to this man but was planning to betray and exterminate him. Although this contention is denied in certain Hungarian accounts, what actually occurred tends strongly to support it.

As a tenet of Magyar policy, Dracula was to be used against the Turks and Laiota like the lethal weapon he was. Then, his task finished, he was to be disposed of as quickly as possible. If events were manipulated in such a way that his death could be accomplished through enemy action, so much the better. It would be a comparatively simple matter. All that would be necessary would be the withdrawal of military protection at the crucial time and place, resulting in what the French might call a *coup de maître*. Master stroke or not, it could hardly fail to be effective. Did Dracula see it coming? There is evidence that he did. Knowing the blow to be aimed would probably be mortal, did he take steps to ward it off? Curiously enough, the answer seems to be no.

In mid-July, 1476, he left Sibiu with a large body of troops and rode north to the waters of the Târnova Mare, then west to the Mures River, then north again, heading for a planned council of war with Báthory in the small Transylvanian settlement of Turda, 15 miles south-southeast of the old German city of Cluj (Klausenburg). Before he left he said goodbye to his family, assuring his wife of their early reunion. He was never to see them again.

It was almost dusk. Once more he bestrode the battered ramparts of the palace at Tirgoviste. Once more it was November, and he wondered why so many of his battles were fought in winter when he had grown to hate the cold and was beginning to suffer from it more and more. Abruptly he stopped, then stood quietly at an embrasure, gazing from his high vantage point across the rooftops. The city was more heavily damaged than he realized; earlier invested by the Turks; never repaired by Radu; taken by Laiota; and now, this very day, captured by the only man in the world who had a right to it, himself, the son of Dracul.

What day was this? It was the eighth day of November. And here he stood in the chill twilight, exhausted, alone but for a quietly pacing sentry, viewing his capital and knowing it would be that no more, that its day in history had passed forever. He would not even tarry here. As soon as the army had been reprovisioned, the men and horses rested, the offensive would sweep onward toward the southeast to hack and smash its way to eternal glory, driving the enemy over the Bulgarian border and beyond. They would *do* it this time. Báthory held nominal command but he, Dracula, was the brains of the thing and Báthory knew it. So did Matei if it came to that. Aye, by the Eternal God, so did they all!

He was looking toward Transylvania now, hazy to the northwest, the line of the snow-crowned alps rapidly deepening in purple. What an epic it had been. Stéfan and his army of 15,000 attacking out of Moldavia;

straight down the Siret River to invade eastern Wallachia. Himself, Báthory, and Brancovic with the main force of 25,000; first marching to the northeast, traversing almost the full length of the great plateau of Transylvania; taking Fagaras, Codlea, Brasov itself by October; then down the Dambovita through Bran and Rucar, across to the Ilfov, with Tirgoviste waiting for them like a ripe plum.

"Oh ye mighty Mars," he muttered, "god of war, patron deity of my household, fail not your son, Dracula, for much is yet to be done. I am tired, Almighty One, and feeling old though but five and forty years of age. Aye, even my blooded steed is tired and my path is long. Great Mars who gave victory to eternal Rome, hear me I beseech thee. What I ask for is much, but have I not waged battle in a way to do thee honor? Succour me now, my lord. Let me chew the bread of ultimate triumph before it be too late."

Only minutes later he entered the great hall, already lighted by many burning torches, and took his position among the men of high rank who were gathering there. Those already seated rose wearily in respectful salute, Stéfan Báthory among them. He saw Matei's liaison man, János Vitéz, more diplomat than soldier, and knew the taking of Tirgoviste would be rapidly reported to Buda. He saw, also, his own political officers, Mihai Log and Ion Polivar, remembering their recent successes with the Brasovian town council. Skilled at molding public opinion, they had perhaps done as much as Vitéz to neutralize Transylvanian opposition, especially among the Saxons, convincing many that the Turks were the prime enemy. They were valuable, even essential, so much so that he raised his gauntleted hand to them in salute, watching them bow and smile in recognition of the honor.

As he sat down, everyone else did likewise. His gaze sought Báthory's and held it. Their relative positions were interesting, he thought. Technically, the Hungarian was his superior officer. Yet this was Tirgoviste, his own capital, this royal edifice both his palace and his court. By the laws of protocol of *any* land he outranked Báthory on this ground militarily and politically.

"My dear count," he said. "As you know, our losses are thus far comparatively light. Prince Stéfan has cut the road to the south and his army lies athwart it. Not that the enemy has the strength for a counterattack, look you. General Harczy here reports moderate casualties. When Brancovic and Luca come in I vow they will say the same. Therefore, relax and rest all of you as my honored guests. It is my hope, subject to your approval, General Báthory, that we will be on the march again within seventy-two hours."

Báthory frowned. He said, "Of course, my lord will realize the necessity to garrison Tirgoviste now that we've taken the place. If we detail enough troops to hold it securely it may well weaken us in the field. May I ask your thoughts on the subject?"

Dracula pondered the question. From the nearby barracks and its parade ground he could hear faintly an occasional anguished cry and even imagined he heard a steady moaning. Most of the wounded would die, he knew, for their injuries nearly always mortified. *Light* casualties still meant scores of dead, possibly several hundred.

"The essential thing is to get on their backs before they can reorganize," he said, "to pound them into the ground like a stake. If we take up the pursuit quickly, look you, time is on our side. If we delay it is on theirs. It is not essential to defend Tirgoviste. The enemy cannot come north again without major reinforcements."

"And what of Mustapha Sinan? Can we *know* he will not reinforce?"

"He has not done so yet. Laiota and the Emir Ilderim are alone—with whatever they have left of 30,000 troops."

"I don't like it," said Báthory. "The whole thing has been too easy. In sooth, my lord, it has the smell of a trap." He paused to gauge the reaction of the others. "Like most others here, I was also under the impression that you planned to be crowned in this place, reinvested as Prince of Wallachia. What of that?"

Dracula could definitely hear the wounded now, so many more than he had realized. "My crowning is preordained by God," he said, "and will come when it comes. Tirgoviste is finished. The Muslims have burned its many churches, a sign of the Almighty's displeasure, the withdrawal of His protection. The new capital of the land will be our next objective, a fortress that was built at my order."

"The Citadel of the Dambovita?"

"It will be called that no more. Henceforth, it shall have but one name. Bucharest."

"And you will make it your capital?"

"I will. Can I be crowned here in a gutted cathedral with no roof? This city is a burned-out shell and was torched for a reason. Predestined."

From the half-exhausted listeners there was a murmur of interest. General Dozsa, a mud-spattered leader of horse, got to his feet and raised his wine glass. "A toast!" he proclaimed, then waited for the rest to rise. "To His Highness Prince Vlad III and his new capital of Bucharest! May it know unparalleled prosperity and eternal greatness!"

"Here! Here!" came the cry as men who longed for sleep joined him in raising their goblets.

Dracula was pleased and somewhat surprised. Clearly, not all Hungarians were against him. He was in the act of drinking when a sudden silence fell on the assembly and all turned their heads to look in the same direction. A giant Magyar infantryman entered the hall, the largest man he had ever seen. He was bedraggled, filthy, showing every sign of prolonged exposure to combat. He stopped in the middle of the room. In his arms he carried a small man, bloody, white-faced, the eyes open and expressionless, wearing a general's uniform.

"It is Luca!" someone exclaimed. "Luca is dead!"

Dracula walked to where the soldier stood with his burden and took it from him. "Vasili," he said softly. "Come you back to me as clay, Vasili?" Then, to the huge one: "How came he by this?"

The man looked half-stunned. He seemed to struggle to get a grip on himself. "I—the casualties are still coming in, my lord. There are many more. I found—I found the general on the main north road. His horse was dead. He—he was pinned under him. I thought—you would want him brought here."

Dracula opened his tightly clenched jaws. "Yes," he said almost inaudibly. "Oh yes. Uh—thank you, soldier."

Unwaveringly watched by all, he walked with unsteady gait to the long conference table and laid the little man on it; removed his own doublet, carefully folded it, placed it under the dusty head. Very gently he closed the sightless brown eyes. Only then did he notice the broken shaft of the arrow an inch of which protruded from the dead man's chest. A Wallachian arrow shot from a bow serving Laiota. Inside he felt empty, as devoid of blood as a flayed and gutted carcass hanging in a marketplace. Fate could *not* do this to him. Not now. Not in such a way. Slowly he took off Luca's gauntlets and laid them down, folded his arms on his breast. Using both hands, with infinite tenderness he stroked the pallid, begrimed cheeks with his fingertips, oblivious to the onlookers.

"Dost leave me now?" he muttered. "Your time of parting was ill-chosen. Don't you think? Such a long trail we rode together, *spatar*, you and I. Like Gilgamesh and Enkidu. Achilles and Patroclus. And will you not see me crowned in Bucharest? I will rename it for you if you want.

Yes. We can call it Luca. Would you like that? Luca, the Citadel of the Valiant One. Vasili... Vasili... Come you back, my general. I—I cannot go on..."

His deeply stricken voice lapsed into silence. Curiously, it seemed to him that his journey had come full circle, that this was where it had begun. Then, as he gazed at it, Vasili's quiet face appeared to dissolve as though in water. Flowing. Disintegrating. Unraveling at the seams like the warp and woof of his prince's life now so blasted. Dracula felt himself choking and fought desperately for control. It was unreal, this scene, a product of exhaustion, a battle-induced phantasm that would vanish like mist with the dawn. Wouldn't it? *Wouldn't* it?

From somewhere afar, as though it came from realms infinitely distant and forever lost, he heard the cry of a loon.

In the flickering light and moving shadows caused by the blazing fires the great limestone cave was a wonder to behold. Some 200 men had taken shelter in it, among them most of the army's leaders, while outside in the darkness of dense, swamp-girded forest were pitched the several thousand tents of the combined Turco-Wallachian forces.

The armed camp was a bristling hedgehog of defense. Pickets were relieved every two hours. Mounted patrols were everywhere. The Dambovita River lay between the bivouacked host and the Hungarian-Moldavian-Serbian coalition. So did the Balteni marshes, mile after mile of tree-interspersed, snow-covered quagmire whose invisible quicksands were a deadly trap for the unsuspecting. Let an assaulting army cross the river; if they were flanked they would be forced into the fatal swamps and sucked under. Let them somehow get through this clutching, shaking death; they would find themselves confronted by a strange Christian-Muslim alliance whose valor was equaled only by its savagery; desperate men who had been driven southward, who had surrendered Tirgoviste, then Bucharest, yet men still imbued with a fanatical will to resist.

That was the thing, the *will* to resist! In the firelit cavern, Basarab Laiota sat on the broad stump of a broken stalagmite and thought about it, his ruddy, black-bearded face a study in grim determination. The enemy was powerful. He gave them that. They were wily beyond belief, more cunning in deception, in the diversionary attack than any he had ever faced. He gave them that, too, crediting it to the rival he hated above all men, the God-accursed Dracula. But it must come to an end soon. On the night of 11 November the foe had slipped out of fallen Tirgoviste under cover of darkness, silently, like the approach of the Black Death. On the sixteenth they had taken Bucharest after fierce resistance. Ten days later, Dracula had been crowned in that city, for the third time usurping the throne of Wallachia and reaffirming the title he richly deserved, that of Pretender.

But now it must *end!* Laiota's infiltrators had reported it. Dracula had enemies in his own camp, Hungarian enemies. His task was done. King Matei had no desire to cross into Bulgaria and fight the entire might of the Porte. They would desert the usurper now. It was almost a certainty. Would he go back to Buda with them and give up his throne? No. Every fiber of his being was wedded to Wallachia, his mind concentrated on the defense of Bucharest against counterattack. But what would he have with which to defend it? A Hungarian army? Never. A death plot aside, Matei would need his troops in the west against Poland. A major force of Moldavians? Impossible. Prince Stéfan could never spare such numbers of men without inviting insurrection at home, a deadly *coup d'état* in his capital of Suceava. Serbians? Vuc Brancovic would simply withdraw. They *must* abandon the foresworn miscreant swine. They *would* abandon him, perhaps leaving a token force but nothing of any account. On this winter's night, the third of December, with icicles festooning the pitched tents of the army, Laiota was ready to wager his future on it. The Wallachians would not fight for Dracula either. Very soon he must stand alone. Then...

Laiota turned to the men at his side. Nicolae Ispirescu, István Eliade, and Barbu Lazan were all Wallachian generals, all boyars owing their rank and their fortunes to their military ability and Danesti royal patronage. Eliade had lost father, mother, and sister on Dracula's brutal death march to Poenari. Ispirescu had lost his young wife during the enforced rebuilding of the Castle of Agrish. Lazan, strangely withdrawn and silent except when commanding his troops, but a devil in battle, nursed some hidden grievance and a hatred for the Impaler bordering on insanity.

"Ispirescu," said Laiota, "do all the commanders know of our meeting here within the hour? The time approaches."

The burly general nodded. He said, "Most of them are here in the cave already, Your Highness, and await the word to foregather. I have sent out riders for the others."

"And what think the three of you? Will they put their hearts into the primitive rite I will propose or hang back from it? Eliade?"

The officer's face, lean almost to emaciation, showed an unexpected eagerness. "They all hate him as much as we do, my lord. I have never seen such black malice in any group of men in my life. On my oath, you'll find them of one mind and that in favor."

"Lazan?"

"Why would they not wish for it, Your Highness?" Lazan, very swarthy for a Romanian, looked almost like a Turk. That he answered in more than his accustomed monosyllables was proof that Laiota's intended ceremony inflamed his imagination. "It will bind us together as nothing else could do," he added. "Like iron."

"So I myself believe," said Laiota.

He was about to add more when a glimpse of men in motion to his left front caught his attention. The summoned officers arriving? No, it was a small body of Turks. The Ottoman commander, Ilderim Effendi, the Emir Kara Ekrem, the Emir Achmed ibn Aziz. The ever-present janissary guard was with them, perhaps a dozen men protecting each of the Muslim leaders. Knowing Laiota's location in the cavern beforehand they approached him directly. He rose with his generals and waited. When they were within a few feet of him they stopped. All three emirs bowed. As they straightened their bodies, they made the Islamic sign of peace, the compressed fingers of their right hands touching stomachs, chests, and foreheads. Laiota and his officers bowed in turn.

"*Salaam aleikum, sidi*," said Ilderim in ceremonial Arabic. "Peace be unto thee, lord. May thy tribe increase a thousandfold in the endless blessing of Allah."

Laiota was watching Ilderim closely. Always the handsome emir made the same impression on him. From his spiked Saracenic helmet with its chain mail neck guard, to his damascened breastplate and jeweled scimitar, to the pointed and turned up toes of his ornate oxhide boots he was the most resplendent military figure the Wallachian had ever seen. That he claimed descent from the conquering Sultan Saladin was unimportant—but the Turkish army he commanded was another matter. Laiota saw in that army his only chance.

"*Aleikum-es-salaam*," he responded in one of his few memorized phrases, and bowed again. "And unto thee also peace, great emir. May the wisdom of the Prophet Mohammed be ever thine."

At a gesture from Laiota, saddlecloths were spread for the visitors who now sat cross-legged in the Muslim fashion. Tea was brewed, for in obedience to Koranic law they drank no spirits. The prince waited politely for the Turkish leader to open the conversation.

"May it please thee, *sidi*," said Ilderim after a pause, "the *spahi* scouts have returned. They report no enemy activity across the river, no sign at all. In the absence of their expected reconnaissance patrols, perhaps we may conclude they've abandoned their offensive. On the other hand, they have proved themselves capable of great guile and this may be only another stratagem. I am inclined to believe the latter is correct. So are my emirs. We think the launching of their attack is therefore only a matter of time."

Laiota was thankful for Ilderim's conversance with Romanian, for his own Turkish was deplorable, the Arabic the other used for giving greeting or quoting the Koran even more so. Yet he was sure the man had not come here to speak of this alone. Each had liaison officers in the other's camp, each officer his own mounted courier, and this means had not been used. It was typical Turkish indirectness, he assumed, an almost Byzantine inscrutability. If this were Constantinople they would sit on silken cushions smoking those cursed water pipes called *nargilehs* and saying very little until the Ottomans were ready to reveal their minds. But this was Wallachia. Laiota tried to probe the other's thoughts.

"I have previously stated my belief that they will not come south of the Dambovita, general. They can avoid the marshes. That devil Dracula knows the terrain very well. But their army isn't large enough to flank us and they cannot deploy for a cavalry charge in the middle of a forest. In my opinion they will abandon the Impaler soon, Hungarians, Serbians, Moldavians, the lot of them. He will find himself holed up in Bucharest with his own personal guard and little else. Then we'll have him."

Ilderim appeared to consider. "Kazîglu Bey—taken as easily as that?"

"As easily as that."

Laiota was smiling. He was aware that the Ottoman spy network was widespread and efficient, that unknown Wallachian traitors in his own army served it secretly. Yet he, too, had his spies. That was how he knew that Ilderim concealed a Florentine stiletto in his right boot.

The Turk's beringed fingers drummed a light tattoo on his sword hilt. "Why should they betray him, *sidi?* He saved them from certain disaster at Vaslui. It was largely his generalship that gained for them both Tirgoviste and Bucharest. Demon or not, he is the best they have. Why would they withdraw after victory?"

"Because, my esteemed friend, their army is too small to do anything else. According to our agents, they had 40,000 men in the beginning. Now they have considerably less. Can they invade Turkish-held Bulgaria with *that?* Can they engage your sultan's main force with a fifth of the Ottoman strength? Matei is fighting the Poles and Bohemians. He does not closely watch the east. Stéfan faces unrest at home. Even Brancovic fears revolt in Sméderevo. Add to that the fact that Buda does not trust Dracula and never has, and you will see they have used him only as a tool to get rid of me."

"But they have let him become Prince of Wallachia again—for the third time."

"An empty gesture, Emir Ilderim, entirely without meaning. Mark you what I say, sir. Within a month they will withdraw the bulk of their forces and leave him dangling like a plucked chicken in the marketplace."

"Your Highness has men in Buda?"

"One man, at the moment. He confirms the existence of a conspiracy to rid themselves of this maggot once and for all."

"The Magyars—"

"They seem to be divided on the point. But all that really matters is Matei. He hates and despises him."

Ilderim pondered this information with pursed lips, glancing first at one of his emirs and then the other. "A cabal at the Hungarian court," he said softly. "Boyar plotters set on this man's death. I have come here tonight to urge a last stand, *sidi*, a final defense on the line of the Dambovita. You must know the reason. Sultan Mehmed, may Allah enrich him, will not suffer the enemy to enter the land of the Bulgars. He has given orders. If they cross the Danube—it is to be over the body of the last of my soldiers. Now—"

"Now you know they will never cross it."

"I would like to be able to believe it, *sidi*."

"You *shall* believe it!" Laiota had seen the remaining commanders arrive. Now he got to his feet as his own generals and the Turks followed suit. "Watch what I do," he said. "By your leave, my emir, I will show you how to light a fire that no power this side of hell can quench! Aye, look you, a conflagration that will burn Kazîglu Bey to ashes!"

As officers of many other ranks gathered round a rapidly forming circle of generals and emirs, Laiota was approached by a captain of horse and a common soldier, both Wallachians and seemingly together. He returned their salutes. He knew the officer by name. Normally, he would have made him wait, but there was something in the look of him—

"Captain Antonescu? You come from the forward area, do you not? Is the enemy on the move?"

The cavalryman made a negative gesture. "No, Your Highness. But this archer, Creanga by name, is the bearer of important tidings. He had a comrade who was wounded when we lost Tirgoviste, a bowman like himself who has since died. He says the man told him that he killed General Luca."

Laiota was not sure he had heard the other correctly. "General—General Luca?"

"General Vasili Luca, my lord. The Pretender's comrade-in-arms from the time of his second reign. Creanga swears that the archer Lucian Costin killed him with a single bowshot."

Aware of the eyes of many army leaders upon him, Laiota turned to the bowman. He said, "You have the look of an honest man, Creanga. What made your friend Costin so sure he had killed General Luca?"

Seemingly overawed in the midst of so much authority the soldier answered nervously. "It was the horse, Your Highness, a big white Arab like no other. Most everyone knows that animal by now. The men used to lay wagers on who would bring him down first."

"Did anyone collect?"

"Your Highness?"

"Was the horse killed?"

"Yes, Your Highness. Costin was sore hit but he remembered that. The stallion took three arrows in the side. The general was lung shot."

"Very well. Thank you, captain. You were right about the importance of this. I charge you to make sure that Creanga gets an extra food ration for the next three days."

Antonescu bowed. "Yes, my lord," he said. "I'll see to it."

Laiota immediately turned to the waiting men who surrounded him and mounted a low prominence. The Turks were on the outside of the ring, he noted, a place they might be glad to be when they saw his intention. He saw Ilderim staring at him fixedly. Why did the man always call him *sidi*, the Arabic word for *lord?* Why not a Turkish title? Then he realized his mind grasped at trivia to avoid the main issue, the question of how his own generals would respond. If they thought what he would propose a fool's notion they would lose all respect for him. It could divest him of moral authority with the Wallachians and cost him his leadership over them.

"Renowned emirs of Islam's glorious Crescent," he said. "Feel free to attend as spectators of what we will do, or to withdraw if you choose, or to join us as our valiant brothers in arms. Wallachians. Commanders of my army. Hear me. On the far side of the Dambovita lies the enemy. They have taken cities from us and forced us into retreat, and now we stand with the Danube and the Bulgarian border not far to our rear. These are *our* lands they wrest from us, not theirs. Some of you have lost your fathers and mothers. Some have seen your sisters raped. Your wives, too. And the stakes, my friends, will you ever forget them? Will you forget who it was who planted them by the thousand in the blood-drenched soil of Wallachia?"

He paused for the effect he knew this would have. Directly before him he saw the rugged faces of two old acquaintances, the *haiducs* Ion Laurianu and Alexandru Millian, robber barons from the depths of the Mad Forests of Vlasie, warlords with their own private armies who had joined him out of hatred of Dracula. He decided to enlist their aid.

"I see two great *haiducs* before me and honor you both. Which of you will tell me the name of the dog who has done this to us?"

Millian answered at once. "Your Highness, it is he who calls himself Wlasislaus Dragwlya."

Laiota was aware that Dracula sometimes signed his name thus in Old Slavic. "Otherwise Dracula, am I right? The self-styled Prince of Wallachia who claims the title of Vlad III?"

"Dracula," said Millian. "Yes, my lord. Vlad Tepes, the madman who impales women and children. We are not likely to forget him."

Laiota drew his poniard and held it aloft in the firelight. Against the high walls of the cave there flickered the immense shadow of an armed giant, a creature out of myth whose silhouette seemed to ebb and flow like a tide among a forest of hanging stalactites.

"Nor have *I* forgotten him!"

Laiota knew that he rose above himself stentorianlike, that never before had he been so commanding, so desperately driven, so like an Olympian god. It was the force of destiny he felt grip him and bear him upward, and somehow he knew instinctively that they, too, would surrender to its mighty surge. Like a man possessing the suppleness of his vanished youth he leaped down from the natural platform and confronted them at close quarters.

"He has lost General Luca," he told them. "A man who saw him killed has just reported it. And Luca was his *luck*. His death is an omen. Draw your daggers!" It was not a request but a command. "Join me hand to hand and brother to brother in a blood oath. We will *kill* Dracula! We will kill him at all hazards! Nothing will stop us! Nothing! Nothing! *Nothing!*"

They responded to a man. Only the Turks held back, staring at them in intense curiosity as officer after officer pricked the flesh of his palm with the point of his blade and brought it against the palm of another, the group quickly forming an extended and unbroken chain around their divinely inspired prince.

"Dracula!" thundered Laiota. "Dracula is his name! The Son of the Devil! The Son of Satan! On the sacred blood of our fathers we swear to kill him! On the graves of our revered ancestors we swear it! On the tombs of the honored dead of Wallachia we swear it! Swear! Swear! *Swear!*"

Like a great sighing exhalation they responded to him.

"We swear!"

"Swear it!"

"We swear it!"

"And when, short of killing him, will we abandon this solemn resolution? I say—*never!*"

In one voice they gave him their answer.

"Never! Never! *Never!*"

Still bleeding, yet highly exhilarated by this scene he rightly regarded as a signal triumph, Laiota made his way through cheering supporters to where the Turks were standing.

"Emir Ilderim, you saw?"

The Ottoman commander bowed to his Wallachian ally with obvious respect. "I saw, *sidi*."

"And do you believe?"

The Muslim smiled. "I believe. I believe, also, that another popular myth was dispelled tonight. The first was that Sultan Mehmed, may Allah defend him, is a coward. That was given the lie at Constantinople, the Trebizond, and Karamania. According to the royal astrologers it will be again—in the Mediterranean."

"And the second myth?"

"That there are weaknesses in your character, *sidi*. I saw nothing but strength."

Now it was Laiota who bowed. "Thank you," he said quietly. "When I bring thee the severed head of Dracula, O Lion of Islam, the world can decide whether or not you are right."

Ilderim glanced at Achmed ibn Aziz, then at Kara Ekrem. Still again he expressed his thoughts in the Arabic of the divine Koran. "*Inshallah*," he said. "As God wills."

11
The Last Battle

In this frozen world of cloud-filtered moonlight the sharp crunch of his boots on the lake's ice was the only sound. He was alone. There was no Vasili now with whom to converse; no Stéfan to remind him of his vanished youth; no wife to warn him in the dark of the night when the demons of hell gathered round his bed to mock him and he felt the coldness of the grave filter slowly into his bones.

He had never once brought Valeria to Wallachia, and on this nocturnal walk above unsounded black depths he at last knew why. Knew it positively. It was because of the strength of his presentiment that death awaited him here. Yes, *here* at the monastic island of Snagov, and very soon; or at his new capital of Bucharest only a few miles away; or between the two, perhaps, somewhere in the Mad Forests of Vlasie hard by the Dambovita; or across that river to the west, near Balteni where they killed his father.

No, he had never brought Valeria. She was Princess of Wallachia but he dared not let her sit beside his throne and share his risk. She stayed in Sibiu with their sons; and his other son, Gherghina, had been found as by a miracle, brought to Bucharest by the peasant who raised him in Arefu; and that was good; and God had been kind; but he, Dracula, was nearly at the end of his long and bloody trail—and he knew it.

He stopped and stood very still. In the shimmering lunar radiance he could see his own exhaled breath. *Why* had the armies deserted him? Had Matei been false from the start, using this whole campaign only as a means of ensuring his destruction? No other explanation fit, did it? Yes, the king was fighting the Poles, even the diehard Bohemians still, but they were at truce now. And Báthory had left him a small contingent, 3800 men, not even enough to expire with gracefully. And Stéfan had left him a personal guard of 200 more, Moldavians sworn to die for him. And that was the lot. Safe in Suceava, Stéfan could congratulate himself. He had lived to see Radu dead, extricated his own force from Wallachia, avoided further conflict with the Turks. He had even assuaged his conscience by providing "protection" for the cousin he had twice betrayed. Two hundred men.

"I am Dracula," he said aloud. "Will I be remembered? Tell me, O ye children of Mars. Give me my due." He spread his arms, raising his outstretched hands to the unresponding skies. "I am Dracula. I've existed since the morning of the world!"

From the shore of the lake he thought he heard the moaning of a light wind. Two hundred men. They were with him still, this gift of Stéfan. Even here they were with him. Looking toward Snagov Island he thought he could see them at the foot of the great wall, *his* wall, built by him as he also had fortified Bucharest. "Let us go with you, my lord," their commander had pleaded. "We are sworn to protect you to the end." And he had replied: "This walk I take alone. Only the stars and moon shall attend me." And now they stood by the wall, like a dark excrescence in their black cloaks; and they thought of home or their women or warm fires; and their teeth chattered; and their lives and their loyalty were his.

As he gazed, the clouds parted and the moonlight increased. Like a misty dream he could see rising above the lofty ramparts the three principal chapels now, including the one he had built. It was not like the others. It had a floor plan like the Moldavian monastery at Voronets, but without that structure's pointed spires and vividly purple wall paintings. It was taller than any of them, taller than the Chapel of the Annunciation that stood near it. That had been built by Vladislav II and he had killed him at Tirgsor twenty years ago, killed his Danesti kin there four years later. Did it matter in the eyes of God? There was *this* monument he would leave behind and there were others. Saint Nicholas Monastery was his work, built at Tirgsor in expiation for the sin of murder. Did the son of Dan II rest the easier for it? Did God add it to the account? Yes. All of it must mean *something*. He always gave them a chance to pray before death, did he not? He had never been a heathen unbeliever or intentional blasphemer. He was Dracula, and his head hurt him, and he was alone. If he stood here long enough, stood very still, maybe his body heat would melt the ice and he would break through it. How deep were the waters of Snagov Lake? How far would he go down into the unimagined watery void...and down...and down?

He began to walk back, trying hard not to slip, yet failing more than once and nearly falling. He was thinking of Laiota now. That Danesti dog was really a cat and had nine lives; or maybe a reincarnation of Fat Frumos, the ancient chief god of the Dacians. How could he have lived so long and survived so much? Was he immortal as some said? No. Only he, Dracula, was that. They could kill Vlad Tepes, yet he would live on as one of the undead, as *moroi*, like the Red Tower, the castle at Turnu Rosu that legend said was indestructible. But Basarab Laiota? He survived because the Turks were loyal to his cause, true to their own cause of crushing the Draculesti. Ilderim Effendi would fight to the end for that and he still had 20,000 troops. Kazîglu Bey had 4000. Nearly inevitable was Mehmed's final victory.

His footfall, breaking the crust of the snow, seemed louder now. December, 1476; a few days before Christmas. Would he live to see the coming year? Why was he visiting Snagov? Did he think they would attack Bucharest and take it, that he was safer in this place? What a cowardly thought. But no poltroon, he; no craven cur; no, not once. He had come here to pray in the chapel he had built, to pray *here* because *he* had built it. In Bucharest he had built walls and embrasures and firing pits for additional cannon, not churches. But here in this great monastic complex he had fortified and expanded he was closer to God. Still, it *could* withstand a siege. It had its own water supply, constantly replenished by springs; tons of dried fish and fruit were stored in its cellars; so was unleavened bread baked by the monks, virtually imperishable. Add to these the numerous stores of gunpowder and—

"We are here, Your Highness! Here! We will light a torch for you!"

As though it came from only a few paces away, he heard the shout very clearly. Captain Victor Cuza's voice. A yellow flame flared in the night. He saw greaves and breastplates; Castilian-type Moldavian morions, the faces beneath them white in the sudden glare; behind them the black prominence of the high, crenellated wall.

"I am here!" he called. Then, coming up to them, "You are late with your flame, Cuza. Why did you not light it earlier?"

The Moldavian officer saluted. "We had flint and steel but the tinder was wet, Your Highness. A soldier had to be sent within the walls for more."

"Attend me," said Dracula.

"My lord."

"How deep is this lake, think you?"

"No one knows, Highness."

"Not even in the villages round about? Calugareni? Vadul Parvului?"

"I think not, my lord. Nor at Stroesti. But they might know at Turbati. They have a soothsayer there, a venerable sage who is very wise. They say he is truly an oracle."

Dracula smiled. "I need no oracle to tell me the depth of a lake. You are shaking. Are you cold?"

"Freezing, my lord. We are all freezing."

"One question more. Radu's boyars took Snagov in 1462, fourteen years ago. They hid their riches in its churches. According to the peasants hereabouts, the monks eventually buried this treasure in the lake to keep it out of Turkish hands. The monks deny it, of course. Those robed and tonsured sons of perdition lie with great finesse. Have you heard aught of this?"

Cuza was plainly puzzled. He said, "Your Highness, we are Moldavians, only visitors here in your land of Wallachia. How can we know what is unknown to you?"

"How would you defend this place, captain? Suppose they were to attack across the ice. Suppose they came in moonlight, just as now."

"I would cannonade them, my lord."

"Men spread out as skirmishers make poor targets for cannon, especially at night. Why not depress your barrels enough to fire in front of them? Why not use heavy shot to break the ice beneath them? Why not drown them?"

Despite his increased trembling Cuza bowed a second time. "Your Highness is plainly a great tactician," he said, his voice sounding thin in the frigid air.

Dracula laughed lightly. "And I will not even charge you for the lesson. Come, let us inside before our guts freeze solid."

Cuza saluted again. "Your Highness." He turned to his company of silent men and bawled a command. "Moldavians! You will follow us at rout step in single file. Close order. You pikemen, take up the rear and stay alert. God of my life, look alive there! Have you forgotten we are still at war? Don't count on the picket line to keep the enemy away from Snagov. The sluggards among you are courting arrows in the back. Close up! Close up!"

Arriving at the postern gate they were challenged by the sentry there, challenged again within the walls before they came to the great keep, the most massive structure of the recently completed fortifications. Here the troops were dismissed to quarters. With Cuza and a subaltern named Rebreanu, Dracula entered the torch-blackened confines of the place and led the way to the guardroom. There he ordered hot wine for himself and the captain as Cuza's subordinate rebuilt the fire on the hearth.

"How fares our Turk-loving robber?" he asked. "Is he ready for the questioning?"

Cuza shook his head. "A henchman of the *haiduc* Millian is not a good subject for it, Your Highness," he said. "They are all arrant knaves and madmen, these mountain brigands, even madder for allying themselves with Laiota. Methinks this one will die under torment before his tongue be loosened."

Dracula frowned deeply. "Is he so stout as that?"

"Aye, my lord. They all are. But what can be expected of murderers and robbers? Stubborn to lunacy."

"And the girl?"

"She is another matter, Highness. We have but to show her the instruments of persuasion and she will chirp like a magpie, my word on it."

"But does she *know* anything, captain?"

"She might, my lord. As field concubine to a *spahi* general she may have heard things. The man may have spoken in his sleep. 'Tis not impossible. I vow she should be carefully interrogated."

They drank slowly. Both were still shaking from the cold. Dracula thought of other times and places where prisoners were to be questioned. But never as now. Never before with so fine a line between life or death hanging in the balance. What were the enemy intentions? When would they come against him? Did they already know that Báthory, Stéfan, and Brancovic had pulled out, that the dreaded Vlad Tepes had almost nothing left with which to maintain his position in Wallachia? When did they plan to move north? His cavalry patrols had discovered nothing. Nothing.

Out of the corner of his eye he saw an Orthodox monk enter the room silently. Father Titu. Taking his position by the wall, the man stood quietly with folded arms under the long sleeves of his robe, a silent reminder of the power of the church he served, a church still holding firm in Wallachia though its prince was now an apostate Catholic. Dracula ground his teeth in suppressed anger. He trusted no cleric of whatever faith, yet the continuing presence of Orthodoxy in his land made him look ridiculous. He had wanted to break them, drive them out, replace them with Augustinians or Benedictines, aye, even Cistercian or Carmelite friars with their insufferable holiness and insane dogma. *Anything!* But the certainty of a peasant revolt held his hand, so nothing had changed. Orthodox monasteries prevailed here as they always had. Their monks were crawling all over the place like ants, nearly three score of them. He wondered how many were the paid informers of Matei Corvinus, hence traitors to Wallachia. How many would willingly collaborate with a victorious Ilderim and Laiota? He imagined them discreetly crossing themselves whenever he appeared, intoning secret incantations as though he carried some dread contagion.

Suddenly he shoved his wine aside, spilling it, and got to his feet, his eyes flashing fire. "This foul sputum of the *haiducs*, is he still in his cell or already with the tormentors?"

Cuza also rose. "In his cell, Your Highness."

"Very well. Have him taken to the dungeons at once. Tell Orszagh to secure him to the rack but to do nothing until I get there. If that Hungarian hellhound and his two loathsome acolytes cannot loosen the dog's tongue, look you, I have some methods of my own that may suffice. There is the *cordeles*, for example, what English seamen call the Spanish windlass. With that we can screw the eyes out of his head."

"I obey, my lord." Cuza seemed to hesitate. "What of the girl?"

"Where is she?"

"Still in your private quarters under guard, Your Highness."

"She can wait." Dracula licked his lips voluptuously. "She will not spoil, I take it?"

"No, my lord."

"Good. I will join you below."

Cuza saluted. "Your Royal Highness."

Dracula delayed only long enough to go to the stable and personally see to the feeding of Icarus, an act that had become a habit with him. He seemed to think more clearly when with his horse, to be unusually calm, as though the warmth of the great animal was somehow transmitted to the body and soul of its owner. Ten minutes later, with Cuza and Rebreanu, the Impaler stood in the torture chamber with its flaming brands, the hideous realm of the muscular Orszagh and his depraved assistants. The prisoner, a wiry, hair-covered Wallachian named Nicolae Sima, lay supine on the rack, shackled and helpless.

"We can take you apart by inches," said Dracula, "remove your eyes, lop off your nose and ears, or do other things of exquisite refinement. Have you noticed my iron maiden standing against the wall? She is beautiful with all her lovely spikes, is she not? German made, you know. She comes from Nürnberg where they make the clocks and she herself moves by clockwork. We simply put you inside her, Sima. Ah the sheer ecstasy of her embrace as she closes upon your body with infinite slowness. The spikes can be adjusted, you see. The eyes and genitals are much favored to receive her caresses. But she will kiss thee only once, thou traitor dog, and that I promise you!"

He paused to let the full import of his words sink in. "Well, speak, man. Will you answer our questions or enjoy the favors of our lady?"

The prisoner was already sweating despite the chill in the air. "I have already told your officer that I know nothing," he said staunchly. "Military plans of the Turks and Laiota? I am not a soldier, Prince Vlad, but only a follower of Alexandru Millian. We are not an army."

"You have 3000 armed men. Horses and weapons."

"These are for protection, Your Highness, to defend our land."

"Oh? And that is why you ride with the Danesti pretender and his Turkish friends?"

"Who else will help us?"

Dracula came close to the captive and laid his fingertips on his naked abdomen. "You are merely flesh and blood," he said ominously. "Do you think you can withstand this?"

Sima closed his eyes, then opened them again. "I can but try. I have said I know nothing. How can I answer you?"

"Have you heard of the Italian despot, Galeazzo Maria Sforza?"

"No."

"He is Duke of Milan. They say he can make a man eat himself. Oh yes. One roasted piece of meat at a time. We also have that capability, for I have studied his methods. I, you see, am no more kind than he."

Sima said nothing. He stared at the high-beamed ceiling now as though his mind were far away. Dracula found him unusual, almost a sort of enigma.

"Of course, you might prefer the greater delicacy of the tyrant called Ferrante. You do know of him, do you not?"

The prisoner said nothing.

"He holds the title of Ferdinand I and has the esteemed privilege of kingship in south Italy. He is a gentle soul, so gentle they call him the Beast of Naples. One of his favorite sports is to starve his victims to death in iron cages suspended above the city streets, an infernally slow process. He also has them mummified and preserved, would you believe that? There is a sequestered hall in his palace where he keeps them on display for his more select guests. Now there is a singular conceit. Just fancy that."

Sima remained mute.

"By God, you have made your decision!" Dracula exclaimed. "Before I am done, my tight-lipped churl, you will wish your horse had carried you to hell instead of so foolishly close to our lines."

"As his grandsire might have carried you."

Dracula was gesturing to Orszagh to prepare the iron maiden for use. Now he turned and stared at the captive. "What did you say?"

Sima jerked against his bonds. He had raised his head and was trying to look at the prince. "You spoke of my horse, Deucalion. As you see, he bears the name of a Titan."

"Deucalion? Yes, a son of Prometheus. And what of that?"

"Do you not think it odd, prince, that a horse breeder knows of such things?"

"A horse—"

"Yes, I breed them, and my father before me. The name was suggested by a learned monk, one Father Grigore. It is because my mount's grandsire was the most noble of them all, a steed you knew once—and honored."

Dracula could hardly breathe. He spoke very quietly. "Name this animal."

Sima nodded. "I will," he said. "Deucalion is out of a thoroughbred mare by a black stallion named Endymion. He, too, came from purebred stock, the finest blacks ever foaled in Wallachia."

"And his sire?"

"Your great warhorse, Strigoi."

"You are a liar!"

"Prove I'm a liar, prince."

"I would have known of this."

Sima lay back and licked at his dry lips. He said, "Strigoi was bred just once before you left for the Dobrogea. You cannot have been unaware of it. The mare's name was Titania, a black like the others. She was purchased in Transylvania by your general, Radului. Her foal was dropped the following spring."

"And you came by Deucalion—how?"

"I saved the *haiduc's* life in battle. He found the horse with a dead officer, who may have found it with yet another. He gave him to me in gratitude."

Dracula sensed the unease of the others in the chamber. Cuza, Rebreanu, Orszagh, all felt the strangeness of the conversation between prince and condemned prisoner. Even Orszagh's dehumanized torturers, so animalistic in their dumb gestures, seemed to share the general puzzlement. Yet it was true. It *had* to be true, and he had seen the huge beast Sima had ridden into captivity. Three hands taller than most of his breed he was. Black as the night he was, from mane to fetlocks. Strigoi his grandsire? Nay, by the eternal God, not so! It was reincarnation. Destiny. The great black now waiting quietly in the stable, waiting for *him*—was Strigoi himself.

He could feel his own body trembling as his eyes fastened on the captive. "I believe you," he said. "I want you to give me this animal."

Sima's back muscles were starting to cramp and his breathing was being affected. "Take what you want," he gasped. "How can I prevent you?"

Dracula felt an intense yearning coupled with a sense of maddening urgency. "You don't comprehend," he said. "I cannot take him by force. You must give him to me of your own free will. Do you agree to that?"

"Your Highness is very persuasive."

"He is mine?"

"Of course."

Instantly the Impaler turned to Cuza. "See that this man is released at once," he said, "and unharmed. Give him hot wine, rations for three days, a warm cloak, and a good horse. A *good* horse, mark you. Detail one of your best men to take him through our lines—and free him."

The captain appeared dumbfounded. "Your Highness, I—"

"You look sick. Can it be I have been obscure?"

Cuza cleared his throat noisily, then seemed to find his voice. "No, my lord. I—understand."

"Then carry out my order."

"Yes, my lord. Uh—what of the girl?"

"What did you say her name was?"

"Anna Olahus, Highness."

"Oh yes. She who wandered too far from the camp for water. The little foolish one. Shall I tell you what she told me? Oh yes, I questioned her. She said she is not the concubine of Emir Ibrahim but an ordinary camp follower he won at a toss of dice. She does not speak Turkish and never understood a word he said."

"Then why—?"

"Why did I not release her at once? Because she is fair to look upon and I am lonely, Cuza. Yes, even I. For a brief moment, an hour perhaps, I may have thought she knew something of enemy intentions. Now I say she does not—nor does Sima here. And I have one other observation to make. Would you care to hear it?"

"Yes, my lord."

"It is simply this. If the two of them knew all of the foe's plans that there is to know—in the end it would make no difference. Do you follow me?"

"I think so, Your Highness."

"Very well. On the morrow, I will take Anna Olahus back to Bucharest with us and install her there as my consort, temporarily."

He waited only until Sima had been unshackled, then left the dungeon and ascended to ground level. Passing between the monks he found conversing, he experienced a nearly overwhelming sense of joyful fulfillment, as though some lost thread of his life had been found again and grasped. Seemingly impervious to the cold now he left the keep unattended, heading for the stable—and Strigoi.

To students of history the year 1476 might well prove fascinating, for by the time it had arrived, many of the movers and shakers of the international scene had arrived as well or were shortly to do so. Soon to grace the world of art as few others, in the village of Caprese in Tuscany, a year-old male infant still suckled at his mother's breast. His name was Michelangelo Buonarroti. In less than a year, the painter Tiziano Vecellio (Titian) would be born in Venice. In only seven years, a creative phenomenon named Raffaello Santi (Raphael) would first see the light in the city of Urbino, a man destined to do great things in a very short span of years.

The time was ripe also for incredibly bold adventure, the founding of vast overseas empires, and the greatest period of exploration in the ages-old human saga. Ponce de León, Diego de Velázquez, and Pedro Cabral were all sixteen years old. Giovanni Caboto (John Cabot) was fifteen. Juan Cabrillo's year of birth is unknown, but he was very young. Vasco da Gama had reached the age of seven. Francisco Pizarro was six. Vasco Nuñez de Balboa was one year old; Ferdinand Magellan would be born in four years; Hernán Cortes in nine. Thanks to the prodigious efforts and sacrifices of men such as these, the foundations of both British and Portuguese power would be laid through the discoveries of Cabot and Cabral, respectively, and in less than two generations the Spanish Empire, rapidly outstripping its rivals, would bestride the world like a colossus.

What, in the meanwhile, was to be the fate of Eastern Europe? Put succinctly, it was to become Turkish. By the year 1481, the Ottoman Empire would include not only Anatolia (Turkey proper), the Trebizond in Hither Asia, and the Khanate of the Crimea, but all of Rumelia (Albania, Macedonia, and Thrace), Bulgaria, Wallachia, Serbia, and Bosnia. By 1520, with the acquisition of Syria and Egypt, it had doubled in size. By 1556, Moldavia and all of Hungary had fallen to Turkish arms in Europe; in the Middle East, Armenia and the western remnants of the Persian Empire in the Tigris-Euphrates Valley; in northwest Africa, the territories ruled for centuries by successive Arab and Berber dynasties, now consolidated under Ottoman rule as the vast Pashalik of Tripoli.

Not until 1571 was Turkish dominance successfully challenged. As might have been expected, the gage of battle was thrown down by the only major sea powers then in Christendom, Spain and Venice, assisted by the papacy and a number of other Italian city-states, primarily Genoa. The fleet of this Holy League, consisting of about 200 galleys (not counting lesser craft) and 30,000 men, met a Turkish fleet of similar size and strength off Lepanto (Návpaktos in the Greek) in the strait connecting the Gulf of Corinth with that of Patras. The result was an overwhelming Christian victory. As concerned the halting of further Islamic expansion in Europe, nothing so decisive had occurred since the year 732 when the Frankish king Charles Martel (the grandfather of Charlemagne) defeated the Moors of Spain in the Battle of Tours or Poitiers.

But in 1476 the victory of Lepanto lay still in the future. What then of the man who alone among Balkan rulers stood like a rock against Muslim expansion for a protracted period of time? To write Dracula off as simply one of history's enthroned madmen is greatly to oversimplify what was in reality an extraordinarily complex personality. Mad he certainly was. Simple he was not. Nor does the truth of his ending, whatever it may have been, lend itself readily to simplistic explanations. For one thing, his death smacks strongly of a peculiar form of self-punishing masochism leading to suicide. For another, he almost certainly could have prevented it.

In his book *The Truth about Dracula*, the Hungarian scholar Gabriel Ronay writes as follows: "Dracula's greed and his indiscriminate butchery of the free people of Transylvanian towns, with their charters of rights and royal tax exemptions, proved his downfall, for eventually the Saxon merchants turned the wrath of the mighty Hungarian King Matthias [Matei] Corvinus against him."

This is true as far as it goes, for there is little doubt that Matei planned to kill the Impaler or that Hungary's sudden withdrawal of support achieved that result in the end. However, it is clear that had there still been a Wallachian army in being under Dracula's command, Buda's treachery would have had small result. In the final analysis it was not the action of foreigners that destroyed Dracula but his abandonment by his own people. For never once down the centuries, from the mad Nebuchadnezzar in his meadow to the brooding Napoleon on his island, was any ruler more totally forsaken. Not only had his own boyars turned against him long before, fighting first for Radu, then for Laiota, and always in alliance with the Turks, but the Romanian common people—who in his twisted way he may have loved—thoroughly and finally repudiated him, only to turn about ultimately and honor him in folklore. Lest anyone be left in doubt, moreover, the greed to which Ronay refers was not primarily for money or material possessions. It was for power.

The behavioral pattern Dracula developed after his defeat in the Dobrogea and the subsequent loss of the remainder of his army was curious to say the least. Geographically speaking, his power base had been founded on an obtuse triangle extending from Tirgoviste to Castle Dracula (the Castle of Agrish) to the ecclesiastical see of Curtea-de-Arges, the latter representing religious authority in the land as the capital city and citadel on the river did political and military. Once this area was overrun by the Turks in 1462 there was nothing left, no core of sovereignty on which to rebuild royal might. A rational man might have retired at this point. Flight not only from the conquered principality but from the country would have been indicated; indeed, as far west as France or even

England, which were both Catholic nations then. For Dracula was a marked man and the arm of his enemies was long.

But what did he do in this most dire and threatening of crises? One has the impression that relinquishing his claim to the throne of his fathers was the furthest thing from his mind. A gambler all his life, at this juncture he wagered yet again, entrusting his future to the very chancy speculation that the Hungarian king would not only offer him asylum and welcome him as an ally but would eventually join him in the reconquest of Wallachia.

If Dracula was psychotic, he was certainly not stupid. In fact, his grasp of both Balkan and Hungarian politics was such that his arrest at Königstein and subsequent imprisonment at Vàcz and Vísegràd must have come as no surprise to him. Yet, given this likelihood from the start and knowing the nature of the odds he faced, he *still* put himself in the hands of a man he had no reason to trust. It was not the first time he had done such a thing. One recalls his flight to Suceava after his first defeat as a youth and his appeal for sanctuary to Prince Bogdan. After the latter's murder he again became a fugitive. This time he sought shelter and aid from a more doubtful source, appearing virtually unattended at Hunedoara Castle to seek the protection of János Hunyadi. In the early years the steadfast fatalism on which his gambling instinct was based proved an occasional advantage. Once his power had been eroded, however, it could serve only to hasten his inevitable undoing, as the event proved.

One cannot help but speculate on the almost mystical relationship between Dracula and the island of Snagov. In the Arthurian legend, one of the most strange and beautiful of Celtic mythology, the saga speaks of the Isle of Avalon (today believed by most historians and archaeologists to have been Glastonbury in Somerset), where the wounded and dying King Arthur was transported by three chimerical queens. It was there that Arthur's deadly sister and Merlin's pupil Morgan le Fay dwelled, and from there that prophecy said he would return. As has been mentioned earlier, in the case of Dracula there is a similar legend. He died of his wounds. He was the savior of his people. At the time of their greatest need he would come back as surely as any miraculous avatar of Hindustan. If Romanian folkloric superstition were ever to be fulfilled, the most logical place for his magical reappearance would be Snagov. Indeed, it is there that peasants now living expect that they or their descendants will some day see him, perhaps emerging phoenixlike from the lake.

With this island and its ecclesiastical foundation the Draculas had long been associated. Most historians believe the original monastery was built either by Dracula's grandfather, Mircea cel Bătrîn (Mircea the Old) or by a powerful contemporary boyar, and it is known from the chronicles that Mircea established a princely residence there. Nonetheless, it was undoubtedly Dracula who fortified the place, just as one of the three chapels that existed in his day may definitely be credited to his founding. From the island's length of roughly a mile to its breadth of half a mile at its widest point, the Impaler raised his fortifications, wall upon embrasure-pierced wall, watchtower upon watchtower, all of it protected by the natural moat of the surrounding lake itself. Did he regard it as an impregnable sanctuary, a last-ditch redoubt to which he could retreat should an enemy army take Bucharest? It is virtually certain that he did. For in him was the knowledge that all tyrants have, the assurance that the chief emotion they arouse in mankind is that of universal hatred. Such men almost invariably plan their retreats in advance.

It was early morning. The winter frost invested the air. Along the crenellated battlements that encircled Bucharest, the sentries paced as always, half-numb with the chill. In the great hall of the fortress Dracula sat alone, confronted by ghosts. Sometimes they came to him singly, forlorn figures out of the grim past who would stand and stare awhile, then disappear. Sometimes there was more than one. Always they were diaphanous, shot through with light, as incorporeal as air. Normally they were mute. Occasionally, it seemed to him, they left behind some tangible manifestation of reality, such as a cold spot in the room that did not dissipate for hours, yet to which only he was sensitive. He wondered if this was how it would end. Visions. Hallucinations. A glass of wine in a hand growing ever more numb. A power from another world that would strike it from his fingers. Then just a tired prince in a high-backed chair, his sightless eyes fixed on the infinite.

Or would he *rise up in glory* and smite his enemies one last time? Would he, like Samson, spread his arms out of the stygian night of his blindness, break their granite columns, and pull down their temple upon them?

He got up and began to pace. One friend had come back as more than a specter. Strigoi. He graced the stables now, the finest of his breed that ever carried Christian knight into battle. Should he bring him to his bedchamber as Caligula had done with Incitatus? No. Why should he ape a Roman emperor? Strigoi would understand. Strigoi waited. He was covered by the richest of blankets embroidered with gold thread but he did not need them. Did gods require protection from the ravages of the elements? Would the winged steed Pegasus have felt the cold? What was Strigoi or himself for that matter but illusion, as Olympus itself had been. Prince and beast existed in time but not in space. Neither had substance or reality. Arrows, spears, scimitars could never harm them, no grave claim them. They were *immortal!* Strigoi and the Son of the Devil would ride forever—far, far into realms of the unknown and beyond to the most distant reaches of the universe. Who then were the Turks or traitor boyars to confront and oppose them? Could man and steed stoop even to war with such mortals? If Mehmed were here in this room with him now, he would reduce him to cinders with his glance. Ah the sight and the feel of it. And men would say: "It was Dracula who did this. Dracula. When cometh such another?"

And the Divine Host would arrive for him and lead him upward through paths of eternal light, ever upward; and such glory would be his as few men envisaged in their wildest dreams.

He staggered and leaned against a table, breathless. He wanted to cry out but his vocal cords constricted in his throat as though he were slowly being throttled. At last he knew he was hopelessly mad. It struck him as monstrous that knowledge of his terrible affliction should seethe within his madness like a stream of cold wine coursing through his boiling blood, flowing relentlessly. Frightful enough it was to be insane, but to *feel* it within oneself was unendurable agony. He wished to weep but that relief was also denied him. He must call for General Kosary, the only officer of that rank in his tiny Hungarian force. Would they fight for him? Or would his call to battle be the prearranged signal for his assassination? It did not matter.

Summoning a steward, he spoke to him briefly. "Lay out my armor in my chamber and prepare to attend me," he said. "The helmet with the dragon crest. The dragon breastplate and shield. The sword with the dragon hilt. Send word to the grooms, also, that Strigoi is to be similarly caparisoned, the crest of my father's order on pommel, blanket, and stirrups."

The attendant bowed. "Will Your Highness dine before your departure?"

"No. No, I think not." Dracula paused. Slowly, deliberately, he raised his right hand and tightened the curl of his broad mustache with his fingers. "They say Hungarians are very astute, my good Jokai, that keen perception is a Magyar trait. Tell me this then. Do you think I am insane?"

The steward's mouth widened in the faintest of smiles. "Certainly not, my lord," he replied. "The mind of a sovereign prince can never be so tainted, for he rules by divine right."

Dracula nodded. "The Magyar reputation for shrewdness is well founded," he observed. "'Tis your honesty that is in question."

"Your Highness?"

"Tell General Kosary I wish to see him."

Jokai bowed again. "At once, my lord."

After the man had left, Dracula remained as motionless as before. In forty-five years of life he had memorized but one quotation from the New Testament, a passage from 1 Corinthians 13. Now, unbidden, it came to his mind. He spoke the words softly.

"When I was a child, I spake as a child, I understood as a child, I thought as a child; but when I became a man, I put away childish things. For now we see through a glass, darkly; but then face to face: now I know in part; but then shall I know even as also I am known."

He closed his eyes. Wandering through some dim recess of his brain other words came slowly to the fore, words for which he at first groped unavailingly. Then he grasped them. They were from a work with which he was less unfamiliar, Khayyám's *Rubáiyát*. These, too, he spoke in a kind of half-comprehended daze.

"I sent my soul through the Invisible, some letter of that after-life to spell: And by and by my soul returned to me, and answered 'I myself am Heaven and Hell.'"

He straightened his body. His eyes opened. "So be it," he murmured, and to his imagination the spacious room with its oaken beams and armorial panelings seemed to fill with tinkling silver bells. "We will ride against them, Strigoi. We will meet them as of old. Aye, though they be a host that blots out the horizon and the world—we will yet prevail."

Had Jokai been there to see and hear him, to judge his condition by the symptoms he displayed, that perceptive steward might have been smiling still.

"We are surrounded, my lord."

From the pale winter sun that gave no warmth, rays of shimmering light were filtering through the trees. In one of those rays General Bela

Kosary stood as though transfixed, his armor agleam with tiny motes of shifting luminescence. His tone seemed matter of fact, almost disinterested.

Leaning against the lightning-blasted trunk of a black oak, Dracula was watching him carefully. "With me it was ever thus," he said. "It was always the enemy who had numerical superiority, never Kazîglu Bey. That is *why* we are surrounded, general, is it not? We are 4000 men against five times that number. We had to give ground or be flanked. Encirclement was inevitable."

Kosary stepped out of the sunbeam, cleared his throat and spat. "'Tis as good a day as any on which to die," he said. "I understand your Moldavian royal guard has sworn to fight for you to the death, Your Highness. Or rather, they were committed to this by Prince Stéfan. I must tell you that my Magyars are not so committed. Be that as it may, they do not relish the thought of Wallachian captivity, still less of Turkish. They will give a good account of themselves."

Dracula snatched at a buzzing fly and missed. He said, "In my youth I would have taken that singing insect on the wing. But we change, you see. We slow down. Perhaps you berate me in your mind."

"My lord?"

"We could have stayed in Bucharest behind our walls. My sortie invites open battle."

Kosary shook his head. "Call it a sortie, a reconnaissance in force, or merely a country stroll, Your Highness, it is all one. A few more days at most. We know that Mahmud Pasha is sending them siege engines, a great array coming by river. They will knock down the walls and gut the place. A sack is not a pretty thing to see. I would rather be here."

"You show a noble indifference to death."

"I am a soldier, my lord, and the son and grandson of soldiers. I am reminded of my lineage. There is Hunnic blood in most Magyars. Aye, dating back to Attila. Death is an illusion."

Dracula wet his lips. "So I have always thought."

He was looking at his Moldavians now, his devoted 200, or the eight score or so who remained. To his right and left and to his rear they were, the nearest of them only a few paces away. They were all skilled archers. Now they used trees as cover and waited, as certain to be overrun as they were to take a heavy toll of the attacking enemy before they died. That enemy was invisible and had been so since the last skirmish. That was the curse of fighting in forest country. And what forest was thicker than the Vlasie? What concealment more total than this, cover so dense the foe could be within easy bowshot yet unseen? He turned to Kosary again.

"Who do we have to our direct front?" he asked. "Turks or Wallachians?"

"Last night it was Turks, Your Highness."

"I know that. I speak of now. This moment."

"I think they are Wallachians. Laiota himself and most of his boyars."

"And why do you think so?"

Kosary unbuckled his chin strap, took off his steel casque and scratched his head. He struck a fly, smashed it, and smiled with satisfaction. "Because, given a choice, the Turks have no taste for a frontal attack. Too wasteful of men. Their greatest victories were won by flank action."

"And Laiota?"

"It boots nothing to him either way, my lord. It has to be foot on this terrain. Cavalry is useless. His chief concern is to make good his boast."

"Which is?"

"That he will kill you, Your Highness. Surely, you have not forgotten the blood oath they swore. Our spies—"

"Oh yes, I remember now. More than mere bravado, think you?"

The general considered. He said, "Yes, more than that. Laiota has been made to look the fool repeatedly, especially when we drove him from Tirgoviste. Now he has his chance. The withdrawal of Báthory and Stéfan—"

"Was treason!"

Kosary blinked. He replaced his helmet and fastened the strap. "An unfortunate decision," he conceded. "We will pay dearly for it."

Dracula stared at him steadily. "They are in violation of their sworn oath. Their signatures and seals were worth less than the vellum they put them to. They are dishonored."

What the officer might have said was left unspoken. Both men turned as Captain Cuza approached and saluted.

"Your Highness, the scouts report enemy movement to the direct and right front," said Cuza. "To all appearances they are massing for an attack."

Dracula regarded the Moldavian levelly. "Fetch my horse," he said.

Cuza glanced quickly at Kosary. "Your horse, my lord?"

"Strigoi, damn you! Get him for me!"

"He is not with us, Highness. All the horses save those of the mounted scouting patrols were left in camp."

"Not with us."

"No, my lord."

For the first time since leaving Bucharest, which still lay so near, Dracula felt the clutch of augury. Inexorably fixed. Implacably hostile. Had he known of this? He could not remember.

"Kosary," he said quickly. "You had best rejoin your troops. I shall expect it of you, that *good accounting*."

The general saluted. "You shall have it, Your Highness," he said.

The Impaler watched the man disappear into dense foliage. "We cannot see, Cuza," he said. "That is our difficulty. 'Tis an old maxim of mine. I cannot fight an enemy unless I can see him."

As though he sensed something extraordinary was about to happen, Cuza's expression became clouded with concern. "My lord, the scouts—"

"Are subject to the handicaps that always plague mounted men in forest country. They see even less than we." Dracula was squinting in the strangely diffused light. Now he pointed. "That hill over there. The one with the very tall black oak at its summit. I will climb it to reconnoiter. You and your men may follow or not as you choose."

Cuza gazed in the direction indicated. "My lord, it is too open," he said in startled unbelief. "You must stay here to command! Suppose the attack comes—"

"The attack will come when I will it to come. Not before. Do you wish to accompany me, captain?"

In Cuza's eyes was the look of a brave man who knows that his fate is sealed. "Yes, Your Highness," he said resignedly. "We are duty bound never to forsake you."

"Good. Then gather your command and fall to."

"Your Highness."

As he made his way along a partially overgrown goat trail, Dracula saw the hill loom larger and knew he could climb it with ease. Once he glanced back to see the Moldavians not far behind him, all of them coming on in the old way, the way the Wallachians had done, their devotion of that high order that only Vlad Tepes could command. It made him proud. Laiota could not attack. Not yet. How could he act before his predestined moment?

In twenty minutes they had reached the hill's base and started up.

But now there was movement where there should have been none, the enemy maneuvering to his left. With most of the slope still above him he stopped and turned to face them. He called to Cuza.

"Kosary was right. That is the Pretender and his boyars out there. Archers at the ready, captain! Single targets as they present themselves!"

Cuza's acknowledgement was drowned in the familiar vibratory whir as the first of the enemy arrows sped toward them. Dracula saw a man pitch backward silently, his vocal cords destroyed by a shaft through the throat. Perhaps a dozen more fell at the same time. But this was folly, he knew. The boyar-led yeomanry was shooting at extreme range, sacrificing their effectiveness, causing nothing like the morale-shattering carnage of bowmen at a hundred paces. He *loved* to see archers duel. Their courage was greater than any man's because in the open they were nearly defenseless. They could not hold shields and shoot bows at the same time.

"Ho there!" he shouted. "Hear me, Moldavians! Wait until they break cover and enter that clearing! Then have at them!"

As he spoke he was moving forward, abandoning his own concealment, coming into the open as though impelled to do so by a force unknown. At the enemy rear there were mounted boyars, he saw, at least four of them bawling orders. Was one of them Laiota? The fools! What good were horses on this terrain? Now the foe was visible. *Highly visible* and advancing. Wait. Wait. He glanced to his right to see Cuza with his arm raised. Yes, be cool, thou paladin of Stéfan. Soft you now. Cuza's mouth was open. His command was a clarion call to battle.

"Archers! Shoot!"

Suddenly, the air seemed full of arrows. Thirty, forty, fifty of the enemy received them in their bodies and went down, leaving irregular gaps in their array. Dracula exulted. They should have been spread wider as skirmishers. Much wider. Their very numbers were a disadvantage. Still he walked forward. Now he, too, began to shout.

"Shoot! Now is your moment! Shoot, I tell you! Shoot! Shoot!"

Abruptly he stopped and stood still. Before him was a figure that gripped him in wonderment, freezing him in his tracks. It was a little girl. He saw her very clearly. She was naked. She had dark eyes that seemed to be full of tears, very large eyes that were fastened on him, in their lustrous beauty a fathomless sorrow that transcended woe itself. She held out her arms to him. Involuntarily, he too opened his arms.

"Don't cry!" he called. "Why weep you, child? I will help you! I am coming, don't you see? I will help you! I will—"

His voice seemed to die within him. She was close when it happened. One moment their gazes were locked in loving embrace. He saw every lineament of her countenance. Then very slowly she was turning. Her feet did not appear to move. She just turned—turned—turned—until her bare back was toward him and he saw what it was she revolved upon. An angel out of heaven—he knew it now—*impaled upon a stake!*

He screamed. He covered his eyes with his hands and screamed and screamed, then fell to his knees.

"Oh Father, forgive! Forgive! Forgive me, for I have *sinned!*"

It was then the first lance hit him. Like a red-hot flame he felt it burn through his left shoulder outside the breastplate. How—? One of the horsemen. He staggered to his feet and braced himself. Leaning forward on the shaft he snapped it off short. The solid thudding of hooves. He could hear them. Another one galloping. Coming at him. He drew his sword. Moisture filled his eyes. He could barely see. Yet out of a shining void the second lance came and like lightning he parried it with his blade; then a third, and he parried that. He was *invulnerable!* They would see. He felt nothing from the shoulder wound. Nothing. He was Dracula. He needed only his horse to cheat the end they had prepared for him, only his winged Pegasus.

"Strigoi!" he shouted. "Strigoi to me! Come you, my steed!"

He did not feel it penetrate. The first arrow was like a caress. It took him high in the right thigh above the steel cuisse. He broke it off and dropped it on the ground. Now infantry rushed him; *him*, the finest swordsman in the Balkans. Disengage. Thrust. Parry the riposte. One man down. Two of them. He gave ground, somehow keeping his feet. It seemed the energy of his youth had returned. Unquenchable. Demoniacal. Still at close quarters, the next enemy appeared literally to spit himself on his reeking blade. So did the next and the next. Then he heard a voice but could not see its owner. Strident. Commanding.

"Get away from him, you fools! Disengage, I say, and give us a clear target! Do you hear me? Stand clear of that man!"

Then there was no one to fight. Like a dispersing mist the opposition faded. Dracula found himself alone. He swayed like a drunken cripple. Looking up, he saw two separate suns, for a battle-ax had cleaved his helmet and its bent rim hung down. The same voice spoke again.

"Take your last look at him this side of hell! You may wish to describe this day to your progeny. Archers at the ready!"

Desperately he tried to hold to his hilt. The Norsemen. What had they believed? What had their *skalds* taught in all their sagas? No Viking could enter Valhalla without a sword in his hand, proof to the war god Odin of his valor. But he could not hold it. From nerveless fingers it fell to the ground, there to join the dark arterial blood still spurting from his thigh with every beat of his heart.

"I am Dracula!" he murmured, reeling to the onslaught of his own sudden feebleness. "I've existed from the morning of the world!"

Then the final command was given. "Archers! Shoot!"

The areas unprotected by armor were hit instantly: neck, armpits, groin. And Dracula fell. Within his seething brain a black, all-encompassing cloud boiled away into nothingness and all his yesterdays rolled into one. It was Basarab Laiota who raised a warning hand and held the others off.

"Touch him not! On your peril be it else! Do you harken to the sounds of battle? List thee well, all of you, for 'tis the last of his infamous cohort being slaughtered. Now stand ye witness to this. I, the Lord Laiota, the anointed and rightful Prince of Wallachia, do hereby keep the sacred oath I swore to the men of my army and our Turkish ally!"

His sword was in his hand. He raised it once and struck. Leaning down, he removed the damaged morion with its dragon crest, then took the head of Dracula by its long, graying hair and held it triumphantly aloft for all to see.

"Look you well upon it," he said. "'Tis the head of the usurper men have called the Impaler. The head of Dracula. Tyrant, apostate, pretender. Do not forget its appearance. It is my intention to send it as a gift to the sultan of Turkey. Very soon, therefore, it will be the chief attraction and amusement of the mighty citadel of Constantinople. God has defended the right!"

The men of the boyar army bowed their heads. Most of them within earshot crossed themselves. That the green banner of the Ottoman Empire would now fly above the Balkans for centuries probably did not occur to them.

In the Black Sea and the Sea of Marmara, in the white-capped Strait of the Bosporus whose tides flowed endlessly between them, even on the battlements of Mehmed's Rumeli Hissar, the mighty fortress he had built as a base for the siege of Constantinople, the rain had begun to fall. It fell indiscriminately. On the storied water crossings it fell, where Darius the Great led his Persian hordes against Miltiades and his Athenians at Marathon. It fell on the sultan's palace. On Emperor Justinian's sublime church of Hagia Sophia, now and since 1453, the greatest mosque in the world of Islam, it fell also.

On the water-girt side of the still magnificent edifice, so changed with its four minarets, lay the extensive quarters of the royal harem; on its opposite that of the city's great square, a drilling ground for Turkish troops, but the setting, also, of state ceremonies and glittering pageants; and occasional executions.

On this winter day the square was all but deserted. Not long ago it had teemed with clamorous humanity, raucous and bent on pleasure through sensation. That was when the head was first displayed. Sultan and emirs had been there, *tsauches* and dervishes and imams, officers of every rank and unit of the army as *azapis* and janissaries cordoned off the designated area in the interests of discipline and crowd control. Not now. On this gray and dripping afternoon but one living man occupied the otherwise empty premises. He was not Turkish. He was a Berber from Bengasi in Cirenaica, a child of the desert on his once-in-a-lifetime pilgrimage to Mecca, a man in the grace of *hajj* who, once he had kissed the black stone of the Kaaba, could ever after claim the venerated title of *hajji*.

This pilgrim was himself a dervish. In the Parsi tongue of ancient Persia the word meant *beggar*. In Turkish it meant the same. But having come from the burning sands of North Africa, *he* was a special kind of dervish, the offspring of supernatural *jinn* called by his people a *marabout*.

All *marabouts* are dancers and this man danced. His movements enlivened by hashish, his blood-inflamed energy redoubled by it, he gyrated and gamboled about the square, spun dizzily in circles, turned and leaped and ever and again prostrated his length upon the soaked and slippery flagstones, but always to the southeast, the direction of Mecca. Closer and closer he came to the head mounted on its stake. Repeatedly he stopped and stood still to gaze upon it. Once he remained motionless long enough to read the large inscription in Turkish, the black letters glistening with raindrops.

KAZÎGLU BEY
TYRANT INFIDEL USURPER
Thus by the Divine Will of Allah will perish all the
enemies of Islam

The man seemed puzzled. He understood Turkish script well enough. Yet to his drug-bedazzled brain it appeared that this Lord Impaler was a great king, even as the sultan who had captured this city.

With small, mincing steps that were part of his mystical frenzy he approached the upright stake through the water now deepening in the square and stood before it. The head had been raised considerably higher than his own. It did not appear lifelike. He noted its mottled gray color, saw also that ravens and gulls had torn away most of the scalp, leaving the skull exposed. A long mustache that might once have been waxed hung straight down, drooping like those of the mandarins on the porcelain the caravans brought to Turkey from far Cathay.

He drew even closer. The eyes were very dark, he observed, of some indeterminate hue, seemingly aglow with an eerie inner light. That decomposition was well advanced he also grasped, for one of them protruded from its socket and the remains stank.

"Whence came you?" asked the Berber in Arabic, then performed a graceful pirouette. "Were you distinguished? Wore you a crown with a scepter in your hand? Or were you peasant-delivered from the breech of a whore rather than her womb? I will pray for you in holy Mecca, brother. I will kiss the stone of the sacred Kaaba twice and the second shall be thine. Oh mock me not with your sly grin, for I am serious. I, Hussayn of the Street of the Cloth Merchants in the Casbah of the blessed city of Bengasi. Aye, ancient Berenice it was, founded by the Ptolemies. Know you of it? I say know you of it, friend?"

The slack mouth with its broken, blood-stained teeth spoke no word. The rain fell harder and harder. Lightning lit up the ancient square and thunder rolled. Wind-driven spume lashed at the silent mosque that was once a church. But although the water soaked through his many layers of clothing and he became as one with the rain—the *marabout* danced on and on.

Epilogue

Historically, there are several opposing versions of how Dracula met his end and not one has been substantiated to the exclusion of the others. Certain facts are known. As has been said, after the taking of Bucharest he was deserted by his erstwhile allies, given only a token force, and left to fend for himself. Of course, it did not take long for the Turks and Laiota to discover this. Quickly they surrounded him. He was then obliged to choose between a protracted defense of his new capital, the outcome of which was nonetheless certain, or a sortie outside the walls which would settle the matter quickly. As all accounts agree that he died in the marsh-laced woodlands of the Vlasie Forest near Bucharest, what he chose to do is obvious. In this case attack and not discretion was the better part of valor.

Some of the tales of his last day of life are intriguing and rather fanciful. In their superlative study, *Dracula: A Biography of Vlad the Impaler, 1431–1476*, the noted Dracula authorities Radu Florescu and Raymond T. McNally consult the *Russian Narrative*, story number 18. After cautioning their readers that the author "was clearly not a participant or a witness but had information from hearsay," they quote as follows:

> Dracula's army began to kill [the Turks] and to pursue them without mercy. Then out of joy Dracula ascended a mountain

> in order to see how his men were killing the Turks. Detaching himself from the army, one of those around him, taking him for a Turk, hit him with a lance. Dracula, seeing that he was being attacked by his own men, immediately killed five of his assassins on the spot with his own sword. However, many arrows pierced him and he died in this manner.

After noting that all but ten of Dracula's Moldavian guard died with him, the scholars add: "We beg to differ from the interpretation of the author of the Slavic story; Dracula's death undoubtedly took place in the course of battle, but likely the assassin was either Laiota or one of his paid hands."

In the companion piece by the same authors, a book entitled *In Search of Dracula* (both books were published in 1973), they write:

> One story has it that at this battle the Turks were beginning to break ranks, and Dracula, confident of victory, climbed a hill in order to observe his army cutting the Turks down. However, he was temporarily isolated from his men and to maintain his safety disguised himself as a Turk. Unaware of this subterfuge, one of his followers came upon him, and thinking he was a Turkish leader, struck him with a lance. Dracula defended himself with his sword as well as he could, killing five assailants, but he soon fell victim to his own men. Another version states that it was a force of boyars and other personal enemies who confronted him and—despite the efforts of the loyal Moldavians—killed him. Thus death came to "the impaler" when he was 45 years old, and when his third reign had spanned barely two months.

On the basis of logic, the passage from the *Russian Narrative* that ascribes Dracula's death to the Turks is not difficult to refute. While there have been instances of commanders mistakenly killed by their own men (Stonewall Jackson at Chancellorsville comes immediately to mind), in the case of Dracula it seems highly improbable. For one thing, even if Turkish raiment had been handy to him, which is unlikely, he would not conceivably have donned it under the circumstances. However, let's say for the sake of argument that he did so. Had he no voice with which to identify himself? Could he not have removed his helmet to reveal his distinctive head with what may well have been the broadest mustache in Christendom? Jackson was caught by surprise in the darkness of night and shot out of his saddle by Confederate rifle fire. But in Dracula's case the light was sufficient for archers to see their targets and bring them down. One is reminded of Napoleon's means of revealing himself to Marshal Ney and the intercepting French Army after his escape from Elba; throwing open his greatcoat as Stendhal wrote and shouting: "Look, it is I, don't you recognize me? If there is one soldier among you who wishes to kill his Emperor let him fire, for now is the moment." Obviously, Dracula could have done the same.

As for the claim of the *Russian Narrative* that Dracula was "confident of victory" in this instance, it is clear that he could not possibly have been so unless he was utterly blind to the facts, and this we know was not true. That he lived in the shadow of death in his last months and was aware of it is clear. He left his wife and sons in Transylvania. He never once tried to bring them to Wallachia. That he realized his end was both inevitable and imminent became more and more apparent as events unfolded.

Some of the points of comparison between certain aspects of Dracula's life and their counterparts in the life of Cesare Borgia have been noted. They were remarkably close. Even their deaths were similar, for Borgia, too, chose a form of suicide at the end, charging alone on horseback against overwhelming numbers. Indeed, the strange affinity is so apparent that one might wonder if Niccolò Machiavelli's philosophy of statecraft as revealed in his famous book *The Prince* (*Il Principe*) was not based as much on the life of Dracula as that of Borgia. It is a philosophy both ruthlessly cynical and intensely pragmatic. The Florentine's credo of *rule by fear* was adopted by both princes, by Dracula long before the book was written. Regardless, in mitigation of that bleak advice Machiavelli also had this to say: "Nevertheless a Prince should inspire fear in such a fashion that if he do not win love he may escape hate." More than any other single factor, perhaps, it was their violation of this precept that spelled doom for the princes in question.

Curiously, less than three generations after Dracula another ruler infamous in history may well have been influenced by the notorious Wallachian. He was Ivan IV of Russia (1533–1584) known as Ivan the Terrible (more correctly, Ivan Grozny is translated as Ivan the Dread), the first grand duke of Moscow to officially bear the title "Tsar of All the Russias." In his hatred for his own boyars and his ferociousness in crushing them, Ivan's wrath knew no bounds nor did his cruelty. In his case, too, it was the murder of a family member, his beloved young first wife Anastasia, that triggered his savagery and madness. "They have murdered my little heifer," he said, referring to the boyars, and for that crime many thousands were to pay horribly with their lives.

In his book *An Illustrated History of Russia*, Joel Carmichael writes of Ivan: "He became known for an extreme kind of sadism while still a boy, and grew up with a combination of intense piety of the Russian type—obsessive devotion to the external observances of the Church and utter indifference to the inner meaning of the religion, to say nothing of its ethics—and extravagant sexual license."

Does it sound reminiscent of Dracula? Carmichael continues:

> Ivan's prey generally met their deaths in churches, quite often during the actual mass. In the midst of the most extravagant blood-baths he kept lists of the people he had murdered, and distributed money to monasteries to pay for their eternal repose. Some 4,000 names of those he killed were actually listed; the true number is thought to have been much larger. Obsessed by terror of plots and political catastrophe in general—doubtless quite rightly—he wrote Queen Elizabeth in 1569 asking for asylum should he be ejected from Russia and offering to make the arrangement reciprocal. She declined.

Again Dracula comes to mind most emphatically. Ivan's appeal to the wily Tudor queen was typical of so guilt-ridden a psyche. Caught in the tangled web of his own progressive psychosis, fearing instinctively the end it presaged, the tsar searched desperately for sanctuary prior to need. His luck was better than some. Defeated by Stéfan Báthory (the famed descendant of Dracula's co-commander) in 1582, and simultaneously losing most of Siberia (the Tatar khanate of Sibir) to the Cossack chieftain Yermak, he somehow survived his military reversals and lived to see his fifty-fourth year. Not so with Dracula. Once defeated in the Dobrogea, though the remainder of his life dragged on for years, he was never again to know real power. As a ruler dependent on foreign armies controlled by alien governments, his ultimate decline and fall was only a matter of time.

To a marked degree Dracula's reputation suffered from the widespread propaganda of his enemies, at least some of which is provably false.

As an example of unscrupulous military censorship based on omission of numerous damaging facts and extreme distortion, we have a passage from *History of Mehmed the Conqueror* by Kritovoulos of Imbros. The Byzantine observer, one of several historians retained by the sultan, dismissed Dracula out of hand with the following paragraphs quoted here for the reader's interest in their entirety. Kritovoulos uses the Greek spelling for Dracula's name and explains in a footnote that he refers to "Vlad the Impaler, Voyvod of Wallachia."

The revolt of Drakoulis (Drakula), chief of the Getae (Vlachs)

In this situation, then, while the Sultan was putting things to rights in the City, in the winter, it was announced that Drakoulis, chief of the Getae, was striving to head an insurrection, and that he had gathered a considerable army, with horses and weapons, to rebel against the Sultan who had previously granted him that principality.

This man and his brother had fled when John the Getan (Hunyadi), ruler of the Paeonians and Dacians, had come in with a considerable force and had killed their father and given the governorship to another man. The father of the present Sultan had then welcomed these two fugitives who fled to him. He very nobly nourished them in the palace while they were yet young boys, and on his death he left them to the Sultan his son. He, too, brought them up with great care and honor, and provided for them royally.

Then when a revolution occurred as to the rulership over the Getae, and the man who had been governing the region was badly defeated, the Sultan took this Drakoulis, and at great expense forcibly set him as ruler over all the country of the Getae. He exchanged pledges and oaths with him, specifying that he should guard unsullied and pure his affection and good will toward the Sultan, and also the promises and treaty which they had made.

How Drakoulis crossed the Ister and devastated the country around Nicopolis and Vidin

But Drakoulis remained faithful to this treaty only a short time. Then, forgetting all and being evil-minded toward the one who had trusted him, he revolted against the Sultan. First, he secretly crossed the Ister with a large and powerful army, and invaded all of the adjacent section of the Sultan's domains, namely, around Nicopolis and Vidin. Then, after capturing much booty and killing many people, he crossed the river again and returned to his own country.

On this, the Sultan sent messages to him to remind him of his obligations, and to try to find out the causes of the revolt. But Drakoulis, even before finding out the object of their coming, seized them and killed them by impaling them, and uttered many blasphemous threats against the Sultan.

Advance of the Sultan against the Getae, his crossing of the Ister, and overrunning of all their country, and devastation of it

The Sultan could not bear this insult, but was justly indignant. He immediately gathered a very large army and, after thorough preparations during the winter, crossed the Ister in the early spring. Once he had crossed, he overran in a few days practically the whole country of the Getae, sacking and plundering it, coming on like a torrent and sweeping all before him. He captured fortresses, pillaged towns, and carried off immense booty.

That rash and arrogant man did not wait for the swift advance of the Sultan, but fled immediately. He occupied the most inaccessible mountainous parts of the country, and awaited the outcome of events. And the Sultan wreaked his will on the country. In the end he appointed Rados, the brother of Drakoulis, as commander and ruler of the Getae. This Rados he had with him.

Drakoulis now gave up all hope for his own situation. Having no prospect any longer of ruling, he decided to kill his enemies by making a desperate attack, and to die in the attempt. Having made this senseless resolve, he decided to attack the camp by night. So about midnight he took his men and attacked one corner of the camp, in disorderly fashion and without any plan. He slaughtered a considerable number of animals, camels, and horses and mules, but he did not succeed in reaching the men.

When the Sultan learned of the attack, he purposely ordered his soldiers to fall back a little, so as to draw the enemy farther forward and make him more vulnerable. Then he gave the army the signal ordering a general attack from all sides. So they rushed in with a shout and with great dash and eagerness, and slaughtered all on the spot except a considerable number whom they took alive.

Defeat and flight of Drakoulis

Drakoulis hid in a certain place, and then fled and got away as a fugitive to Paeonia. The Paeonians (Hungarians) arrested him and shut him up in prison. And the Sultan, as I have said, appointed Rados as ruler of the Getae and gave over to him all rule and authority over them, taking pledges from him. Then he recrossed the Ister, taking with him an immense quantity of booty, prisoners, and cattle which he distributed to the army. He reached Adrianople in the fall and gave his army a brief rest there.

So much for Dracula, and was ever the disposal of an antagonist so neat and simple? One wonders why Mehmed needed two mighty armies to contend against so *contemptible* an enemy, why so great a force was delayed for months on the Danube (Danubius or Ister on ancient Roman maps, the latter meaning *lower course*), and why it was necessary to fight that same thoroughly "slaughtered" foe all over again in the Dobrogea. So much, also, for the veracity of the Porte's honored scribes and historians. Although he wrote five centuries ago, Kritovoulos might have done just as well as a propagandist for Mussolini, Hitler, or Stalin. Indeed, the German Führer's paragon of the art of deceiving the masses, Dr. Paul Goebbels, could possibly have learned something from him.

The riddle of the burial of Dracula's headless body is one of the most mystifying in the annals of Eastern Europe, and once again it takes us back to the island of Snagov, a place in peasant tradition long associated with dark tragedy, events ranging from individual murder to the drowning of a group of fettered convicts under whom a pontoon bridge broke up in the 1860s. The lake in which the island lies is located 12 miles west of Bucharest, modern Romania's capital city. Now, as then, there are rustic settlements near its shores. There are also sumptuous villas, most of them the residences of high-ranking members of Romania's Communist Party; power boats for their recreation; at least one launch used to commute between the island and the lake's primary docking facility.

Curiously enough, of all the extensive complex of structures that existed at Snagov in Dracula's time—the monastery with its cloisters and three distinctive chapels, a keep, a prison, a mint, farmhouses, stables, cattle sheds, and royal hunting lodge—nothing remains today save one small church, and that the very one that folklore and historians alike agree is a Dracula foundation. It is here the Impaler is believed to have been buried, his corpse secretly laid to rest by monks loyal to his house, men who in addition may have been grateful to the benefactor who so liberally endowed them despite his involuntary apostasy. If this is true, if Dracula really was interred at Snagov, then his last battle must have been fought not far away. Why this conclusion? Because the monks who lived there and are said to have found the body and buried it were not itinerant and very seldom traveled more than a mile or two from the monastery.

It was in 1931 that the Romanian government's Commission on Historic Monuments authorized an archaeological dig on the island of Snagov that was to include certain minor excavations in and around the existing church. Although it was not officially stated, the chief purpose was to find Dracula's body if possible and to confirm or refute the tale of his burial once and for all. Interested experts were chosen for the mission. Chief among them were George Florescu, one of Romania's foremost genealogists, and the noted archaeologist Dinu Rosetti. The History Museum of Bucharest, of which Florescu was then director, later published a compendium on their finds entitled *Diggings at Snagov*.

This dig, which continued into the year 1932, was doubtless one of the strangest in the history of archaeology. Legend had it that Dracula's tomb was situated in front of the altar and had always been there, a site selected by sympathetic monks and their Orthodox abbot who daily prayed for his soul. This grave was distinctly peculiar. For one thing, its location was contrary to all church practice and violated both Orthodox and Catholic precepts. For another, although it was larger and more imposing than every other tomb in the chapel's precincts save one, the great stone slab laid over it bore no inscription whatever, a circumstance likewise at odds with canon law. These factors alone led the investigators to expect much.

What must have been their surprise and disappointment when, on removing the tombstone they were sure had covered the Impaler, they discovered instead a mere hole in the ground. Undignified by even so much as a crumbling casket, instead of a human skeleton they found the bones of several animals, some antique ceramic pieces, and a few Iron Age artifacts that anteceded Dracula by centuries. What was the meaning of it? Clearly, the remains of the original occupant had been removed. Apparently, also, the conversion of the site into what amounted to a refuse pile was intended as a dire insult. The inference seemed obvious. The person important enough to have earned such hatred *could* have been Dracula. Taken together with the legend concerning the unique altar site it probably *was* he. But to where had those who had desecrated this resting place transported the dead man's bones?

Other graves were opened. In most of them human skeletons were found intact, legs straight, feet together, arms crossed in solemn repose at abdomen or rib cage, each of them laid out on pieces of coffin-shaped stone. The legs of one, a female, had been turned gracefully to her right side and bent at the knees while her hands were folded at her throat, a very unusual way of preparing a body for burial. But of Dracula's unknown plot there was no sign among the rest. Not until the expedition leaders decided to open *the other* grave site, shown on their floor plan of the church as Tomb B, did they uncover something that stirred their imaginations more than anything they had yet seen.

This grave was on the north side of the chapel close to the entrance, if possible a more curious location than that of the one in front of the altar. An unmarked crypt of carefully mortared bricks had been built around it. It was oriented east and west, the precise opposite of the first. However, the most singular thing that was noticed at first investigation was that its stone appeared identical with that of the altar tomb, similarly uninscribed, of exactly the same shape and size. Now the scientists really did believe they were on to something.

Entry into this nameless crypt proved startling. There was a badly deteriorated coffin inside. Around it, still showing traces of gold embroidery, were the tattered remains of a shroud in faded purple, the color of royalty. The gold crown they found, studded with cloisonné work, bore a large gem clutched by feline claws. There were scraps of red silk, much faded; a woman's jewel-set ring sewn into the remnants of what had been a sleeve; a necklace on which the outline of a snake could still be vaguely discerned. And the occupant of the rotted casket? He was still there. However, the skeleton had been reduced virtually to powder, the bones so minutely granulated as to make it impossible to determine whether or not a skull had ever been among them. Could this have been the result of natural degeneration? It is not likely. Immersed in seawater, bones will in time dissolve. In either air or a vacuum, however, they normally stay intact almost indefinitely unless in some corrosive medium, a fact proven by skeletal remains dating all the way back to the Pleistocene Epoch and the very earliest *Homo sapiens*.

What had happened here? In all probability a hammer had been used. And the motive for pounding a skeleton into dust? Were it not for the royal cerement, the crown, the necklace, and the ring, it could be attributed to hatred, the implacable malice that might have been gratified through the deceased's pulverization. But the articles placed in the casket would seem to denote esteem, possibly even love. Could they have been sent to the monastery by the widow for this purpose? Do we see in them the hand of Dracula's Magyar wife? She knew he was deeply hated. Did she order the destruction of his bones to conceal his identity and prevent their despoilment, the dishonor of having them cast out into potter's field? Or was it a mistress who did this, lovingly, or an enemy acting in wrath *before* the reburial? It is unlikely that anyone will ever know.

Why may we assume that this was the skeleton of a man rather than a woman? There are several reasons. First, the disintegrated coffin was of a size and type normally used to bury males; indeed a royal male, hence the purple shroud. Second, the gold circlet was not a feminine tiara but a true crown. Third, the serpent motif of the necklace was definitely masculine, akin in Romanian heraldry to Dracula's dragon emblem. And the woman's delicate ring sewn into the shredded sleeve? As concerned the sex of the once-existant corpse, it is the most convincing evidence of all. In Western Europe it had been the romantic practice of knights to carry such things on their persons as tokens of a lady's favor, particularly in battle or tournament. Would Dracula have adopted the custom? In the impressionable days of his childhood he had been in the Germanies with his father, especially in the imperial city of Nürnberg where the significance of such a ring was well known. And youth often remembers.

In the opinion of the leaders of the dig at Snagov, Dracula has been found. They conclude he was originally buried in Tomb A by the altar, then later moved to Tomb B by a person or persons unknown. Just when or for what reason the skeleton was destroyed remains conjectural, as does the motive for the reburial itself. Speculation is endless. According to Florescu and McNally, an Orthodox priest from one of the lakeside hamlets, the Reverend G. Dumitriu, believes not only that the church contains the remains of Dracula but also those of his second wife. Perhaps the lady with the gracefully curved legs? But then there are many beliefs.

In thinking about it all, one is tempted to compare this ill-fated tomb of evil reputation with that of the Taj Mahal in India. In that white marble edifice on the Jumna River near Agra, a thing of incredible beauty, the Moghul emperor Shah Jahan lies side by side with his beloved wife Mumtaz in peaceful and venerated majesty, their gorgeous marble coffins perfectly intact. This seems quite fitting. For unlike his treacherous son Aurangzeb, who overthrew him and imprisoned him for life, Shah Jahan was a good man and just, and would appear to deserve this sweet repose in such a setting. And Dracula? Considering the life he led and the suffering he caused he too would seem to be where he belongs. *Requiescat in pace*.

The Romanians made Dracula into a national hero; the Russian accounts say he was harsh but justified; the Turks, Hungarians, and Saxons say he was an unmitigated swine and a devil incarnate. Out of all the conflicting information that has filtered down to historians, I have at all times sought to find the inner man, to bring him to life through an admittedly unusual interpretive style based on existing evidence. This has not been simple and there are no guarantees of accuracy. As with any study of an individual dead for centuries, particularly one as shadowy as this, both the psychological and historical conclusions are, to a degree, open to challenge. Of the numerous possibilities with all their shadings and nuances of character, it remains my hope that the portrait created is not too far off the mark.

Perhaps a few words should be said about strict authenticity as distinguished from imaginary license. Where history has not recorded the names of individuals I have seen fit to supply them. This was true in the case of Dracula's two wives, for example, in that of the Wallachian and Turkish generals with Laiota; and even in the case of Vasili Luca, a man whose existence may be inferred, though the proof is lacking. No one knows the names of the Hunyadi henchmen who destroyed Dracul. I've supplied them, too. And the mighty steed Strigoi is fictitious, at least as to name. For in a certain sense history is merely a series of impressions. The historian grasps what he can. If he is honest with himself he admits that all of them are open to various interpretations.

Are the remains of Dracula really at Snagov today? Probably. The winter storms still rage over the lake. At Poenari the silent ruins stand on both sides of the storied Arges, while the Chindeia Tower in the rubble of Tirgoviste's haunted palace may serve as a haven for lovers. All has changed. Nearly all that was familiar in the days of the Impaler has passed away never to come again. It is better thus. And the moon rises eternally above destroyed Castle Dracula, and the bats fly through its mist-filtered light, and over the fabled Borgo Pass of the Carpathians the spectral wolves howl. How was it that Omar put it?

They say the Lion and the Lizard keep
The Courts where Jamshyd gloried and drank deep:
And Bahrám, that great Hunter—the Wild Ass
Stamps o'er his Head, but cannot break his Sleep.

It is finished. Even the soulless dust is quiet. And the actor Bela Lugosi, by his own wish, dreams his endless dreams still wrapped in his vampire cloak.

Glossary of Foreign Words and Guide to Pronunciation

Amlas (Áam-laas): Duchy in Transylvania.

Agrish (A-grish): Dracula's castle on the Arges River.

Arges (Ár-ges): A Wallachian tributary of the Danube.

azapi (a-źa-pee): Ottoman ordinary infantry, as distinguished from the crack Janissary Corps.

Basarab Laiota (Bas-a-rab Lay-ó-ta): Prince of the Danite line, twice ruler of Wallachia.

Bela Lugosi (Báy-la Loo-gosh-ee): Hungarian actor, star of first American Dracula film.

Bran (Braan): German-built castle in eastern Transylvania belonging to János Hunyadi, then to his son, King Matei.

Brasov (Brah-soff): German-built city in eastern Transylvania devastated by Dracula.

Caligula (Ca-leeg-you-la): Third Roman emperor, an insane tyrant and debauchee.

Carpathians (Car-pa-thee-ans): Central European mountain system between Czechoslovakia and Poland extending into Romania via the Transylvanian Alps.

Cesare Borgia (Chez-a-ray Bor-zha): Italian Renaissance prince and conqueror, a son of Pope Alexander VI.

Curtea-de-Arges (Coor-taya-day-Ár-ges): Ecclesiastical see on the Arges River, seat of the Wallachian metropolitan.

Dambovita (Dam-b́o-vi-ta): Tributary of the Danube in Wallachia.

Dobrogea (Do-bro-źhaya): Black Sea coastal area south of the Danube in southeast Romania.

Dracul (Dra-ćool): Prince Vlad II of Wallachia, Dracula's father.

Egrigöz (Eh-gree-ǵoz): Site of castle in Ottoman province of Karaman, in southwest central Turkey.

emir (ee-ḿeer): Ruler of an emirate or province in the Ottoman Empire, often with high military rank.

Fagaras (Fa-ǵar-aas): Duchy in Transylvania.

Gherghina (Ǵare-gee-na): A presumed illegitimate son of Dracula.

haiduc (h́y-dook): Romanian warlord commanding a private army, much like a cossack hetman (chief) in tsarist Russia.

Hunedoara (Hoon-ay-do-á-ra): Castle of János Hunyadi in west central Transylvania.

Ialomita (Ee-a-ĺo-mee-ta): Tributary of the Danube in Wallachia.

Ilfov (Eel-f́ov): Another Wallachian river flowing southeast.

inshallah (een-śhal-lah): Arabic for "As God wills."

Ivan Grozny (Ee-v́aan Ǵroz-nee): Ivan the Terrible (more accurately Ivan the Dread), Tsar Ivan IV of Russia.

janissary (j́an-is-sar-y): Crack infantry corps of the Ottoman Turks mainly comprised of Christian captives.

János Hunyadi (Ýa-nosh Hoon-ýa-dee): Famed Hungarian crusader against the Turks and father of King Matei Corvinus.

Karaman (Ḱa-ra-maan): Province and town of southwest central Turkey.

Kazîglu Bey (Kah-źeeg-loo Bay): Turkish for the "Lord Impaler," the Ottoman name for Dracula.

Königstein (Ḱur-nig-stine): German-built Wallachian castle (Piatra Craiului in Romanian) belonging to King Matei.

Koran (Ko-ŕaan): Muslim holy book, its writing accredited to Mohammed.

Mahmud Pasha (Ḿah-mood Ṕaa-sha): One of Sultan Mehmed II's more successful generals.

marabout (ḿar-a-bout): North African name for Muslim dervish, believed to possess supernatural power.

Matei Corvinus (Ma-t́ii Cor-v́ee-nus): King of Hungary, son of János Hunyadi.

Mehmed (Ḿech-med): Sultan of Turkey, responsible for the fall of Constantinople, known to history as Mehmed the Conqueror.

Mihnea cel Rau (the Evil) (Mee-ńay-a cel Ŕaa-o): Dracula's eldest surviving son, who ruled briefly in Wallachia in 1508 and again in 1509.

Mircea cel Bătrîn (the Old) (Mer-śay-a cel Ḃah-treen): Dracula's grandfather and Wallachia's seventh prince; reigned from 1386 to 1418.

Moldavia (Mole-d́ah-vi-a): Easternmost region of Romania, ruled in Dracula's time by his cousin Stéfan cel Mare (Stephen the Great).

Murad (Ḿoor-adh): Murad II, Sultan of Turkey, father of Mehmed II.

Pest (Pescht): City founded by the Romans, separated from Buda by the Danube River; today, as the unified Budapest, it is Hungary's capital.

Radu cel Frumos (the Handsome) (Ŕa-doo cel F́roo-mos): Wallachian prince who became a Turkish general and fought his half-brother, Dracula.

Sforza (Sfórt-za): Noble family in Italy during the Renaissance; ruled as dukes of Milan from 1450 to 1535.

Sibiu (Śee-bee-yew): German-built city in south central Transylvania, site of Dracula atrocities.

Sighisoara (See-gee-so-ár-a): City in Transylvania 45 miles northeast of Sibiu; birthplace of Dracula.

spahi (śpa-hee): Turkish cavalryman.

spatar (spah-t́aar): Wallachian army commanding general, second in rank only to the prince.

Stéfan Báthory (Śtay-faan B́aa-tor-ee): Hungarian general; theoretically Dracula's superior during the Impaler's final campaign.

Stéfan cel Mare (the Great) (Śtay-faan cel Ḿar-ay): Prince of Moldavia and Dracula's cousin; his ally during his third and last reign.

Strigoi (Stree-ǵoy): Romanian for "demon bird of the night"; Dracula's warhorse.

Tirgoviste (Teer-go-v́eest): Dracula's capital city in central Wallachia, on the Ialomita River, 45 miles northwest of Bucharest.

Transylvania (Tran-syl-v́an-ee-a): Region of northwest and central Romania; in Dracula's day a Hungarian province.

Vaslui (V́aas-loo-ee): Moldavian city of eastern Romania, site of Christian Pyrrhic victory over the Turks on January 10, 1475.

Vladislav (V́laad-ee-slaav): Vladislav II, son of Dan II, twice ruler of Wallachia; killed by Dracula at Tirgsor, August 20, 1456.

Vlad Tepes (Vlaad Seh-ṕesh): Romanian for Vlad the Impaler, one of Dracula's sobriquets.

Vlasie (V́las-ee-yeh): Dense forest of the lower Arges and Dambovita rivers.

voivod (Voy-vóde): A warlord, primarily in Hungary and Romania.

Vuc Brancovic (Vook Bŕaan-co-vitch): Serbian despot and Tyrant of Smédérovo who was allied with Dracula during his final reign.

Wallachia (Wah-ĺach-ee-a): Region of southeast Romania between the Transylvanian Alps and the Danube, ruled as a principality by the Draculesti.

Bibliography

Balfour, John (Baron Kinross). *The Ottoman Centuries*. New York: Morrow, 1977.

Carmichael, Joel. *An Illustrated History of Russia*. New York: Reynal & Co., 1960.

Chamberlin, E. R. *The Fall of the House of Borgia*. New York: Dial Press, 1974.

Creasy, E. S. *History of the Ottoman Turks*. London: Cambridge University Press, 1906.

Davis, R. H. C. *A History of Medieval Europe*. London: Longmans, Green & Co., 1957.

Dedijer, Vladimir; Božić, Ivan; Ćirković, Sima; Ekmečić, Milorad. *History of Yugoslavia*. New York: McGraw-Hill, 1974.

Eversley, G. J. S. L. *The Turkish Empire*. London: Macmillan, 1923.

Florescu, Radu, and McNally, Raymond T. *Dracula: A Biography of Vlad the Impaler, 1431–1476*. New York: Hawthorn Books Inc., 1973.

Frazer, James G. *The Fear of the Dead in Primitive Religions*, 2 vol. London: Macmillan, 1934.

Glut, Donald F. *True Vampires of History*. New York: Citadel, 1971.

Halecki, Oscar. *The Crusade at Varna: A Discussion of a Controversial Problem*. New York: Praeger, 1943.

Inalcik, Halil. *The Ottoman Empire*. New York: Praeger, 1973.

Khayyám, Omar. *The Rubáiyát of Omar Khayyám*. Translated from the Persian by Edward Fitzgerald. Philadelphia: David McKay Company, 1942.

Kritovoulos of Imbros. *History of Mehmed the Conqueror*. Translated from the Greek by Charles T. Riggs. London and New Jersey: Princeton University Press, 1954.

Lamb, Harold. *Genghis Khan: Emperor of All Men*. New York: Doubleday and Co., 1927.

———.*Omar Khayyám*. New York: Doubleday and Co., 1934.

———.*The Crusades*. (Originally published in two volumes as *Iron Men and Saints* and *The Flame of Islam*) New York: Doubleday and Co., 1945.

Le Fanu, Joseph Sheridan. "Carmilla" from *In a Glass Darkly*. New York: Warner Paperback, 1970.

Lennig, Arthur. *The Count: The Life and Films of Bela "Dracula" Lugosi*. New York: Putnam, 1974.

Lucas, H. S. *The Renaissance and the Reformation*. London: Macmillan, 1935.

Ludlam, Henry. *A Biography of Dracula: The Life Story of Bram Stoker*. London: Fireside Press, W. Foulsham and Company, 1962.

Machiavelli, Niccolò. *The Prince*. Translated from the Italian by Hill Thompson. New York: Heritage Press, 1954.

Mallory, Thomas. *Le Morte D'Arthur*. New York: Heritage Press, 1955.

McNally, Raymond T. and Florescu, Radu. *In Search of Dracula: A True History of Dracula and Vampire Legends*. New York: The New York Graphic Society, 1973.

Miller, Charles. *Khyber: British India's North West Frontier*. New York: Macmillan, 1977.

Mohammed (Mohammed bin Abdul-Muttalib). *The Koran*. Translated from the Arabic by N. J. Dawood. New York: Heritage Press, 1956.

Morris, Donald R. *The Washing of the Spears*. New York: Simon and Schuster, 1965.

Pius II (Enea Silvio Piccolomino). *Memoirs of a Renaissance Pope: The Commentaries of Pius II*. Translated from the Latin by F. A. Gragg. New York: Praeger, 1959.

Ronay, Gabriel. *The Truth About Dracula*. New York: Stein and Day, 1972.

Rudorff, Raymond. *The Dracula Archives*. New York: Arbor House, 1971.

Seton-Watson, R. W. *A History of the Roumanians*. London: Cambridge University Press, 1934.

Shaw, Stanford Jay. *History of the Ottoman Empire and Modern Turkey*. New York: Cambridge University Press, 1977.

Suetonius (Caius Suetonius Tranquillus). *The Lives of the Twelve Caesars*. Translated from the Latin. Introduction by Joseph Gavorse. New York: Random House, 1931.

Stevenson, Robert Louis. *The Strange Case of Dr. Jekyll and Mr. Hyde.* New York: Airmont Publishing Company, 1964.

Stoker, Bram. *Dracula.* New York: Dell Publishing Co., 1965.

Sugar, Peter F. *Southeastern Europe under Ottoman Rule, 1354–1804.* Seattle and London: University of Washington Press, 1977.

Wolf, Leonard. *A Dream of Dracula: In Search of the Living Dead.* New York: Little, Brown and Co., 1972.

INDEX

Abdu-l-Khalid, 143, 147, 152
Abdur Rahman Khan, 105
Achilles, 44, 131, 225
Achmed ibn Aziz, 228, 234
AEIOU, 203
Aeschylus, 16, 84
Agrish, Castle of, 87, 137, 139, 143–144, 149–150, 156, 157, 158, 171, 172, 180, 194, 227, 246
Al-ad-Din, 40, 126
Albania (*see* Scanderbeg)
Albrecht of Austria, 52
Alceste, 65–73, 193
Alexander the Great, 44, 119, 122
Alexandru, 144
Alexandru I (Aldea), 35, 50, 82
Aminah, 37
Amlas massacre, 100–101, 148
Anastasia, 262
Anghel, Nicolae, 142, 148–150
Antonescu, Captain, 231
Antoninus, Marcus Aurelius, 32
Arabian Nights, 21
Arany, Ferenc, 26–29
Arghezi, 11–13
Arnim, Helmut von, 93
Arnim, Karla von, 93–97
Aron, Petru, 59, 62, 63, 145, 205
Arpadian kingdom (*see* Hungary)
Arthur Pendragon, 22, 247
Asachi, Titu, 82
Attila, 92, 100, 135, 153, 251
Attrition warfare, 121, 128–129
Aubusson, Pierre d', 219
Augustus Caesar, 18
Aurangzeb, 269
Aurelian, 32
Avalon, 247
Ayesha, 37

Balassa, General, 169
Balbi, Venetian envoy, 127
Balboa, Vasco Núñez de, 10, 245
Baleanu, General, 143, 147, 194
Barbarossa, 22
Barbo, Pietro (*see* Paul II)
Basarab, House of, 7, 46, 49, 152, 191, 195

Basarab Laiota, 98, 181, 204, 206, 209, 211, 214, 216, 218, 220, 221, 222, 224, 225, 226–234, 237, 239, 240, 241, 246, 252, 253, 254, 256, 259, 260, 269
blood oath to kill Dracula, 231–234, 252
and death of Dracula, 255–256
Basarab cel Mare, 33
Basarab II, 53, 82
Basarab the Young, 98
Bastards, 145
Báthory, Elizabeth, 221
Báthory, Stéfan, 221, 222, 223–224, 236, 239, 252
Báthory, Stéfan (the later), 262
Bats, 13, 14, 19, 193, 270
Bayar, Ismet, 109, 112
Bayezid I, sultan, 34
Beast of Naples, the (*see* Ferdinand I)
Beheim, Michel, 154–155, 180, 181
Berserkr, 44
Bisexuality, 44, 60–61
Black Death, 10, 64, 135, 227
Black Prince (*see* Edward)
Blaga, Titu, 84
Blondel, 44
Blood feud, 88
Bluebeard, 10, 104
Bogdan II, 56, 58, 59–60, 62, 63, 120, 205, 219, 247
Bohemia, 147, 164–165, 178, 182, 185–186, 187, 190, 203–204, 220–221
Bonfini, Antonio, 168, 181
Borgia, Cesare, 6, 9, 10, 131, 200–201, 261
Brancovic, George, 57, 62, 210
Brancovic, Vuc, 210, 211, 215, 216, 218, 223, 227, 230, 239
Brasov massacre, 91–97, 99, 101, 132
Bratulescu, 80
Bubonic plague (*see* Black Death)
Bucephalus (horse), 122
Bucharest, 224–226, 227, 229, 235, 236–237, 244, 248, 251, 253, 259, 266
Burton, Sir Richard, 21
Cabinet of Dr. Caligari, The (film), 20
Cabot, John, 10, 245
Cabral, Pedro Alvares, 10, 245
Cabrillo, Juan, 245
Calga, 174–176
Caligula, 79, 103–104, 122, 123, 192, 193, 198, 201, 248–249
Calinescu, Petru, 11–13
Calixtus II (pope), 76, 132
Caltuna, 60, 98
Cantemir, 80
Cantharides, 166–167, 175–177
Capone, Al, 102
Carmichael, Joel, 262
Carmilla (Le Fanu), 20–21
Carradine, John, 16
Casimir IV, 133, 182, 204, 221
Castle Dracula, 155, 158, 246, 270 (*See also* Agrish, Castle of)
Catavolinos, Toma, 134
Cesarini, Giuliano, 28, 54
Chalkokondyles, 133, 134, 154
Chamberlin, E. R., 201
Chaney, Lon, Jr., 16
Chapel of Balteni, 49
Charlemagne, 245
Chilia, 121, 130, 131, 134, 136, 148, 218
Chindeia Tower, 72, 84, 270
Cîrstian, 220
Clive, Colin, 4
Clive, Robert, 221
Colet, John, 10
Coligny, Gaspard de, 100
Columbus, Christopher, 10, 74–75
Commission on Historic Monuments (Romania), 266
Commodus, 32
Conduratu, G. C., 180
Conduratu, Miron, 47–48, 85
Constantine XI Paleologus, 28–29, 63
Constantinople, fall of, 9, 28–29, 42, 62–63, 74, 106, 111, 133, 154, 203, 219, 233, 256
Cordeles, 240
Cortés, Hernán, 10, 245
Corvinus, Helena, 163, 169, 181
Corvinus, House of, 181, 192

Corvinus, Mathias, 78
(*See also* Matei I)
Cosbue, Barbu, 82
Costin, Lucian, 231
Council of Basel, 31
Count, The: The Life and Films of Bela "Dracula" Lugosi (Lennig), 17–18
Crasna, Battle of, 120–121
Creanga, 231
Crusade at Varna, The (Halecki), 5
Crusades, crusading orders, 8, 131–132, 140
Cuza, Victor, 237–241, 243–244, 252–254
Czabai, Micaela, 197–199, 200

Dacians, 11–12, 13, 18–19, 32–33, 123, 237
Dan II, 35, 82, 237
Dan III (Danciul), 98, 99–100, 237
Danesti, 35, 52, 53, 57, 58, 60, 62, 63, 67, 69, 72, 81–82, 98, 99, 181, 204, 218, 220, 227, 236–237, 241
Danube ports, 127–128, 130, 131, 133–134, 135
Darius the Great, 119, 256
Decebal, 18
Despina, Maria, 204
Deucalion (horse), 242, 243
Diggings at Snagov, 266
Dingane, 103
Dobrogea, 46–47, 52, 53, 55, 136–137, 143, 148, 155, 170, 193, 200, 206, 243, 246
Dr. Jekyll and Mr. Hyde (Stevenson), 20, 200
film, 16, 20
Domitian, 18
Donanyi, Imre, 188
Doukas, Michel, 154
Dozsa, General, 224–225
Dracul (*see* Vlad II)
Dracula (*see* Vlad III)
Dracula (film), 3–4, 17, 20
Dracula: A Biography of Vlad the Impaler (Florescu & McNally), 5, 259–260, 269
Draculesti, 33–35, 218, 221
Dragon, the, 7–8, 18–19
Dragos, Prince, 33
Drusilla, 122–123, 139–141, 144, 145–146, 151–154, 155, 157, 193, 194
Dumitriu, G., 269
Dushan, 188–189, 194–199, 215

Edward the Black Prince, 9, 58
Edward IV, 185
Efrosin the sinner, 199
Eftimiu, Eliade, 86
Egrigöz, 1–3, 7, 54, 55, 60, 161
Ekrem, Kara, 228, 234
Eliade, István, 227–228
Elizabeth I, 262
Endymion (horse), 242
Enkidu, 225
Enveri, 154
Erasmus, Desiderius, 10
Eugene IV (pope), 27, 31, 55
Eupraxia, 50, 51, 60
Euripides, 84
Evil, will to, 103

Fagaras, 100, 101, 130, 148, 158, 180
Fall of the House of Borgia, The (Chamberlin), 201
Fall of the House of Usher, The (film), 20
Faludi, Michael, 164, 168
Faludi, Militsa, 168–171, 172
Farma, Radu, 130
Fat Frumos, 237
Faust, 23
Faustina, 145, 177, 193
Feliciana, 66–71
Feraru, Dinu, 82
Ferdinand I, 10, 242
Florescu, George, 181, 266
Florescu, Radu, 5, 181, 259–260, 269
Frankenstein, 4, 20
Friedrich III, Emperor, 99, 130, 133, 154, 164, 202–203, 221
Frumos, Fat, 237

Gales, General, 117–119, 123–124, 127, 143

Gama, Vasco da, 2, 10, 245
Gane, C., 181
Genghis Khan, 38
Geopolitics, 131
George of Podebrad, 133, 164, 178, 182, 202, 203–204, 221
Gherghina, 144–146, 156, 157, 235
Gilgamesh, 225
Gilles de Rais, 10, 104
Giotto di Bondone, 193
Giskra, Jan, 148, 159
Giurescu, Constantin, 5
Goebbels, Paul Joseph, 266
Goethe, Johann Wolfgang von, 23
Gragg, F. A., 5
Grecu, General, 144, 146, 194
Greek tragedy, 15–16, 84–85
Grigore, Father, 242
Guerrilla, 121, 128–129
Guesclin, Bertrand du, 128
Guise, Henri Duc de, 100

Habsburg, Rudolf von, 191
Habsburgs, 191–192, 203
Hadrian, 37
Haiduc (horse), 207
Halecki, Oscar, 5
Hamid, Celal, 142–143
Hamza, Pasha, 134
Hannibal Barca, 71
Hanseatic League, 76
Harczy, General, 223
Harker, Jonathan, 13–15, 16–17, 19–20, 21
Harold II, 145
Haroun-al-Rashid, 36
Harsanyi, Anna, 168
Hashish, 174–175, 257
Haushofer, Karl, 131
Heliogabalus, 201
Henry V, 9
Henry VII, 9
Henry VIII, 9
Hephaestion, 44
History of Mehmed the Conqueror (Kritovoulos), 5, 113, 263–265
History Museum of Bucharest, 266
History of the Romanians, A (Seton-Watson), 5
Hitler, Adolf, 131, 265
Holy League, 245
Holy Roman Empire, 202–203
Homer, 166
Homosexuality, 1–3, 40, 43–44, 65–68, 107, 129, 201
Hope, Anthony, 7
Horror film, the, 15–21
Horthy, General, 169
House of Wax (film), 20
Howling, The (film), 16
Huguenots, 100
Hulagu Khan, 38
Hull, Henry, 16
Hundred Years' War, 9, 128
Hungary, 36, 49, 50, 52–53, 55–56, 58, 60, 63–64, 74, 77, 78, 98–99, 111, 129–131, 133, 147–148, 158, 167, 172, 251
  and Bohemia, 164–165, 178, 182, 185–186, 187, 190, 203–204, 220–221
  and Dracula, 224–234, 246, 247–256, 269
    exile of, in Pest, 185–212
    imprisonment of, 158–183, 265
    military use of, 202–226
    and Varna, 25–31, 42, 54–55
    (*See also* Hunyadi, János; Matei I; Transylvania)
Hunyadi, János, 9–10, 25–31, 34, 45–47, 50, 52–53, 54, 55–56, 57, 61–62, 63, 64, 76, 77, 78, 99, 111, 130, 131, 132, 161, 178, 181, 203, 210, 217, 219, 247, 263, 270
Huss, Jan, 164, 202
Hussayn of Bengasi, 257–258
Hussites, 164, 202
Hyde, Edward, 200

Icarus (horse), 198, 206, 213, 240–241
Ilderim, Emir, 38, 39–40, 41, 224, 228–230, 231, 233–234, 237, 240
Illegitimacy of birth, 145

Illustrated History of Russia, An (Carmichael), 262
Impalement, 103
(*See also* Dracula)
Incitatus (horse), 122, 192, 248
Incubus, 15
Inhumanity, 103
Inonu Pasha, 106–112
In Search of Dracula (McNally & Florescu), 5, 260
Iron Maiden, 241
Islam (*see* Koran; Mohammed; Ottoman Empire)
Ispirescu, Nicolae, 227
Issus, Battle of, 119
Ivan III, 132, 168
Ivan IV ("The Terrible"), 261–262
Ivascu, 12

Jackson, Thomas Jonathan ("Stonewall"), 260–261
James, Henry, *The Turn of the Screw*, 20
Janissaries, 38–41, 43–44, 54, 63, 107, 108, 116, 123, 125, 126–127, 129, 142–143, 147, 148–149, 152, 155, 178, 228, 257
and homosexuality, 40, 43–44, 129
Janissary of Ostrovita, The, 154
Janosi, Sandor, 207, 208
Jaszi, General, 169
Jekyll-and-Hyde syndrome, 102
Jihad, 35–36, 41–44, 55
Joan of Arc, 8–9, 10
Jokai, 250
Justinian, 257

Karadja, 26, 29
Karamania, 219, 233
Karla, 93, 94–97
Karolyi, General Bela, 164, 169, 211, 216–217, 218–219
Katana, 167
"Kazîglu Bey," 108, 127, 159, 161, 179, 229, 237, 251, 257–258
Khadija, 37
Khalil, Grand Vizier, 41, 106
Khayyam, Omar: *Rubaiyat*, 122, 162, 182–183, 250, 270
Khyber (Miller), 105
King, Stephen, 20
Knights Hospitalers, 8, 219
Kodály, János, 168
Königstein, 159, 160, 247
Koran, 32, 35, 41, 43, 112, 229, 234
Korjus, General Erno, 207–212
Kormendi, Eva, 169
Kosary, General Bela, 169, 249, 250–254
Kosovo, Battle of, 34, 57, 62, 63
Kossuth, Countess Ilona, 168–171
Kritovoulos of Imbros, 5, 113, 133, 154, 263–265
Kuprili, Ismet, 144, 147, 152, 178, 210
Kurytsin, Feodor, 168, 219
Kutuzov, Field Marshal Prince Mikhail Ilarionovich, 128

Ladislas, son of Hunyadi, 77
Ladislas Posthumus, 64, 74, 77, 98, 99, 203
Ladislas II, 204
Ladislas III, 25, 31
Langella, Frank, 16
László V, 203
Laurianu, Ion, 232
Lazan, Barbu, 227, 228
Lee, Christopher, 16
Le Fanu, Sheridan, 21
Lennig, Arthur, 17
Leo I (pope), 92, 135
Leonardo da Vinci, 10, 185
Leonidas, 64
Lepanto, 245
Lessing, Father Heinrich, 91–97
Log, Mihai, 223
Louis IX, 8, 131–132
Louis XI, 104, 202
Luca, Vasili, 83–85, 86, 109, 112, 117, 119, 143, 146–147, 189–193, 194, 207, 208, 210, 213, 214, 215–216, 217, 223, 225–226, 231, 233, 235, 270

Ludendorff, General Erich Friedrich Wilhelm, 221
Lugosi, Bela, 3, 16, 17–18, 270
Luther, Martin, 10
Lycanthropy, 13

Machiavelli, Niccolò: *The Prince*, 131, 261
McNally, Raymond T., 5, 181, 259–260, 269
McNee, Patrick, 16
Mad Forests of Vlasie, 235, 251–252, 259
Mafia, 88, 102
Magellan, Ferdinand, 10, 245
Magyars (*see* Hungary)
Mahmud of Ghazni, 36
Mahmud Pasha, 251
Malipiero, Bianca, 168
Marabout, 257–258
Marathon, 256–257
Martel, Charles, 245
Martin, Frank, 105
Mary of Burgundy, 203
Matei I, 78, 99, 104, 130, 144, 147, 158–160, 162, 163–166, 167, 168, 170, 174, 176, 177, 178–179, 180, 181–182, 186, 190–191, 194, 199, 201–202, 203, 204–205, 206, 207, 208–209, 211, 216, 220–221, 222, 227, 230, 236, 240, 246
Matelots, 44
Matusa, General, 116–117, 119, 120, 143, 194
Maximilian, Prince, 203
Medici, Catherine de, 100
Medusa, 15
Mehmed II, Sultan ("Wolfeyes"), 3, 5, 9, 27, 28–29, 30, 37–38, 39–42, 61, 62–63, 74, 76, 78–79, 98, 143, 146, 170, 191, 209, 210, 219, 230, 233, 237, 249, 256, 263–265
  on the Danube, 107, 107, 111, 112–113, 115, 116, 117, 119–120, 121, 122, 123, 126, 127, 134, 135–137, 143, 265
  and siege of Constantinople, 9, 28–29, 42, 62–63, 74, 106, 111, 133, 219, 233, 256
Memoirs of a Renaissance Pope: The Commentaries of Pius II, 5
Mephistopheles, 171–174
Merlin, 247
Mezid-Bey, 30, 53
Michelangelo Buonarotti, 20, 244
Midhat, Abdullah, 112
Mihail (Dracula's son), 193, 198, 199
Mihail I, 35, 82
Mihnea, 156, 200
Mille, Octavian, 82
Miller, Charles, 105
Millian, Alexandru, 232, 239, 241
Miltiades, 256
Mircea cel Bátrîn, 33–35, 36, 81–82, 127, 129, 248
Mircea, Prince (Dracula's brother), 26, 30–31, 45–49, 50, 51, 54, 55–56, 58, 59, 60, 62, 74, 78, 82, 85, 118, 130, 193
Mircea, Prince (Dracula's son), 156, 193
Modrussa, Nicolas (Niccolo Modrussiense), 104–105, 135–136, 168–169, 181
Mohammed, 31, 35, 37, 42, 43, 44, 110, 228
Mohammed II (the Conqueror) (*see* Mehmed II)
Moldavia, 33, 50, 56, 59, 62, 74, 86, 103, 129–130, 131, 134, 136, 204, 205, 216, 219, 220, 227, 245, 251
  (*See also* Stéfan cel Mare)
Mongols, 34, 38, 52, 77, 88, 142, 215
Monk's Rest, The, 139, 153
Montenegro, 76, 133
More, Sir Thomas, 10
Morgan le Fay, 247
Mumtaz, 269
Murad I (sultan), 43
Murad II (sultan), 1–2, 3, 9, 26, 27, 28, 31, 35–36, 37–43, 52, 53, 55, 60–61, 62
Murnau, Felix, 15
Mussolini, Benito, 265
Mustapha Inonu Pasha, 106–112

Nadasdy, 216–217, 218
Nana Sahib, 104
Napoleon, 128, 135, 221, 246, 261
Nazism, 131, 265
Nebuchadnezzar, 246
Nelson, Horatio, 135, 221
Nero, 104
New Testament, the, 250
Ney, Marshal Michel, 261
Night of Terror, 120–127, 134, 135–136, 143, 170, 219
Normans, Normandy, 145
Nosferatu (film), 15–16, 20

Odin, 44, 256
Olahus, Anna, 244
Oltea, Princess, 58, 60
Olteanu, Alceste, 65–73, 193
Order of the Dragon, 8, 50
Orkhan (sultan), 43
Orlock, Count, 15
Orszagh, 240, 241, 242, 243
Osman, Emir, 39, 41
Ottoman Empire/Turks, 3, 5, 7, 142–143, 190, 204–205, 219–220
  advance into Europe, 9–10, 22, 25–44, 52–56, 61–64, 75–76, 78–79, 104, 106–137, 143–144, 147–148, 178, 209–212, 233, 245–246, 256
  (*See also* Kosovo; Night of Terror; Varna; Vaslui)
  and fall of Constantinople, 9, 28–29, 42, 62–63, 74, 106, 111, 133, 154, 203, 219, 233, 256

Panaitescu, Grigore, 109
Panaitescu, P. P., 180
Panu, Theodoru, 146
Patroclus, 44, 225
Paul II (pope), 164, 202, 219
Peace of Seghedin, 54
Pegasus, 117, 249, 255
Perseus, 15, 117
Pest, 185–189
  (*See also* Hungary, Dracula, exile of, in PestVlad III, exile in Pest)
Phased withdrawal, 128–129
Piccolomini, Enea Silvio de (*see* Pius II)
Pius II (pope), 5, 22, 104, 130, 131, 135, 159, 160, 202
Pizarro, Francisco, 10, 245
Plague (*see* Black Death)
Plutarch, 119
Poe, Edgar Allan, 20
Poenari, Bluff of, 142–143, 147, 148–150, 153, 155, 227, 270
Poland, 133, 182, 204, 221
Polivar, Ion, 223
Polyzoides, Stavros, 186–189
Ponce de León, Juan, 245
Price, Vincent, 20
Prisoner of Zenda, The (Hope), 7
Prometheus, 242
Pyrrhic victory, 217
Pyrrhus of Epiros, 217

Radu cel Frumos (Dracula's half-brother), 1–2, 7, 46, 51, 54, 60–61, 62, 98, 121, 135, 136, 137, 140, 143, 144, 146, 148, 152, 155, 157, 158, 161, 162, 164, 178, 181, 182, 183, 190, 202, 204, 206, 220, 222, 236, 238, 246, 264, 265
  death of, 220, 236
  defeated and deposed by Stéfan, 204, 206
  estranged from Dracula, 60–61, 62, 121, 161
  hostage of the Porte, 1–3, 46, 54, 60–61, 161
  and rule of Wallachia, 98, 137, 161, 202, 222, 246, 264, 265
Radu cel Mare, 157
Radu Negru, 33
Radu II, 35
Radului, General, 119, 143, 194, 243
Raphael Santi, 10, 244
Realpolitik, 131
Rebreanu, subaltern, 239, 241
Red Emir (*see* Sinan, Mustapha)
Red Tower, 237
Rhodes, 219
Richard I (Lion-Heart), 44, 79
Richard III, 6, 9, 185

Riul Doamnei, 155
Robber's Roost, The, 186–189
Robert the Devil, 145
Ronay, Gabriel, 246
Rosetti, Dinu, 266
Rudolph the Black, 33
Ruritania, 7
Russian Narrative, 201, 259–261

St. Bartholomew's Eve massacre, 100, 101
Saint Louis, 8, 131–132
Saint Nicholas Monastery, 236–237
St. Valentine's Day massacre, 102
Saladin, 2, 228
Saltykov-Shchedrin Public Library (Leningrad), 201
Samson, 118, 248
Sappho, 172
Satan, 171–174
Savonarola, Girolamo, 10, 74
Scanderbeg, 57, 58, 64, 75–76, 108–109, 132, 133, 160, 219
Schreck, Max, 15
Scorched earth policy, 121, 128
Scorzeny, Miklos, 186–189, 195–196, 201–202
Selim Mejid, Emir, 41
Serbs, 52, 188, 194, 197, 213, 214, 215, 227
Seton-Watson, R. W., 5
Sforza, Francesco, 168
Sforza, Galeazzo Maria, 241
Shah Jahan, 269
Shaka, 103
Shelley, Mary, *Frankenstein*, 4, 20
Sibiu, 62, 77–78, 98, 100, 101, 204–212, 220, 222, 235
Siegfried, 206
Sigismund, Emperor, 4, 8, 49–50, 52
Silistria, pasha of, 135
Sima, Jon, 81
Sima, Nicolae, 241–244
Sinan, Mustapha, 210–211, 214, 215, 224
Sixtus IV (pope), 219
Slavici, Nicolae, 81–82
Snagov Island, 49, 235, 236, 237–240, 247–248, 266–269, 270
Solomon, 197
Solomon's Tower, 161, 171, 177, 180, 200
(*See also* Vísegràd)
Southeastern Europe under Ottoman Rule (Sugar), 129
Spahis,38–39, 41, 61, 106, 108, 116–117, 125, 147, 213, 229, 239
Spanish Inquisition, 74
Speke, John Hanning, 21
Stalin, Joseph, 265
Stéfan cel Mare of Moldavia, 56–60, 62, 74, 103, 120–121, 130–131, 132, 134, 136, 159, 202, 204–205, 208–211, 216, 217–219, 220, 222–223, 227, 230, 235, 236, 239, 251, 252, 254
Stendhal, 261
Stevenson, Robert Louis, *Dr. Jekyll and Mr. Hyde*,16, 20, 200
Stoker Bram, *Dracula*, 3, 4, 5, 7, 13–15, 16–17, 19–20, 21–22
Strategic retreat, 128–129
Strigoi (horse), 122, 124, 125, 126, 127, 206, 242–243, 244, 248–249, 250, 253, 255, 270
Succubus, 15
Suetonius, 104
Sugar, Peter F., 129
Suleiman the Magnificent, 219–220
Szilagy, Count, 164
Szilagy, Ferenc, 169
Szilagy, Michael, 99
Szilagy, Valeria, 163, 165, 169–170, 172–177, 178–179, 193–194, 195, 196, 197, 198–199, 200, 207, 211, 235

Taj Mahal, 269
Tamerlane, 34, 52, 153
Tirgoviste, 49, 50, 52, 53, 54, 57, 60, 62, 66, 77, 78, 87, 98, 106, 111, 116, 119, 134, 137, 141, 143, 155, 156, 199, 220–222, 270
Muslim destruction of, 222, 223, 224, 226, 229, 231, 246

Titania (horse), 243
Titian, 10, 244
Titu, Father, 240
Tommasi, Pietro, 132, 133, 159, 168
Torquemada, Tomás de, 10, 74
Tracy, Spencer, 16
Trajan, 18
Transylvania, 7, 13, 25, 29, 33, 47, 50, 52, 53, 55, 62, 63, 76–78, 98, 99, 100, 102, 106, 129, 130, 132, 142, 147, 148, 152, 160, 161, 178, 188, 204, 205, 207, 222–223, 246, 261
Transylvania in the History of Romania (Giurescu), 5
Trebizond, 106, 167, 233, 245
Tripoli, 245
Truth about Dracula, The (Ronay), 246
Turhan, Imam, 41, 42–43
Turks (*see* Ottoman Empire/Turks)
Tursun Bey, 133, 154

Undead, the (*see* Vampirism)
Universal Studios, 17

Valens, 37
Valeria (*see* Szilagy)
Valerian, 32
Valhalla, 44, 256
Valley of Retribution, 86, 91–97, 134
Vampirism, cult of, 3–4, 11–22, 122, 147, 172, 237, 270
  and Dacians, 18–19
  fascination of, 17–18, 20
  and films, 15–18
  right of passage, 19
  and women, 17–18
Van Helsing, Abraham, 21
Varna, Battle of, 25–31, 34, 37, 40–41, 42, 45, 47, 54–55, 57, 63, 217, 221
Vaslui, Battle of, 213–219, 220, 229
Velázquez, Diego, 245
Vendetta, 88
Venice, 76, 127, 133, 159, 168
Verrocchio, Andrea del, 185
Vísegràd, 161–166, 180–181, 193, 200, 247
Vitéz, János, 223

Vlad the Monk, 51, 98, 121, 200
Vlad II (Dracul), 4, 7–8, 26–27, 29, 30, 31, 35, 36, 46, 47, 48, 49–56, 60, 61, 67, 73, 74, 78, 82, 130, 160, 200, 206, 210, 222, 235, 270
  "apostate," 52–54
  death, 49, 56, 58, 59, 60, 62, 63
  illegitimacy, 145
  Order of the Dragon, 8, 50
Vlad Tepelus, 156
Vlad III (Dracula), 1–3, 4–10, 21–23, 30, 46
  an anachronism, 131–132
  apprehension of damnation, 212, 254–255
  birth, 9, 50
  and the boyars, 75, 78–89, 109, 124, 127, 129, 134, 246, 260
  Brasov massacre, 92–97, 99, 101, 132
  and Bucharest, 224–226, 227, 229, 235, 236–237, 244, 248, 251, 253, 259
  builds castle, 87–89
  burial and remains, 265–269, 270
  in Castle of Agrish, 137, 143–159, 172, 180, 194, 227
    escape 151–159, 180
  character, 5–6, 21, 22, 32, 51–52, 75, 77, 156–157, 245–247
  consolidating despotic rule, 76–101, 105–106, 129, 132
  conversion to Catholicism, 163–164, 167, 181–184, 202, 240, 266
  cruelty in historical perspective, 103–106
  Danube campaign, 106–137, 140, 143, 154, 155, 160, 170, 210
  death, 6, 200, 246, 254–256, 259–261
  defeat of Danesti, 56, 61–64, 66–67, 71–72, 73–74, 75, 77
  and Dobrogea, 46–47, 52, 53, 55, 136–137, 143, 148, 155, 170, 193, 200, 206, 243, 246
  early life, 50–51
  "enemy of all mankind," 101
  exile in Pest, 189–200, 201–202, 204, 215

Vlad III (Dracula) (*Cont.*):
first reign, 62
forsaken, 246
frightening power, 69, 71, 72–73
greed for power, 246–247
and *guerrilla*, 121, 128–129
his head exhibited, 257–258
in historical perspective, 8–10, 32–44, 103–106
homeland, 6–7
hostage to Porte, 1–3, 30, 46, 54, 55, 60–61
in Hungarian army, 202, 204–224
impaler, 77–78, 84, 85–87, 91–97, 98, 100, 101, 102, 103, 104, 105, 106, 107–108, 109, 110, 111, 127, 134, 136, 159, 161, 207, 232
imprisoned in Hungary, 159–183, 193, 200, 247
last days, 235–244, 246–256
legend in Romania, 22, 102, 155, 157–158, 246, 247–248, 269
madness, 6, 10, 75, 89, 101–103, 128, 131, 140, 192–194, 232, 245–246, 247, 248–250
marriages, 109, 122–123, 139–141, 144–146, 151–154, 155, 157, 163, 165, 181, 182, 191, 193–194, 235, 261, 269
multiple personality, 101–103
his name, origin and meaning of, 7–8
and possible historical influence, 261–263
propaganda against, 101, 159–160, 161–162, 171, 262–265
second reign, 65–137

Vlad III (Dracula) (*Cont.*):
sexuality, 68–73, 102, 140–141, 163, 165, 172–177, 178–179, 244
at Snagov, 235, 236, 237–240, 247–248, 266–269, 270
his sons, 144–146, 156, 193, 196, 197, 198, 199–200, 235, 261
spy network, 75, 82, 106
and Stoker, 21–22
terrible change in, 74–75, 77
third reign, 180, 224–234
Vladislav II, 29, 57, 61, 62, 63, 66, 67, 71–72, 73, 75, 77, 99, 236
Vlahuta, Tudor, 47, 85
Vlasie, 235, 251–252, 259
Voichita, Maria, 204

Wallachia, Wallachians, 7, 9–10, 13, 22, 26, 30, 33–36, 45, 46, 48, 49–53, 55–61, 63, 64, 76–79, 88, 98, 99, 105–106, 118, 122, 129, 131, 136, 147, 152, 157, 158, 161, 163, 180, 181, 182, 195, 200, 204, 206, 208–212, 218, 220, 224, 232, 240, 245, 256, 261
Wars of the Roses, 9, 185
Werewolf of London, The (film), 16, 20
Werewolves, 13
Wilde, Oscar, *The Picture of Dorian Gray*, 20
William the Conqueror, 145
Wolfeyes (*see* Mehmed II)

Yermak the Cossack, 262

Zapolya, Erno, 169
Zundi, 162–167, 173–174, 177–179

WITHDRAWN